Literature of the
Romantic period,
1750—1850

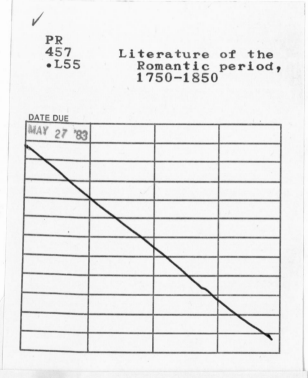

DATE DUE

MAY 27 '83			

Literature
of the Romantic
Period
1750-1850

ENGLISH TEXTS AND STUDIES

General editor: PHILIP EDWARDS

Literature of the Romantic Period

1750-1850

EDITED BY R.T.DAVIES
AND B.G.BEATTY

*Department of English Literature
in the University of Liverpool*

BARNES & NOBLE BOOKS · NEW YORK
A division of Harper and Row Publishers, Inc.

Published in the U.S.A. 1976 by
HARPER & ROW PUBLISHERS, INC.
BARNES & NOBLE IMPORT DIVISION

ISBN 0-06-491614-6

First published 1976

SET IN MONOTYPE BASKERVILLE BY
THE LANCASHIRE TYPESETTING COMPANY LIMITED, BOLTON
PRINTED AND BOUND IN GREAT BRITAIN AT
THE ALDEN PRESS, OXFORD

This volume is dedicated to
KENNETH MUIR
by his former colleagues in honour of a
distinguished scholar, critic and teacher,
and in gratitude for his kind leadership and
counsel in the exceptionally happy department
over which he presided for twenty-three years.

Preface

This volume offers a variety of approaches to the literature of
of the Romantic period in England and Scotland. Most of the
essays centre in what are customarily accounted the Romantic
decades, 1790–1830: that some give a sense of the antecedents
and consequences of Romantic writing explains the larger
period defined in the title. Individual essays aim to be of use to
those with specific interests in particular aspects of the period,
and the collection as a whole invites, and should promote,
enquiry into the problem of the homogeneity of Romantic
literature.

The reader may welcome an outline of the topics discussed.
In the opening essay, R. T. Davies explores some senses in
which Johnson and Boswell use the word *romantic* and some in
which it may be used of them. Nick Shrimpton is concerned
with the vexed question of the meaning and tone of the *Songs
of Innocence*: an answer emerges when the poems are seen in the
context of the eighteenth-century children's hymn. Vincent
Newey concentrates on two preoccupations of Wordsworth,
man's vulnerability and need of inner strength, in order to
establish a closer definition of his poetic personality. Brian
Nellist argues that Scott's Waverley Novels arbitrate between
the rival claims of novel and romance, and he maintains that,
especially in *Redgauntlet*, Scott tries to find some resolution of
this conflict in the irony and resigned acceptance of the
narrator's voice. It is the claim of N. F. Blake that a study of
Coleridge's diction suggests he never ceased to be a late
eighteenth-century poet. Hermione Lee examines the relationship between Jane Austen's satirical criticism of contemporary
fashions in taste, and her endorsement of the eighteenth-
century alignment between taste and morality which lay
behind such fashions; she pays particular attention to *Mansfield Park*. In an article based on early nineteenth-century
periodicals, N. W. Bawcutt sees the Romantic re-appraisal of
Shakespeare's contemporaries as leading to helpless admiration

rather than fruitful imitation of Elizabethan drama. Ann
Thompson discusses Shelley's political satire and the difficulty
it posed for the author (and still poses for the reader) of
reconciling Shelley's positive view of the poet's role with the
apparently negative nature of satire. Bernard Beatty makes
large claims for Byron's calculation as a thinker about the
nature and transmission of poetry: *Don Juan* and the Spenserian
stanzas of *Childe Harold's Pilgrimage* are Byron's attempts to
transmit an older poetic practice. Miriam Allott sees Keats and
Shelley travelling at a different pace to a similar rejection of the
Romantic dream: for example, although *Endymion* constitutes
a kind of reply to Shelley's 'Alastor', these two youthful
attempts to grapple with the dream have common features and
a common direction. It is the argument of S. J. Newman that,
in *Barnaby Rudge*, Dickens sought to resolve the conflicting
claims on his imagination of two great Romantic historical
writers, Scott and Carlyle, but that, in failing to achieve this
synthesis, he nevertheless established the foundation of his
mature art. Kenneth Allott, who had originally shared the
general editorship with Bernard Beatty, unhappily died early
in the preparation of this volume. His wife has devotedly undertaken the task of editing a lecture of his which, whilst quite
other in form and finish from the article which he would have
written, catches something of his sparkle and his authority in
this area. His glance at the 'worried art' of the major Victorian
poets, especially their difficulty as legatees of the neo-
Elizabethan diction of some Romantic poets, indicates the lines
he would have followed had he lived to write his projected
study of Victorian poetry.

The inspiration behind this volume is Kenneth Muir, one of
whose particular interests is the literature of the Romantic
period. Our enterprise will be more than justly rewarded if this
volume succeeds in taking its place among the writings on a
period to which Kenneth Muir has himself contributed with
such distinction.

Contents

Acknowledgements

The editors would like to thank their fellow contributors for their patience and ready co-operation, and also Joyce Bazire, Janet Montefiore, A. D. Mills, and N. Greene, and other members of the Department of English Literature who have encouraged the contributors with their company and by their wish to be associated with our congratulations and thanks to Kenneth Muir. We wish to thank in particular Professor J. E. Cross, head of the Department of English Language, and Professor P. W. Edwards, Kenneth Muir's successor as King Alfred Professor of English Literature in the University of Liverpool. We appreciate their generous advice and their help in the preparation of this volume.

We are particularly grateful to Dr. T. C. Thomas, Vice-Chancellor of Liverpool University, and to Professor E. G. White, Chairman of the Members of Liverpool University Press for their personal interest, and to the University of Liverpool for generous financial support which has made publication of this volume possible. From J. G. O'Kane and M. V. Holland, of the University Press, we have received most helpful professional advice.

We are grateful to our secretaries, Margaret Burton, who administers the School, Christine Moneypenny, and especially Joan Welford who typed the original drafts, deciphered the various corrections, and produced the final typescript.

Samuel Johnson, James Boswell, and the romantic

R.T.DAVIES

In this exploratory essay I shall be concerned with the romantic in various senses. Should the reader be led to conclude, however, that some things in Johnson anticipated, or distinguished him from, writers of the Romantic age proper, my essay will have served a further useful but incidental purpose.

Sitting on a bank 'in the bosom of the Highlands', on 1 September 1773, 'such as a writer of Romance might have delighted to feign', Johnson so passed the time that he modestly wondered a year or so later, as he recounted his experience in *A Journey to the Western Islands of Scotland*, 'whether I spent the hour well . . . for here I first conceived the thought of this narration'.

I had indeed no trees to whisper over my head, but a clear rivulet streamed at my feet. The day was calm, the air soft, and all was rudeness, silence and solitude. Before me, and on either side, were high hills, which by hindering the eye from ranging, forced the mind to find entertainment for itself.[1]

Within two or three weeks of this experience he had written about it in a letter to Mrs Thrale:

I sat down to take notes on a green bank, with a small stream running at my feet, in the midst of savage solitude, with Mountains before me, and on either hand covered with heath. I looked round me, and wondered that I was not more affected, but the mind is not at all times equally ready to be put in motion. If my Mistress, and Master, and Queeney had been there we should have produced some reflections among us either poetical or philosophical, for though *Solitude* be *the nurse of woe*, conversation is often the parent of remarks and discoveries.[2]

1. R. W. Chapman (ed.), *Journey to the Western Islands of Scotland* (Oxford, 1924) [*Journey*], pp. 33, 35. Throughout this book the word in square brackets following the first full mention of a work is that by which subsequent reference will be made.

2. R. W. Chapman (ed.), *The Letters of Samuel Johnson* (Oxford, 1952), 3 vols [*Letters*], no. 326.

I

What we learn clearly from the letter is what is only half said in the *Journey*: the romantic spot had not much moved him. More than that, he wondered that it had not done so. In his account of the same Scottish travels, Boswell said that he had 'a notion that [Johnson] at no time has had much taste for rural beauties';[3] and the lightly sardonic representation in *Rambler*, no. 135, of summer in the country, for 'the greater part of those who waste' it there, as no occasion for 'loitering in woods or plucking daisies' but rather, at best, a repetition in a different and less convenient place of the social pleasures of the town, is certainly rooted in Johnson's own experience: Boswell, with characteristic percipience, observed that Johnson's 'melancholy mind required the dissipation of quick successive variety', so that living in the country he 'had habituated himself to consider as a kind of mental imprisonment'.[4] But, had the Thrales been with him among the inhibiting Scottish hills, in such animated company all four would have found themselves full of ideas and observations, 'poetical or philosophical', whereas, left alone, he was made to realize yet again that he never received 'instantaneous infusions of wisdom from the Dryads'.[5]

It could well be said that it is a Johnson who is the object of Wordsworth's 'The Tables Turned'. The 'spontaneous wisdom' commended in it, 'breathed by health,' the 'impulse from a vernal wood' that

> May teach you more of man,
> Of moral evil and of good
> Than all the sages can,

is what Johnson had no personal possibility of conceiving, let alone feeling on his own pulses. The Wordsworth of 'Expostulation and Reply' who sat half a day upon an old grey stone among the mountains of Esthwaite, feeding his mind in 'a wise passiveness', naturally appeared to the man of learning and will to be an idle dreamer, for a Johnson has had no experience of 'a heart that watches and receives', nor come to distinguish and value the 'feeling intellect', 'Imagination . . . but another name for . . . reason in her most exalted mood'.[6]

3. G. B. Hill (ed.) and L. F. Powell (rev.), *Boswell's Life of Johnson* (Oxford, 1934–50), 6 vols [*Life*], v. 112 and cf. i. 461.
4. *Life*, iv. 338.   5. *Rambler*, no. 135.
6. *The Prelude* (1805–6), xiii. 205, 167–70.

'The mind is not at all times equally ready to be put in motion', said Johnson, and, to arouse it on the romantic bank in a Scottish glen, his recourse was to animated and sympathetic company. His object was intellectual and cultivated, to 'produce some reflections'. The part the Thrales would have played is further developed in a letter about another occasion in the Hebrides, when he does not talk of repairing his psychic immobility in terms of deepening his feelings, opening his heart, dispelling his mood or even correcting his taste, but entirely in terms of 'attention', 'observation', 'conversation', all intellectual, active, and more or less willed.[7] What he looks for is help in applying his mind, just as, having suffered a stroke, his first thought after prayer was to 'try the integrity of my faculties' by translating the prayer into Latin verses.[8]

What Johnson does not contemplate is the kind of experience Boswell describes himself enjoying in Iona. Typically, Johnson was 'inspecting and measuring several of the ruins', so that, says Boswell,

my mind was quiescent; and I resolved to stroll among them at my ease, to take no trouble to investigate minutely, and only receive the general impression of solemn antiquity, and the particular ideas of such objects as should of themselves strike my attention.[9]

Such acceptance of mental quiescence is inconceivable in Johnson, liable, rather, to Wordsworth's criticism of the man of 'meddling intellect' who 'murders to dissect', or, as he inspects and measures the revered ruins of an ancient culture, of the 'philosopher' who is

> a fingering slave,
> One that would peep and botanize
> Upon his mother's grave.[10]

Breakfast followed the early morning tour of the antiquities of Iona, but Boswell 'stole back again to the cathedral, to indulge in solitude and devout meditation'.[11] Boswell's self-knowledge and candour is invariably impressive: had Johnson realized what he was doing he would have been censorious. But his reference to Boswell's reaction in general is neutral and, like Boswell and any other eighteenth-century man of sensibility,

7. *Letters*, no. 329.   8. *Letters*, no. 850.   9. *Life*, v. 335.
10. 'The Tables Turned'; 'A Poet's Epitaph'.   11. *Life*, v. 336–7.

he himself twice makes reflections in his *Journey* on these solemn scenes:

We now left those illustrious ruins, by which Mr *Boswell* was much affected, nor would I willingly be thought to have looked upon them without some emotion. Perhaps, in the revolutions of the world, *Iona* may be sometime again the instructress of the Western Regions.[12]

In this conspicuously indirect reference to his own reaction he does not tell us what emotion it is he would not wish to be thought to have lacked, and, in the final, nobly reflective sentence, only partly suggests what it might be. In no way does he cause us to feel the emotion. The reason for this may be quite simple and give rise in so honest a man to his roundabout way of speaking: he may, in fact, have felt no emotion at all. Boswell said that Johnson was no less affected than he was:[13] but when Johnson visited St Andrews, though he was moved to see the University at that time 'pining in decay and struggling for life [which] fills the mind with mournful images and ineffectual wishes', he said,

Had the University been destroyed two centuries ago, we should not have regretted it [for] the distance of a calamity from the present time seems to preclude the mind from contact or sympathy.[14]

In his other reflective passage on the ruins of Iona his reference to the emotion that should be felt is pompously circuitous and again communicates little or nothing of it, though it may be important that the sentence is of a piece with what we shall observe later[15] to be the other grandly rhetorical turns of phrase:

Far from me and from my friends, be such frigid philosophy as may conduct us indifferent and unmoved over any ground which has been dignified by wisdom, bravery, or virtue.[16]

If we may regard 'dignified by wisdom, bravery, or virtue' as affirmative or positive, then the greater part of the sentence is, significantly, couched in terms of denial or negation, 'Far from me', 'frigid philosophy', 'indifferent and unmoved'.

There are, then, some reasons for thinking that Johnson realized he was sometimes deficient in appropriate feeling, and that he was not altogether at ease that this was so.[17] Even when

12. *Journey*, p. 138.   13. *Life*, v. 334.   14. *Journey*, p. 8.
15. p. 11.   16. *Journey*, pp. 134–5.
17. Cf. Coleridge's 'Dejection': 'I see, not feel, how beautiful they are', etc.

the description of the romantic scenery, as he rode through the night to Inverary, communicates more feeling than most, he suggests no abandonment to it. Instead he records how he again applied his mind by counting the torrential streams. The action was typical of his obsessive temperament,[18] and, presumably, the knowledge of how many streams there were augmented for such a man the feeling aroused by them, but use his mind he did.

On the other hand, in the paragraph of reflections which follows the description of the Highland bank that a writer of romance might have delighted to feign, 'imaginations' are said to be

excited by the view of an unknown and untravelled wilderness . . . The phantoms which haunt a desert are want, and misery, and danger; the evils of dereliction rush upon the thoughts; man is made unwillingly acquainted with his own weakness.[19]

If these were the gloomy traffic of his mind on that occasion it is no wonder that he wished the Thrales had been there to draw him out of himself: but we cannot be sure that these reflections did not, instead, come to his mind as he was writing his *Journey*. In any case, the important thing is that he is not here applying his mind, for imaginations are being 'excited' and evils 'rush upon' the thoughts. Perhaps we are here brought quite close to a state of his mind which explains why Johnson strove always for control of it or to fly from it and why he could not be passive or quiescent, watchful or receptive. 'The great business of his life', so Boswell reported that Johnson had told Sir Joshua Reynolds, 'was to escape from himself; this disposition he considered as the disease of his mind, which nothing cured but company.'[20]

Johnson's dynamic understanding of his own mental pathology was in countless respects remarkable, and, in all likelihood, in part, self-healing. Take, for example, the disquisition by Imlac in *Rasselas*, chapter 44, which will recall several of the Johnsonian characteristics we have been observing.

Disorders of intellect . . . happen much more often than superficial observers will easily believe . . . There is no man whose imagination does not sometimes predominate over his reason, who can regulate his attention wholly by his will, and whose ideas will come and go at his command . . . All power of fancy over reason is a degree of insanity; . . . it is not pronounced madness but when it comes un-governable . . . To indulge the power of fiction and send imagination out upon the wing is often the sport of those who delight too much in silent speculation . . . He who has nothing external that can divert him must find pleasure in his own thoughts, and must conceive him-self what he is not; for who is pleased with what he is? . . . fictions begin to operate as realities.

This passage helps us to understand why Johnson felt so ill-at-ease in the romantic spot in the Highlands. Bearing in mind his particular symptoms, it also helps us to understand why he could not tolerate any romanticization of melancholy, madness, or imagination. So too, does a letter of 1754 to Thomas Warton, written two years after the death of his wife. It is about his con-tinued suffering because of it: a man who writes thus is unlikely to romanticize the image of the outsider, so popular in our own day.

I have ever since seemed to myself broken off from mankind [,] a kind of solitary wanderer in the wild of life, without any certain direction, or fixed point of view. A gloomy gazer on a World to which I have little relation. Yet I would endeavour by the help of you and your brother to supply the want of closer union by friendship.[21]

I know no earlier description of such a psychic condition and certainly not of one following the death of a wife. It seems to me possible that what Johnson sees in himself is filtered through such traditional images as those of Cain or of the Wandering Jew, but, even if this is so, the total representation of desolate, personal alienation entirely subsumes them. In this private letter to a friend one feels no trace of that uneasiness we have so far sensed in Johnson's references to his emotions, let alone any sign that he had difficulty in conveying them. He opens his heart and speaks as directly and simply as anyone can, so that what he does here with utter convincingness enables us, by comparison, to see better the nature of what he does or does not do elsewhere.

Such a comparison between this letter and *The Vanity of Human Wishes* tends to confirm a sense one has in reading the poem. Time has supported the approval given it by Byron who

21. *Letters*, no. 56.

called it 'a grand poem—and so *true*!' and by Scott who said 'that he had more pleasure in reading *London*, and *The Vanity of Human Wishes*, than any other poetical composition he could mention'.[22] And it is obvious that no simple comparison of two kinds of literature so different as a personal letter and an imitation of a Juvenalian satire can be made with propriety or, unless we are quite clear about the limitations of what we are doing, to any critical advantage. One may wonder, however, whether the letter does not throw into relief what may be an element of romanticization in the poem, whether there is not, in the poem, such a relish for the illustration of its theme as is unwarranted, morally or aesthetically. The theme is the negative one of life's hopeless emptiness (except, of course, as only the concluding lines say, in relation to Christian faith), but effective examples of it are worked up with an elaborate oratorical positiveness that conveys pleasure in the successful preaching, and with a poetical sensuousness that, to a degree, suggests these sad instances are substantially savoured. The inflated magniloquence of the first two lines may point in this direction. In them Johnson is, of course, aiming at 'the grandeur of generality'[23] as well as establishing his characteristically magisterial mode, and any artist might be forgiven for a false step or two at the outset of his work. But one wonders whether what is defective in these lines, the conspicuous disproportion of expression to content, does not adumbrate what we are suggesting may be felt as soon as this major poem gets so splendidly under way, its romanticization of the theme.

The point I am trying to make will, perhaps, be made better if we turn to a work of Johnson's in which the same theme is treated quite differently. That Johnson might himself have acknowledged my point is there suggested by the way he represents with quiet irony the amusement which, in chapter 2, the discontented Rasselas finds in the plaintive utterance of observations

that discovered him to feel some complacence in his own perspicacity and to receive some solace of the miseries of life from consciousness of the delicacy with which he felt and the eloquence with which he bewailed them.

22. Quoted in *Life*, i. 193–4, n. 3.
23. G. B. Hill (ed.), *Lives of the English Poets* (Oxford, 1905), 3 vols [*Lives*], i. 21, 45.

But what is more important is that, in *Rasselas*, the theme of the deflation of all human aspiration and endeavour is matched by the deflation of the style. Occasions which the rhetorician might consider it appropriate to play up in order to move our hearts, the better to persuade us, or the novelist to develop in order to make his world more real, the more richly to involve us, are underplayed and undeveloped. To the artist, eager to make the most of his materials, what episode would be more stimulating than that of chapter 6 in which the mechanist fails to fly? But the greater part of the chapter called 'A dissertation on the art of flying' comprises unexcited talk about flying in the abstract, and such action as there is, and such mention (let alone representation) of the aviator's feelings of expectation and disappointment, is entirely contained in the last paragraph, and even then there is no more description of the actual attempt to fly in its positive aspects than in the twenty-seven words,

on a morning appointed, the maker appeared furnished for flight on a little promontory; he waved his pinions awhile to gather air, then leaped from his stand.

It would be hard to write more emptily of empty endeavour. Its uselessness is immediately confirmed in words equally undramatic: 'in an instant [he] dropped into the lake'. Even the irony of the final sentence is not pointed up and sharpened but allowed to speak for itself in neutral terms:

His wings, which were of no use in the air, sustained him in the water; and the Prince drew him to land half dead with terrour and vexation.

So it is again when Rasselas and Imlac, in chapters 13 and 14, dig their way out of the Happy Valley. The account is bare of almost all physical detail so that the achieving of their incredible feat has little reality for us: it is treated as the irrelevance it is. What are relevant, and what are treated at length, always with incisive turns of phrase and often with care for picturesque detail, are the moral observations of the aristocratic labourers. Thus, when they are made, in twenty-nine words, to discover 'a fissure in the rock, which enabled them to pass far with very little obstruction', it is the cue for Imlac to expatiate in seventy-eight words on the proper way to respond to such a pleasing surprise, and to conclude with the elegant aphorism, 'Many things difficult to design prove easy to performance'. Moralizing of this kind came to Johnson naturally and at every opportunity: the telling of a gripping tale did not.

If *The Vanity of Human Wishes* is Johnson's most romantic work, *Rasselas* is his most unromantic. Repeatedly and consistently it represents and acts out the flattening of human hope, joy, ambition, effort, and success. As we have seen, Rasselas himself is not allowed, without ironic comment, even the poet's consolation of eloquence and self-knowledge as he articulates his disquiet. And, though almost every point that Imlac makes about poetry in chapter 10 could be supported from Johnson's other writings, so that one can say that his dissertation is as much Johnson's as his, this noble and compelling defence ends with a gently deflating, ironic detachment from Imlac, on the part of both the narrator and the Prince, that points in some degree to Johnson's own inability to sustain without scepticism his belief in being a literary man as it does also to the way Imlac is carried by his ridiculous 'enthusiasm' beyond Johnson's own reasonable opinion of the poet's role.

There are in the *Journey to the Western Islands* further instances of such deflation or reduction. It was in no state of spiritless depression, in this work any more than in the earlier, that Johnson wrote with light and springy self-deprecation of hardships crossing the sea to Mull.[24] Such making light of an experience that could have been written up and treated as an emotional drama is very frequent in the *Journey*. It is, in part, of course, evidence of that quality in Johnson which so much impressed his wife-to-be on their first meeting: 'this is the most sensible man that I ever saw in my life'.[25] This is the *sense* as opposed to the *sensibility* of Jane Austen's novel. But it is, also, in part, a reaction specifically in a literary context: Johnson is aware with what exaggerated feeling he thinks such an episode might be described in a romance and is adjusting down what he has to say in relation to that expectation. The same literary reference modifies the experience described in the passage with which this essay began, sitting on the bank 'such as a writer of Romance might have delighted to feign'.

Another kind of adjustment occurs in the description of the visit to Slanes Castle.

24. *Journey*, pp. 108–9.   25. *Life*, i. 95.

We came in the afternoon to Slanes Castle, built upon the margin of the sea, so that the walls of one of the towers seem only a continua-tion of a perpendicular rock, the foot of which is beaten by the waves. To walk round the house seemed impracticable. From the windows the eye wanders over the sea that separates Scotland from Norway, and when the winds beat with violence must enjoy all the terrifick grandeur of the tempestuous ocean. I would not for my amusement wish for a storm; but as storms, whether wished or not, will sometimes happen, I may say, without violation of humanity, that I should willingly look out upon them from Slanes Castle.[26]

In this passage, though the subject is singular and wonderful, up to 'Norway' the description is plain and flat: the reader is not stirred nor is he caused to see the phenomenon. The verb 'seem' occurs twice, of all the words used the one with the most potential resonance, whereas in practice it reduces effect by pointing out illusion. Not for Johnson any attempt at generating a willing suspension of disbelief! From 'Norway' to 'ocean', the generalized, semi-poetic words 'terrifick', 'grandeur', and 'tempestuous' are all, to a degree, appropriately suggestive but have none of that particularity whose incomprehensible magic could make the object real.[27] In the last third of the passage two things are important, the modest and humane reservation, which is significant for having been made at all quite apart from what the reservation is, and the giving to the experience of the storm no loftier name than that of an amusement. In what, of course, are a traveller's records, the storm is not claimed, in the manner of poets such as Thomson, Blake, Wordsworth, or Shelley, to be educative, symbolic, or revelatory: Johnson has to make an adjustment because of his inhibited sense that the experience would be only an entertainment, and the reservation then made, that for such a purpose one should not incon-venience other human beings, follows most properly.

Such humanity, honesty, good sense, and ordinariness are, of course, evinced by Johnson time and again.[28] But passages evincing them are often characteristic of the *Journey* in the aspect I am considering, in that, with various effects as we have seen, an undertow repeatedly pulls the swelling spirit down.

26. *Journey*, pp. 16–17.

27. How much of the detail of ocean and storm would Johnson's bad eye-sight have permitted him to see? But he could make distinctions in this sphere and is not merely conventional: cf. *Letters*, no. 326.

28. Cf. *Journey*, pp. 127–8.

Even where Johnson is obviously and frequently thrilled and fascinated by the contrast of wilderness and civilization, for example in the household of the Laird of Raasay set in the barren waste, so that 'Romance does not often exhibit a scene that strikes the imagination more', he writes about it with only the usual limited detail, the usual generalities and abstractions, and the typically literary image.[29] Even here, where he does seem momentarily to escape the undertow, the only feeling directly mentioned, and that once only, is delight. One thing the passage lacks is demonstrated by a comparison with an earlier description of the same phenomenon when he found that a

general air of festivity . . . so far remote from all those regions which the mind has been used to contemplate as the mansions of pleasure, struck the imagination with a delightful surprise, analogous to that which is felt at an unexpected emersion from darkness into light.[30]

That final image gives the writing a rare extra dimension, just as another such does in this passage about Skye where frustration and resentment have found full, sardonic expression without inhibition or stylistic reduction:

No part that I have seen is plain [:] you are always climbing or descending, and every step is upon rock or mire. A walk upon plowed ground in England is a dance upon carpets, compared to the toilsome drudgery, of wandering in Skie.[31]

An expansive passage which Boswell esteemed is, however, of a very different character. It is one of a number in which Johnson is obviously writing more ambitiously, not only in that its reflections are lofty and noble but also in that high rhetoric is conspicuous in its style. Boswell called it 'sublime' and reported that the 'present respectable President of the Royal Society was so much struck on reading it, that he clasped his hands together, and remained for some time in an attitude of silent admiration'.[32] It is that passage about Iona in which Johnson wrote of his sentiments on walking 'over any ground which has been dignified by wisdom, bravery or virtue'.[33] Such set-pieces stand out, and the reaction of Boswell and the enrapt President

29. *Journey*, pp. 129 and 59: cf. *Letters*, no. 326, and, in no. 332, the quotation from Pope's 'Eloisa to Abelard' (l. 134) when the ladies read the evening service at Inch Kenneth (cf. Milton's *Paradise Lost*, iv. 131 ff., and Isaiah 51:3). 30. *Journey*, pp. 52–53. 31. *Letters*, no. 326. 32. *Life*, v. 334, n. 1. 33. *Journey*, pp. 134–5; cf. p. 4 above.

point to their nature: they are the performance by Johnson of what is expected of him as the supremely great writer and moralist. Something in him compelled him to act this part and something in his public made them look for it from him, even though in the complexity of his soul something quite as powerful resisted it and, sometimes perversely, was partly responsible for the reductive passages we have examined. Though it may also be that Johnson, is, in his flat, reductive mode, denying what Boswell recorded was the typical character of his conversation, that it 'teemed with point and imagery', and what Boswell said of his mind in general, that it 'was so full of imagery that he might have been perpetually a poet',[34] I certainly see no reason to think that Johnson associates such imaginative amplitude and fecundity with the romances themselves, nor that he eschews it as he eschews their other wild extravagances.[35] Indeed, Boswell records his saying that one good reason for reading romances is their 'beauty of style and expression'.[36]

There were other 'good reasons for reading romances; as— the fertility of invention, . . . the curiosity of seeing with what kind of performances the age and country in which they were written was delighted: for . . . the people were in a barbarous state'. Here he describes them as 'very wild improbable tales', and, in his *Dictionary*, defines *romance* under two heads, 'A military fable of the middle ages; a tale of wild adventures in war and love', and 'A lie, a fiction. In common speech.' What Johnson so defined he himself read both as a child and as an adult, and Boswell reports Bishop Percy's information that he had heard 'him attribute to these extravagant fictions that unsettled turn of mind which prevented his ever fixing in any profession'.[37] According to Mrs Thrale, Dr Levett said that Johnson's wife, too, was fond of romances and, in her case, was always reading them in bed.[38] It is clear that Johnson, never-

34. *Life*, iii. 260; iv. 428.
35. Cf. A. Johnston, *Enchanted Ground: The Study of Medieval Romance in the Eighteenth Century* (London, 1964) [Johnston], pp. 199, 201.
36. *Life*, iv. 17.
37. *Life*, i. 49, esp. n. 2; J. Hardy, 'Johnson and Don Bellianis', *RES* xvii (1966), pp. 297–9; Johnston, pp. 28 ff.; cf. *Rambler*, no. 4; *Journey*, p. 69; 'Preface to Shakespeare' in A. Sherbo (ed.), *Johnson on Shakespeare*, (New Haven and London, 1968), 2 vols [*Shakespeare*], pp. 64, 82.
38. K. C. Balderston (ed.), *Thraliana, the Diary of Mrs Hester Lynch Thrale, 1776–1809*, 2nd edn (Oxford, 1951), 2 vols, p. 178.

theless, regarded them as, properly, what they were in his day, children's reading.[39] Thus it is is logical for him to account for their popularity among adults of a previous age by saying that 'Nations, like individuals, have their infancy', whereas, in Johnson's own day,

A poet who should now make the whole action of his tragedy depend upon enchantment . . . would be . . . banished from the theatre to the nursery, and condemned to write fairy tales instead of tragedies,[40]

for no grown-up any longer believes in magic and fairies, or in gods and goddesses, and to adults in a Christian, refined, en-lightened, and rational age, they are all a bore. It is incon-ceivable that Johnson could sense the spiritual poverty of an increasingly commercial, materialistic, and scientific civilization which made Wordsworth cry that he would

rather be
A Pagan suckled in a creed outworn,

knowing again Proteus and Triton, than be so 'out of tune' with 'everything' that we find 'It moves us not', or that Johnson could feel and, even more, value, not only the uninhibited imaginative satisfaction of Keats in his re-creation of Endymion and Hyperion, but also his need of them as symbols in his philo-sophy. Like God for many a modern man, Proteus, Triton, Endymion, and Hyperion are, for Johnson, dead, and they have no more significance than rhetorical apparatus. Nor do we ever sense that he felt any inadequacy for what he wanted to say in such limited myth as he uses. In respect of symbols, his mode is that of the didactic allegory and with it he was content.

Whatever may have been Johnson's private pleasure in ro-mances—the evidence that he read them much as a grown-up is limited—his official attitude was uncomplimentary. He praised Fr Lobo's *Voyage to Abyssinia* because it was free from 'romantic absurdities or incredible fictions. Whatever he re-lates, whether true or not, is at least probable'; and he praised the fiction of his own day, the nascent novel, because it was free from the irresponsible 'incredibilities' of the 'heroic romance'.[41]

39. Cf. *Tatler*, no. 95.   40. *Shakespeare*, pp. 82, 752.
41. Fr Jerome Lobo's *Voyage* partly reprinted in R. T. Davies (ed.), Samuel Johnson, *Selected Writings* (London, 1965), pp. 71–72; *Rambler*, no. 4.

The remoteness of the romances from everyday reality, their 'extravagance of fancy', such as Addison admired in Shakespeare, was what Johnson found absurd. Not for him 'the fairy kind of writing which depends only upon the force of imagination', applauded by Dryden and which, according to Addison, brings 'into our memory the stories we have heard in our childhood and favour[s] those secret terrors and apprehensions to which the mind of man is naturally subject'.[42] It was precisely such effects that Johnson could not bear and against which he felt compelled in his own defence to exercise all the power of his intellect.

So he did, also, with respect to any extraordinary claim or remarkable fact. Thus Boswell could say in his *Tour to the Hebrides*, 'My easiness to give credit to what I heard in the course of our Tour was too great. Dr Johnson's peculiar accuracy of investigation detected much traditional fiction, and many gross mistakes.'[43] It was not that Johnson never felt the seduction of the extraordinary and incredible: he acknowledged, 'That which is strange is delightful, and a pleasing error is not willingly detected.'[44] But whatever pleasure he may have taken in the strange work of Macpherson and Chatterton, never mind how 'extraordinary' and 'wonderful' he felt Chatterton, 'the whelp', to be, neither was able to fool him.[45] It was not only that the increasingly fashionable taste in the bardic and twilit, the wild and medieval was as remote from his own as anything could be, and not only that he was the realist who kicked a stone to disprove Berkeley's idealism and, possessed by bad dreams and anxiety, made himself sit up in bed at night and put on the light, but also that, excellent (though amateur) lawyer that he was, and scholar, vastly learned and experienced, he knew the right questions to ask to elicit the convicting answers, and naturally asked them. Of the Highlanders he said percipiently and justly, 'They are not much accustomed to be interrogated by others; and seem never to have thought upon interrogating themselves.'[46] And, after all, such was his readiness to believe, when he considered he enjoyed the support of reason, that,

42. Dedication of *King Arthur* (1691); *Spectator*, no. 419.
43. *Life*, v. 336; cf. ii. 247.   44. *Journey*, p. 26.
45. *Journey*, pp. 106–7; *Letters*, no. 766; *Life*, iii. 50–51.
46. *Journey*, p. 106.

where such extraordinary matters as ghosts, miracles, and second sight were concerned, he was far from their spontaneous rejection, and such was his trust in reason that he could argue convincingly against rationalists.[47]

For Johnson what mattered was that it should be his own senses and his own reason that he had convinced with the result that the things he did and said bear his substantial, personal mark. Who but he would have written, 'The use of travelling is to regulate imagination by reality, and instead of thinking how things may be, to see them as they are.'[48] One could have forecast that no noble savages would have been found in Scotland by one who had asserted that 'Children are always cruel. Savages are always cruel', and that there 'can be nothing more false' than 'to argue for the superior happiness of the savage life'.[49]

Realism of this kind is Johnson's peculiar strength. In an Augustan age which one might have expected to be significantly dominated by a reverence for form and kind and propriety, by classical imitation, and the sophisticated refinement of conventional art, the greatest critic is primarily concerned with none of these things. The 'basis of all excellence', he writes, 'is truth', and there is no doubt what he means by that difficult word: 'he that professes love ought to feel its power. Petrarch was a real lover . . . Cowley . . . in reality was in love but once.'[50] If, despite what I have been claiming, for this once we set aside his superbly and uniquely authoritative formulation, what other is Johnson saying than is said by those so characteristic of our own age—which is sometimes argued to be suffering in this the degenerate consequences of the Romantic era—who profess no interest in technique or tradition or convention but passionately insist on the sincere, the personal, and the true? Johnson's one argument against those who criticize Shakespeare's mixed drama, neither tragic nor comic, but both, is that life is like that: it is mixed.[51] The appeal is not to form and precedent, the pleasures of the imagination or even the needs

47. *Life*, i. 444–5; ii. 150; iii. 188; *Journey*, pp. 97–100.
48. *Letters*, no. 326; cf. *Journey*, p. 28; *Letters*, no. 329.
49. *Life*, i. 437; ii, 11, 73–74, 228; iii. 49–50; iv. 210.
50. *Lives*, i. 6, and cf. 163.
51. *Shakespeare*, p. 66; cf., however, p. 80.

of instruction, but to truth. 'Fine fabling'[52] could not ever have been an ideal of Johnson's, not only because he was incapable of telling a story anyway and not only because of his fear of fantasy, but also because of his incapacity for creative or critical sophistication.

Thus it was, quite simply, to discover whether Homer and the romances were true that Johnson went to the Highlands and Hebrides. He wanted to see for himself a culture they had so far enabled him only to read about. Curiosity, always insatiable in Johnson, was to be entertained.[53] But, in particular, what fascinated him was the resemblance between what he found in the Highlands and Islands and in ancient and medieval literature. 'The fictions of the *Gothick* romances were not so remote from credibility as they are now thought', he concluded, and, unlike Addison, Hurd, and J. Warton, plainly found this evidence of unromantic realism gratifying.[54]

Intending to understand and assess a 'peculiar and discriminative form of life, of which the idea had delighted our imagination', he was disappointed to find that, following the Jacobite uprisings, Hanoverian government had destroyed most of what he sought: 'Such is the effect of the late regulations, that a longer journey than to the Highlands must be taken by him whose curiosity pants for savage virtues and barbarous grandeur.'[55] Yet, of course, mountains and sea were unchanged, and the changed culture that he found in their setting was still interesting because distinctive, and also because its problems were topically controversial and involved gentlemen in whose homes they stayed and whom Boswell knew. He examines why the Scots emigrate, he approves that good lairds are newly learning to farm from English examples, and praises the present skills of one laird in navigation and the domestic elegance of another. He neither patronizes nor scarifies. Boswell rightly quoted the opinion of his friend, Dempster:

There is nothing in the book . . . that a Scotchman need to take amiss. What he says of the country is true; and his observations on

52. R. Hurd, *Letters on Chivalry and Romance* (1762) [Hurd], Letter xii.

53. *Journey*, pp. 17, 97; *Letters*, no. 316; *Life*, iv. 133; *Letters*, no. 329.

54. *Journey*, p. 69 and cf. p. 141; *Spectator*, no. 419; Hurd, Letter x; *An Essay on the Genius and Writings of Pope* (1756).

55. *Journey*, pp. 100, 51, 35, 102.

the people are what must naturally occur to a sensible, observing, and reflecting inhabitant of a convenient metropolis, where a man on thirty pounds a year may be better accommodated with all the little wants of life, than Col or Sir Allan.[56]

Johnson even goes so far as to consider prudently whether it might not be wise to let the military spirit continue in so remote an area of empire as the Highlands, 'where it can commonly do little harm', for he questions 'whether the pride of riches must not sometimes have recourse to the protection of courage'.[57] It is for this expedient reason and no other that he asks 'whether', in its own defence, 'a great nation ought to be totally commercial?' Compromise and adaptation are what he looks for here, just as he did also in those parts of Scotland that, as a consequence of religious reformation, had suffered an 'epidemical enthusiasm' and then, as a consequence of intercourse with England, going to the other extreme, had suffered 'laxity of practice and indifference of opinion', and not yet achieved between them 'the middle point'.[58]

Compromise and adaptation are what circumstances continually effected in Johnson's own life, too. He was a man profoundly driven to excel, whose great and independent soul admired those with ambition to achieve the difficult and the original rather 'than those who never deviate from the common roads of action'.[59] But in the essay I have quoted, after he has illustrated what he means—'many valuable preparations of chemistry are supposed to have risen from unsuccessful inquiries after the grand elixir'—he goes on to accommodate his praise of the aspiring and unorthodox to his more usual mode not only of sense and propriety but also of balanced utterance: 'It is, therefore, just to encourage those who endeavour to enlarge the power of art, since they often succeed beyond expectation, and, when they fail, may sometimes benefit the world even by their miscarriages.' On the one occasion when he talks romantically of 'the dreams of a poet' he is referring to the exceptionally ambitious plans he had for making a dictionary, but we learn that his ideals proved in practice impossible so that he was 'doomed at last to wake a lexicographer'.[60] But what

56. *Life*, ii. 303.   57. *Journey*, p. 83.   58. *Journey*, p. 6.
59. *Adventurer*, no. 99, and cf. no. 138.
60. E. L. McAdam and G. Milne (eds), *Johnson's Dictionary, A Modern Selection* (London, 1963), p. 21.

scholar would mind waking to life's realities if he were to discover that he was to wake to Johnson's *Dictionary*?

One reality that Boswell never thought to see was Johnson himself in the flesh in a Scottish setting. When it happened, he called it 'romantick' because so 'improbable' and so 'wonderful', and described with what 'enthusiastick happiness' he anticipated seeing this unromantic figure 'walking among the romantick rocks and woods of my ancestors at Auchinleck'.[61] Johnson, too, appreciated, with irony, how incredibly incongruous was his presence in Scotland, and, whereas he had felt his fancy little affected by the wild scenery and the romantic bank with which we began, it was quite otherwise when this extraordinary thought about himself came to his mind!

You remember the Doge of Genoa who being asked what struck him most at the French Court, answered 'Myself.' I cannot think many things here more likely to affect the fancy, than to see Johnson ending his sixty fourth year in the wilderness of the Hebrides.[62]

---

61. *Life*, v. 347, 348; *romantick* (*rocks and woods*)—'wild, rough, such as in the romances'.

62. *Letters*, no. 329; cf. no. 323.

Hell's Hymnbook: Blake's *Songs of Innocence and of Experience* and their models

NICK SHRIMPTON

Blake's strangeness is of two kinds. There is first the strangeness of creative originality, of genius, a peculiarity which, in Eliot's words, 'is seen to be the peculiarity of all great poetry'. But even after we have made this recognition there remains an oddness. This second, enduring strangeness is one of form. Having come to realize that Blake's literary manner is not merely idiosyncratic and spontaneous we are left with the fact that the public and, in the best sense, conventional forms which he uses are now unfamiliar ones. We can sense the imaginative vitality of *The Marriage of Heaven and Hell* without knowing that it is an imitation of a Swedenborgian treatise. We cannot, however, properly understand or enjoy it without realizing that the form is not arbitrary but referential and that such reference is part of its meaning. Similarly our reading of the so-called Prophetic Books depends in important ways upon our appreciation of the extent to which their form is derived from the Ossianic epic or the Bible. As we begin to understand the nature and the contemporary currency of such modes we begin to appreciate how Blake uses them. Most important of all, because it is the least conspicuous and therefore potentially the most deceptive, we are beginning to understand the form of Blake's lyrics. They remain strange poems in my second sense if we come to them with expectations derived only from what the anthologies present as the mainstream of the English lyric. Diverse as that lyric form may be, and broadly as any general tradition must be conceived, the *Songs of Innocence and of Experience* still stand outside, still seem different.

The reason for this is simple. They spring from an exceptionally specialized branch of the lyric which happened to be
very active in the latter part of the eighteenth century: the
children's hymn. The genre can be traced back at least as far as
Bunyan, received its greatest impetus from Isaac Watts's *Divine
Songs Attempted in easy Language for the use of Children* (1715) and
subsequently flourished in the hands of such writers as Charles
Wesley (*Hymns for Children*, 1763),[1] Christopher Smart (*Hymns
for the Amusement of Children*, 1770), and Mrs Barbauld (*Hymns
in Prose for Children*, 1781). One of Blake's very few contemporary
reviewers, writing in the *Monthly Review* in October 1806, was,
however inept in other respects, at least in no doubt that the
literary company in which Blake's *Songs* should be set was that
of Dr Watts.[2] In terms of quality there is a great gap between
Blake and contemporary hymn-writers, but this does not mean
that, in so far as our response to the *Songs of Innocence and Experience* depends upon a correct sense of form, we can afford to
ignore this peculiar tradition. Accordingly there has in recent
years been no shortage of work upon this topic of the precise
genre of Blake's *Songs*. What is curious is that such work has
been undertaken in isolation from the very vexed question of
the meaning of the *Songs of Innocence and of Experience*, a question
which depends essentially upon the interpretation of certain of
the *Songs of Innocence* and the consequent tone of that book. I
would like to suggest that a reading of other poems of this particular kind can help us to understand what Blake is saying.

What I have called a tradition is itself twofold. John Holloway has both paid close attention to Blake's use of hymn metres
and usefully extended the comparison beyond the customary
authors to the hymns of Philip Doddridge.[3] But he simultaneously reminds us of the importance to Blake's poems of 'the

1. Wesley's 'Hymns for the Youngest' is sometimes cited as a separate
work. It is, in fact, simply a section of *Hymns for Children* (Hymns LXXII–
CV). Seven of the 'Hymns for the Youngest' (Hymns LXXII–LXXVIII)
had, however, appeared previously in *Hymns and Sacred Poems* (1742).

2. Reprinted in G. E. Bentley Jr, *Blake Records* (Oxford, 1969), p. 181.
The *Monthly Review* was, of course, commenting only on the selection of
Blake's poems printed in B. H. Malkin's introductory letter to his *A Father's
Memoirs of His Child* (London, 1806), which includes 'Laughing Song',
'Holy Thursday' (*Innocence*), 'The Divine Image', and 'The Tyger'. Malkin
himself initiates the comparison with Watts, though for purposes of contrast.

3. *Blake, The Lyric Poetry* (London, 1968) [*Lyric Poetry*].

impress of popular verse tradition'.[4] One might add that it is
not only Blake who draws on popular literature. All these hymn-
writers, particularly when they address children, deliberately
exploit a popular medium. General Booth was by no means the
first Christian to feel that the devil should not have all the best
tunes. In the last decades of the eighteenth century a flourishing popular form was being re-orchestrated by the godly with
extraordinary energy. In numerical terms the most startling
manifestation of this enthusiasm came in 1794 when Hannah
More founded the *Cheap Repository Tracts*, with the intention of
rescuing the new readers produced by Sunday schools from the
vulgarity of popular chapbooks and the subversive influence of
cheap editions of Paine. With characteristic thoroughness Miss
More assembled a collection of penny literature and imitated
the stories and ballads which she found there. She wrote to
Zachary Macaulay:

Vulgar and indecent penny books were always common, but speculative infidelity, brought down to the pockets and capacity of the
poor, forms a new aera in our history. This requires strong counter-
action.[5]

And to a Mrs Bouverie she explained her methods:

. . . it has occurred to me to write a variety of things somewhere
between vicious papers and hymns, for it is vain to write what people
will not read.[6]

Between 1795 and 1798 one hundred and fourteen tracts were
published, with phenomenal success. By the March of 1796
over two million copies had been sold. Hannah More had
achieved, in material terms at least, the supreme success in a
genre which had been active in other hands as well as hers
throughout the 1780s and 1790s, an art strenuously devoted to
religious and political persuasion and aimed with a significant
lack of discrimination at both children and the poor. Whether
Blake shared William Cobbett's ungallant opinion of Miss More

4. *Lyric Poetry*, p. 20.
5. Letter, 6 January 1795. William Roberts, *Memoirs of the Life and
Correspondence of Mrs Hannah More* (London, 1834), ii. 458. Quoted in
M. G. Jones, *Hannah More* (Cambridge, 1952), pp. 140–1.
6. Letter, 24 January, [1795]. Henrietta Georgiana, Lady Chatterton,
Memorials Personal and Historical of Admiral Lord Gambier G.C.B. (London,
1861), i. 275.

('an old bishop in petticoats') we do not know. What is certain, however, is that his decision to write children's hymns was not an eccentric one. It was a decision to participate in what was to be the most prolific and controversial literary form of the decade.

Our knowledge of this form provides an immediate explanation of Blake's choice of topics. The animal poem, the flower poem, and the insect poem were all traditional features of collections of children's verse, in which such objects functioned as moral exempla. Similarly Blake's poems about lost children are using a fairy-tale situation immensely popular in contemporary ballads.[7] Blake is not inventing, he is transforming a convention. And the word 'transforming' is important. He is not like his contemporaries simply exploiting a popular form for didactic purposes. Neither is he merely working in the popular medium. If one wanted a diagram it would have three stages: Blake is parodying the imitation of a popular form. But the parody, which is at the same time both mockingly derivative and seriously original, is a form very much his own. A great virtue of such a mode is that statements do not have to be made directly. Meaning can emerge from what is not said, from the disappointment of expectation, from the ways in which poems significantly do not altogether resemble their models.

A contemporary example can perhaps sharpen our sense of how such a literary stratagem works. In 1973 Charles Causley published a poem singularly apposite to the discussion of Blake's *Songs*, entitled *On Being Asked to Write a School Hymn*.[8] It goes, we are told, in a way in which Blake's contemporaries might not have needed telling, to the tune Buckland ('Loving Shepherd of Thy Sheep'). Causley's sheep are in the abattoir:

> On a starless night and still
> Underneath a sleeping hill
> Comes the cry of sheep and kine
> From the slaughter house to mine.

The form refers us to familiar ideas, the statement rejects them. The point that emerges from the specifically parodic aspect of the poem is that while the conventional symbolism of God as a

7. See, for example, *The Children in the Wood*, republished in V. E. Neuberg (ed.), *The Penny Histories* (Oxford, 1968).
8. *Sunday Times*, 21 October 1973.

shepherd provides a very effective manifestation of care and compassion it does so only at the cost of seriously distorting the nature of that God's involvement in the world: conventionally, the symbolism is truncated, the shepherd postpones the job of turning his sheep into cutlets. In Causley's poem a God who is present everywhere is present in the slaughterhouse:

> But who wields that knife and gun
> Does not strike the blow alone,
> And there is no place to stand
> Other than at his right hand.

A reader with no experience of English hymn-singing would doubtless find some meaning in the poem, although the verse form and diction might appear eccentric. But such a meaning would be a peculiar and limited one compared with that available to readers who have dutifully sung their way through *Hymns Ancient and Modern*. The situation is precisely analogous to that of Blake's *Songs*. The eighteenth-century children's hymn may now seem a negligible literary fossil, but its presence is essential to the life of Blake's poems.

Parody of this serious kind can work either by inclusion or by omission. Causley's method is inclusion: he puts into his poems facts about the world which more conventional users of the form choose to overlook. Blake's *Songs* use both inclusion of this kind and its reverse: significant omission of conventional details or attitudes. In the *Songs of Experience* Blake's inclusions or additions are obvious. But what are the differences that constitute so large a part of the meaning of the *Songs of Innocence*? On the face of it there has been no shortage of commentary. Vivian de Sola Pinto has set 'A Little Boy Lost' against Watts's Song XXIII with the suggestion that Blake's poem is surely intended as a reply to the 'fierce Old Testament morality' of this reproach to childish misbehaviour.[9] D. V. Erdman has compared Mrs Barbauld's *Hymns in Prose* with Blake's poems, suggesting rather unspecifically that Blake echoes them with gently parodic intention.[10] M. W. England has compared Blake and Wesley

9. 'William Blake, Isaac Watts, and Mrs Barbauld' in V. de S. Pinto (ed.), *The Divine Vision: Studies in the Poetry and Art of W. Blake* (London, 1957), p. 78.
10. *Blake, Prophet Against Empire: a Poet's Interpretation of the History of his Own Times* (Princeton, 1954) [*Blake, Prophet Against Empire*], pp. 113-15.

and in the process has suggested several differences between Blake and other writers.[11] Bunyan, Watts, and Mrs Barbauld she declares to 'abound in moralistic injunctions'. Watts and Bunyan are preoccupied with instilling a fear of hell. Smart and Mrs Barbauld present a world in which fear has no place at all. 'Blake', she declares, 'offered his little lambs no such bland and Rousseauistic picture of life. Certainly Wesley did not.' There remain, however, differences between Blake and Wesley. John Holloway indicates one of them simply by quoting a stanza from Wesley's 'Hymns for the Youngest':

> O Father, I am but a child,
>   My body is made of the earth,
> My nature, alas! is defiled,
>   And a sinner I was from my birth.[12]

An uneasy hesitation between children as a symbol of innocence and a conviction that children's nature 'is defiled' is an integral part of the tradition and is something that Blake's poems conspicuously omit. Holloway's own study of 'considered and intended difference' between Blake's work and that of his predecessors produces two main conclusions. First he argues that while other writers impose an adult morality upon children Blake was writing songs, '. . . such that, in a sense, they could come spontaneously from children'.[13] Secondly he suggests that while Blake retains the 'pastoral and beatific side' of the other writers' religious feelings he 'totally repudiates the sin-and-retribution side'.[14] How can these scattered judgements best be organized? Perhaps the least confusing method is to revert to my two categories of parody. Blake does omit 'sin-and-retribution' or 'fierce Old Testament morality' but it is important to recognize the way in which he does so. He presents pleasure as something self-justifying. There are a number of poems in the *Songs of Innocence*, most notably 'Spring' and 'Laughing Song', about which it is genuinely hard for critics to find anything to

11. 'Wesley's Hymns for Children and Blake's *Songs*' in M. W. England and J. Sparrow, *Hymns Unbidden: Donne, Herbert, Blake, Emily Dickinson and the Hymnographers* (New York, 1966) [*Hymns Unbidden*], p. 56.

12. Hymn C of *Hymns for Children* (see above, n. 1). G. Osborn (ed.), *The Poetical Works of John and Charles Wesley* (London, 1869), vi. 462. Quoted in *Lyric Poetry*, p. 49.

13. *Lyric Poetry*, p. 47.

14. Ibid., p. 52.

say. They seem simply expressions of mood. But in the context of the tradition we can see that to present this mood of pleasure without any attendant moralizing does in itself constitute the expression of a moral attitude. Children's hymns were written to improve children, not to celebrate their instinctive behaviour. Compare Blake's two poems with Watts's Song XX ('Against Idleness and Mischief'):

> In Works of Labour, or of Skill,
>   I would be busy too:
> For *Satan* finds some Mischief still
>   For idle Hands to do.

> In Books, or Work, or healthful Play,
>   Let my first years be past,
> That I may give for every Day
>   Some good Account at last.[15]

Even when Watts unbends sufficiently to write a poem supposedly praising play, as in his song 'Innocent Play', he is still essentially preaching. John Holloway suggests that Smart's poem 'Mirth' more nearly approaches Blake's *Songs* than almost anything else in the genre.[16] Yet even here there is an intrusion of a kind which significantly does not occur in 'Spring' or the 'Laughing Song':

> With white and crimson laughs the sky,
>   With birds the hedge-rows ring;
> To give the praise to God most high,
> And all the sulky fiends defy,
>   Is a most joyful thing.[17]

The difference also affects the way in which the traditional exempla, especially animals, are used. In most children's hymns animals simply perform ethical object lessons, either of dreadful warning ('Let Dogs delight to bark and bite') or of corrective encouragement like Watts's doves and lambs. Blake's animals do not come from this moral circus ring. The children in the 'Nurse's Song' of *Songs of Innocence* are not, for once, exhorted to improve themselves on the model of ideal

15. *Divine Songs Attempted in easy Language, for the use of Children*, 13th edn (1735) [*Divine Songs*], p. 29. I quote stanzas 3 and 4.

16. *Lyric Poetry*, pp. 49–51.

17. N. Callan (ed.), *The Collected Poems of Christopher Smart* (London, 1949), ii. 989.

birds and sheep. Rather they themselves use the behaviour of real sheep and real birds as an argument with which to contradict an adult opinion. The sheep endorse the children's instincts. And this omission of preaching involves a preliminary omission of the belief that children are unredeemed sinners. Children's instincts are significantly not reproved. Simultaneously the importance of children is actively heightened. Christ is so much identified with children that adults must feel humble. In 'A Cradle Song' the mother states:

> Sweet babe, once like thee,
> Thy maker lay and wept for me.[18]

'Wept' not just 'for thee' but 'for *me*'—the detail is minute, but the contrast with, say, Watts's 'A Cradle Hymn'[19] is marked. The lesson is for adults as well as for children.

Omission in fact adds up into an argument. What is more, the argument is one which strikes at the heart of the form in which it is presented. The children's hymn and the moralized ballad for the poor (forms which, as I suggested while discussing Hannah More's tracts, often overlap) were essentially designed to keep children and the poor in their place. The form is characteristically a repressive one. Blake's *Songs* were certainly written for children, though not exclusively so, but like all children's literature they had to be bought by adults who wished to teach or improve. Yet Blake's poems encourage children to believe their own instincts to be superior to any adult instruction. The poems implicitly reject the very act of teaching. A habitual customer of Mrs Barbauld or Miss More who, with educative intention, bought a copy of the *Songs of Innocence* for his children would have been the victim of a gigantic confidence trick, a trick fully worthy of a man who would write a Swedenborgian treatise in refutation of Swedenborg. At the end of that treatise, having already produced the Proverbs of Hell, Blake threatens to give us yet another inversion of a familiar form: 'The Bible of Hell.'[20] It is I think not altogether fanciful to suggest that in the *Songs of Innocence and of Experience* he is, in the same sense, offering us the children's hymns of Hell.

---

18. G. Keynes (ed.), *The Complete Writings of W. Blake, with Variant Readings*, 2nd edn (Oxford Standard Authors, London, 1972) [Keynes], p. 120.   19. *Divine Songs*, p. 47.   20. Keynes, p. 158.

I have not, however, yet mentioned the way in which Blake's *Songs of Innocence* are parodic by inclusion. The most useful example is the poem 'Night' and the most relevant comparison is here with Mrs Barbauld. Her *Hymns in Prose for Children* are designed to be devotional rather than doctrinal but that choice of emphasis is no excuse for the fact that when doctrine does emerge, as inevitably it must, it is heavily censored. Her fifth hymn is, like Blake's poem, about night. The difference between the two poems arises when they come to the question of the dangers of the night. Mrs Barbauld, as M. W. England has pointed out, pretends that such dangers do not really exist:

> You may sleep, for he never sleeps: you may close your eyes in safety, for his eye is always open to protect you.
> When the darkness is passed away . . . begin the day with praising God, who hath taken care of you through the night.[21]

In Blake's 'Night' the angels are equally protective but they are not always successful. As in Charles Causley's poem, suffering and death, which the form habitually ignores, are included. Blake presents, however simply, an unusually full version of one Christian explanation of pain. God does not protect us in this world, his consolation is a posthumous one:

> When wolves and tygers howl for prey,
> They pitying stand and weep;
> Seeking to drive their thirst away,
> And keep them from the sheep;
> But if they rush dreadful,
> The angels, most heedful,
> Recieve each mild spirit,
> New worlds to inherit.[22]

In the *Songs of Experience* Blake is to question the adequacy of this doctrine in 'The Tyger' and 'Ah! Sun-Flower'. In the *Songs of Innocence* he simply states the doctrine in full, an activity which seems unspectacular only as long as we are unaware of its literary context. Blake's statement raises questions which children's hymns normally attempt to suppress.

The scale of the questions thus raised brings one necessarily to the problem of the political poems, the poems upon which

21. A. L. B. (Mrs Anna Letitia Barbauld), *Hymns in Prose for Children*, 4th edn (London, 1787), p. 41.
22. Keynes, p. 119.

our conception of the structure and meaning of the *Songs of Innocence and of Experience* ultimately depends. In a sense, such division of Blake's poems by topic is misleading. Fundamentally they cohere around the single theme of protection. Blake's interest is in the relationship between protection and oppression, in asking at what point loving care becomes possession or tyranny. This act of protection underlies many different relationships: parent protects child (the paradigm), ruler protects subject, philanthropist protects pauper, priest protects believer, lover protects lover, God protects his creation. Once the *Songs of Experience* are added to the account the same acts become acts rather of oppression and domination. All Blake's *Songs*, however diverse their immediate topics, address themselves to this problem, with, I think, the single exception of the subsequently added 'To Tirzah'. None the less the surface topics remain diverse and one is politics, the relationship between ruler and ruled, between employer and employee. And at this point I think I should explain what I meant when I said initially that work on the genre of Blake's *Songs* had been undertaken in isolation from the question of their meaning. In view of my obvious debt to M. W. England and John Holloway in what I have said so far it may well be asked why I should make such a suggestion. The point is that these crucial political poems, above all 'The Chimney Sweeper' and 'Holy Thursday', have not, with the exception of a brief, and I think misleading, note by R. F. Gleckner,[23] been considered in the context of the hymn tradition.

A great deal has been written to show, by historical evidence, just how horrific was the treatment of chimney-sweeps and of children in Charity Schools. Such critics have assumed, quite justifiably, that Blake was in the 1780s fully aware of such facts, and they have then gone on to assume, with altogether less justification, that 'The Chimney Sweeper' and the 'Holy Thursday' of the *Songs of Innocence* are therefore ironic. How could a man who knew these things, the argument runs, have

23. 'Blake and Wesley', *Notes and Queries*, NS iii (1956), pp. 522–4. Gleckner compares the two 'Holy Thursday's with Wesley's hymns for charity children (eight hymns in *A Collection of Psalms and Hymns* (1741), which he attributes to John rather than to Charles Wesley. His argument, however, is for a simply ironic reading of the 'Holy Thursday' of *Innocence*, and in the course of it he seriously misrepresents D. V. Erdman's position.

uttered the pious and contented morals of these poems without ironic intention? The argument is supported by two important pieces of evidence. 'Holy Thursday' first appeared in the satirical *An Island in the Moon* in the mouth of the ridiculous Mr Obtuse Angle. Secondly, Blake continued for many years after the completion of the joint *Songs of Innocence and of Experience* to issue separate editions of the *Songs of Innocence*; which contradicts suggestions either that Blake simply changed his mind[24] or that he originally wrote the *Songs of Innocence* as a mere target for *Experience*. The objection to these ironic interpretations of the *Songs of Innocence* is essentially a literary one. Why, when you have written a work of subtle and brilliant irony, add a further section saying the same things in a manner which must by comparison seem lumberingly direct and explicit? I do not believe that the two books are merely repetitive. They offer, in Blake's own word, 'contraries'. 'Night' is not an ironic poem, though it is parodic in the sense that it makes implicit criticism of the inadequacies of conventional versions of what it has to say. Rather it gives a sincere and carefully complete account of what Blake believes to be the Christian position against which are subsequently set the views of 'The Tyger' and 'Ah! Sun-Flower'. All the *Songs*, in my opinion, including the political ones, present just such a tension between contradictory but independently coherent views. But what then, the question remains, is the independently coherent view expressed in 'The Chimney Sweeper' and the 'Holy Thursday' of *Innocence*? What makes it possible for Blake to go on issuing, without correction from a 'contrary', these seeming endorsements of a cruel social *status quo*?

D. V. Erdman has offered the most satisfying account of the way in which Blake's two sets of songs interact as 'contraries'. Discussing those Songs of Innocence which first appear in *An Island in the Moon* he observes that,

24. E. D. Hirsch has advanced a more sophisticated version of the biographical theory which outflanks this objection by positing not one but two changes of mind (*Innocence and Experience: An Introduction to Blake*, New Haven, 1964). Blake, he suggests, celebrates a suprasensible visionary faculty in *Innocence*, enters a phase of 'radical naturalism' for *Experience*, and then reverts to a belief in vision. The immediate objections to this theory must be firstly that it is questionable whether what we see in *Innocence* is 'vision' or simply the presentation of a conventional Christian position, and secondly that the theory is unable to explain 'The Chimney Sweeper' of *Innocence*. Hirsch has to dismiss the last line as 'a flaw'.

. . . the same songs removed from this matrix . . . are plainly not
presented as satire. Their social purpose is larger—to construct one
of the foundations of an imaginatively organized and truly happy
prosperity.[25]

He adds that Blake,

. . . having set out to present the obtuse view as something he could
see beyond . . . discovered through his own mockery that he could
see much *through* the shut eyes of 'the Good' who 'think not for themselves'.[26]

He adduces in support of this contention those annotations to
Lavater's *Aphorisms on Man* in which Blake calls true superstition 'ignorant honesty . . . beloved of god and man' and
praises Lavater's declaration that the saints of humanity are
those who practise unconscious goodness, 'heroes with infantine
simplicity'.[27] This goes a long way towards providing us with
an explanation of 'Holy Thursday'. The innocent speaker of
that poem is certainly simple. Quite apart from any abuses in
their management, the Charity Schools were more than a little
suspect in their claim to altruism. They were carefully designed
not to educate children above their station and thereby provided society with a steady supply of soldiers and domestic
servants. Yet Blake can celebrate the instinct of charity which
prompts the speaker's delight, however ill-informed that delight
may be. The speaker is profoundly wrong in his analysis of what
Charity Schools are like. But he is profoundly right in his naive
sense of what Charity Schools should be. And the 'Holy
Thursday' of the *Songs of Experience* confirms this reading. For
the logical structure of that poem depends at a crucial point
upon just such an innocent intimation. The declaration,

> For where-e'er the sun does shine,
> And where-e'er the rain does fall,
> Babe can never hunger there,
> Nor poverty the mind appall,[28]

is not a deduction from experience. On the contrary it flies in
the face of observed fact. The moral impulse is an instinctive
one and can express itself whether one is making the best or the

25. *Blake, Prophet Against Empire*, pp. 115–16.   26. Ibid., p. 116.
27. See Keynes, p. 75.   28. Keynes, p. 212.

worst interpretation of an existing institution or doctrine (that being the difference between the two 'Holy Thursday's as it is between so many of the directly contrary *Songs*). Yet convincing as Erdman's analysis may be we remain rather unclear as to just what this 'organized innocence' is that the *Songs of Innocence* are so sincerely advocating. In 'Holy Thursday' it is perhaps a question of the moral instinct. But what about 'The Chimney Sweeper'? Erdman states merely: '. . . all that the happy piper can provide for comfort is the inner warmth of faith'.[29] What does that mean? In what way can innocence here hold its own against the acute sociological analysis of *Experience?* It is here I think that the hymn tradition can once again help us.

The only book of Wesley's hymns which we certainly know Blake to have read is *Hymns for the Nation* (1782). His copy survives, autographed and dated: 'W Blake 1790'.[30] But whether or not he ever read Wesley's *Hymns for the use of Families and on Various Occasions* (1767) the book provides us with an illustration of contemporary attitudes which clarifies our understanding of 'The Chimney Sweeper'. The hymns in this collection which we now find hardest to accept are those designed for a group of people no longer found in the average family, the servants. But in 1767 servants were an inevitable part of a literate household and Wesley's hymnbook reflects the fact. Essentially these hymns suggest that servants are working not for their immediate, earthly master but rather for the God who has called them to their station:

> Come, let us anew
> Our calling pursue,
> Go forth with the sun,
> And rejoice as a giant our circuit to run:
> Whom Jesus commands
> To work with our hands,
> Obeying his word,
> We a service perform to our heavenly Lord.
>
> While we labour for Him
> And each moment redeem,
> His service we own
> Our freedom indeed, and our heaven begun:

29. *Blake, Prophet Against Empire*, p. 117.
30. See M. W. England, '*Hymns for the Nation* and *Milton*' in M. W. England and J. Sparrow, *Hymns Unbidden* (New York, 1966), p. 63.

> If he give us a smile
> We are paid for our toil,
> If our work He approve,
> 'Tis a work of the Lord, and a labour of love.[31]

If that seems startling then its effect is rapidly eclipsed by a subsequent hymn written for the servant who is subject to a tyrannous master:

> Lord, if Thou hast on me bestow'd
> A master, not humane and good,
>   But froward and severe,
> Assist the servant of thy will
> With grace and wisdom to fulfil
>   The Christian character.
>
> Trampled as dirt beneath his feet,
> O may I quietly submit
>   To all his stern decrees,
> Insults and wrongs in silence bear,
> And serve with conscientious care
>   Whom I can never please.
>
> Under the gauling iron yoke
> To Thee my only Help I look,
>   To Thee in secret groan:
> I cannot murmur or complain,
> But meekly all my griefs sustain
>   For thy dear sake alone.[32]

Our most immediate hostility to such writing probably springs from a suspicion that a self-interested upper class is cynically putting words into servants' mouths. Blake attempts to avoid this effect, and thereby to improve upon Wesley's expression, by making his poem a dramatic incident, a dialogue between chimney-sweeps in which morals are expressed by the class for whom they are intended. But before we simply condemn Wesley's work I would like to quote a single verse of another of the *Family Hymns*, no. LXXXV:

> Welcome incurable disease,
> Whate'er my gracious God decrees
> My happy choice I make,

31. Hymn CXXXIII ('Before Work'), stanzas 1 and 2: Charles Wesley, *Hymns for the use of Families and on Various Occasions* (Bristol, 1767) [*Family Hymns*], p. 140.
32. Hymn CXLI, stanzas 1–3: *Family Hymns*, p. 149.

Death's sentence in myself receive,
Since God a man of griefs did live,
And suffer for my sake.[33]

Our first response is probably laughter—it is not an attractive
piece of poetry, overstrenuous perhaps and indelicate. But such
laughter is largely an effect of shock and cannot long be justified.
For if in such a situation this hymn is a comfort, who are we to
withhold it? And the same thing can in fact be said of the hymns
for servants. It requires an effort of the historical imagination to
grasp how comforting a Methodist conversion must have been
for an eighteenth-century servant who one week was simply
serving 'A master, not humane and good' and the next was, in
his sincere belief, serving God. But that effort must I think be
made if we wish to understand Blake's 'The Chimney Sweeper'.
Of course Blake's poem, with brutal frankness, stresses the importance to such beliefs of reward in an after-life. But Blake is
also concerned with the active and present comfort brought by a
sense that labour, though arduous, is at least not pointless: in
Wesley's words, '. . . a work of the Lord, and a labour of love'.
We cannot, of course, call this a conventional belief, except in
the sense that it was part of the hymn convention that Blake
inherited. Such Wesleyan convictions were still in the 1780s
exceptional rather than customary. Blake is once again choosing
the best available defence of the *status quo,* just as he had given
the most generous interpretation of Charity Schools in 'Holy
Thursday' and the fullest version of one Christian explanation
of pain in 'Night'. Radicals, naturally, came to hate such
Methodist attempts to make the poor contented even more
violently than they hated the merely cynical or expedient defences of the social system (one thinks perhaps of Cobbett's
Sermon to Methodists)[34] and 'The Chimney Sweeper' of the
Songs of Experience expresses just this response. But such hatred
arises precisely because this is the most adequate defence of the
system, the only defence which itself incorporates something
humane and vital. With this belief one might well be harmed
but in a very real sense one need not, even in the extreme
circumstances of being a chimney-sweep, *'fear* harm'. Wesley
in the third stanza of Hymn CXXXIII makes the point
through paradox:

33. *Family Hymns*, p. 89.   34. *Political Register*, 13 January 1821.

> . . . . we cannot complain
> Of our daily delight as a wearisome pain.[35]

In this conception harm is a spiritual delight. Certainly this attitude is an acceptance of existing explanations—in the words of the unused 'Motto to the Songs of Innocence & of Experience',

> The Good are attracted by Men's perceptions,
> And Think not for themselves.[36]

But it is also the case that such attitudes when properly and fully articulated, when chosen in their best expression, are a response to the facts not an evasion of them. As Blake put it in that difficult note written in the margin of the manuscript of *The Four Zoas*:

> Innocence dwells with Wisdom, but never with Ignorance.[37]

Merely incomplete or evasive explanations of the world do not constitute 'Innocence'. The *Songs of Innocence* discriminate between the good and bad defences of the established order, presenting in their most adequate form those best defences which themselves incorporate something of value in the human spirit.

Blake's book is therefore both parodic and deeply serious. It makes constant reproachful reference to a literary tradition and in so far as it transforms the attitude to children which lies at the heart of that tradition it stands the form on its head. But in another sense Blake's *Songs of Innocence* simply do very well what most children's hymns had done badly. The *Songs* present the best possible defences and interpretations of the act of protection in its familial, religious, and political contexts, providing for example an account of the protection of children which, unusually, allows them free expression of their instincts (a conception much richer than the protective attitude which produces children's hymns). The strength of the arguments is essential to the achievement of a real tension between contraries. Yet I hope it is also now clear why it is that Blake could continue to issue the *Songs of Innocence* independently. Having chosen to work in a form which is characteristically devoted to

35. *Family Hymns*, p. 140.
36. Blake, *Note-Book* (*c.* 1793): Keynes: p. 183.
37. Keynes, p. 380.

the maintenance of the *status quo* Blake is in a sense conforming to its bias. But in doing so he is carefully setting very exacting standards for conservative argument. By making the best defences he suggests the inadequacy of the customary defences. We can, for example, accept the employment of children as chimney-sweeps if we, and they, seriously and consistently believe in a sacramental concept of work—but not otherwise. Even before the *Songs of Experience* are added to the debate, the implication that is beginning to emerge, by simple statement rather than by irony, is that if we cannot in fact have protection of this quality then perhaps we should not have 'protection' at all.

The steadfast self: an aspect of Wordsworth

VINCENT NEWEY

'I long for a repose that ever is the same.' ('Ode to Duty', 1804)

A sense of man's vulnerability to influxes of anxiety and disturbed emotion is recurrent in Wordsworth's poetry. It finds expression, for instance, at the end of the First Part of 'The Ruined Cottage'[1] where the Pedlar, reduced to sorrow by a specially painful memory, breaks off his story of tragedy:

> 'Tis now the hour of deepest noon.
> At this still season of repose and peace, . . .
> Why should a tear be in an old man's eye?
> Why should we thus with an untoward mind,
> And in the weakness of humanity,
> From natural wisdom turn our hearts away,
> To natural comfort shut our eyes and ears,
> And, feeding on disquiet, thus disturb
> The calm of Nature with our restless thoughts?
> (ll. 187–8, 192–8)

We are somewhat surprised to find this state of uncertainty and incipient grief in the Pedlar, though inasmuch as the speech insists upon the primacy of self-control and inward composure it is entirely in keeping with his character. The Pedlar has been presented from the outset as a figure of mature acceptance who

---

1. I refer to the version established from manuscript by Jonathan Wordsworth in his invaluable study *The Music of Humanity* (London, 1969) [*Humanity*], and to the text printed there at pp. 33–49. Composed in 1797–8, the poem gives the story of Margaret—later adapted as part of Book I of *The Excursion* (1814)—in what was probably its earliest completed form. For poems other than this and the related fragment 'The Pedlar' (in *Humanity*, pp. 172–83), references are to E. de Selincourt and H. Darbishire (eds), *The Poetical Works of William Wordsworth*, 5 vols (Oxford, 1940–9) [*Poetical Works*], and E. de Selincourt (ed.), *William Wordsworth, The Prelude*, 2nd edn, rev. H. Darbishire (Oxford, 1959). References to *The Prelude* are to the 1805 text.

can wholly, unfalteringly, embrace the bleakness and impene-
trable ironies of existence:

> We die, my Friend,
> Nor we alone, but that which each man loved
> And prized . . .   (ll. 68 ff.)

> Oh Sir, the good die first,
> And they whose hearts are dry as summer dust
> Burn to the socket. . . .   (ll. 96 ff.)

This tone, in which the pressure of feeling is balanced and
moderated by a wise philosophic detachment, typifies the
Pedlar's customary equanimity, and points to what Wordsworth terms elsewhere 'a just equipoise' in his inner life.[2] On a
symbolic level, in contrast to the young Poet's feverish wandering upon a 'bare wide Common' (ll. 18–26), the Pedlar is associated at once with images of calm, rest and contentment
(ll. 43–48). In the 'Pedlar' fragment in MS D of *The Excursion*
he is formally described as one 'serene . . . unvexed, unwarped',

> alive
> To all that was enjoyed where'er he went,
> And all that was endured; and in himself
> Happy, and quiet in his chearfulness,
> He had no painful pressure from within
> Which made him turn aside from wretchedness
> With coward fears.   (ll. 277–83)

But facing the tragic spectacles of life can never be as straightforward as this passage suggests. The significance of the moment
at the end of the First Part of 'The Ruined Cottage' is that it so
strikingly concedes the force and unreliability of the emotions.
There can be no absolute immunity from disquiet; even the
Pedlar, the exemplar of 'quiet . . . chearfulness', remains in
practice always threatened from within. At this point in the
poem his 'equipoise' is shown to be precarious: emphasis falls
upon his conscious need to surmount an innate 'weakness' and
upon the capacity to be steadfast and to reassert the worthier
side of one's personality.

Wordsworth was to remark late in his life that the Pedlar had
been 'an idea of what I fancied my own character might have
become in his circumstances'.[3] Clearly, within 'The Ruined

2. 'The Pedlar', l. 268.
3. Note dictated to Isabella Fenwick (1843) in *Poetical Works*, v. 373.

Cottage', if the Poet who reacts with 'heartfelt chillness' (l. 213) to Margaret's suffering, and has finally to be rescued from 'the impotence of grief' (l. 500), is an inadequate self that Wordsworth was himself striving to surpass, the Pedlar represents, in general, an ideal union of tenderness and strength, a sensitive but impregnable spirit, to which he aspired. By 1800, in 'Michael', Wordsworth was able, instinctively it seems, to display all the Pedlar's qualities in his own person. However, the matter is again not so simple. Just as the Pedlar, notably at the end of the First Part, has to reaffirm his stability, so Wordsworth had constantly to rediscover his own 'just equipoise' throughout his career. In 'Resolution and Independence', for example, two years after the apparently decisive self-confidence of 'Michael', we find him suddenly beset by an onslaught of despondency: the youthful Poet reappears, baffled and exposed, and must once more be admonished and surpassed. The assurance and self-possession that are main features of Wordsworth's poetic personality are something worked for rather than given. His poetry is at bottom a poetry of struggle. It is hardly surprising that he should have come openly to protest a desire for some inner state beyond all challenge, 'a repose that ever is the same'.

Whereas, then, one of Wordsworth's main themes is man's vulnerability to 'painful pressure from within'—pressure which can take many forms, whether of personal loss, vague despair, an impulsive or haunted awareness of suffering and death, or even, as in Margaret's case, too great a hope—a corollary is man's ability to contain and transcend it. Indeed, his poetry is a feat of that ability in Wordsworth himself. The restoration to the Pedlar of his usual 'easy chearfulness' at the opening of the Second Part of 'The Ruined Cottage' (ll. 200–4) might be interpreted as such a feat on a small scale—as an expression of faith in the 'wise' man's tenure of an abiding spiritual health and as an act of rationalization by which the poem can be continued, having been halted at an image of self-conscious disquiet, itself provoked by an image of cruel suffering, of Margaret's 'bleeding' heart. One remembers 'Incipient Madness' (?1795) where Wordsworth had actually lost himself in the morbid reflections of a 'sickly heart'—that of the poet-narrator—feeding its own desperate melancholy upon the misery of another, namely, the figure who was to become Margaret. The difference between this incoherent fragment and the poem which grew out of it brings home to us the crucial importance, both personal and poetic, of Wordsworth's ability to sustain a thorough steadfastness and resilience.

The conclusion of 'The Ruined Cottage' suggests that behind the Pedlar's equanimity lies ultimately an unquestioning faith in the inscrutable 'purposes of wisdom'. He thinks in terms of Nature's total pattern, the Beauty and Permanence of which Margaret has become a part:

> Be wise and chearful, and no longer read
> The forms of things with an unworthy eye.
> She sleeps in the calm earth, and peace is here.
> I well remember that those very plumes,
> Those weeds, and the high spear-grass on that wall,
> By mist and silent raindrops silvered o'er,
> As once I passed, did to my mind convey
> So still an image of tranquillity,
> So calm and still, and looked so beautiful
> Amid the uneasy thoughts which filled my mind,
> That what we feel of sorrow and despair
> From ruin and from change, and all the grief
> The passing shews of being leave behind,
> Appeared an idle dream that could not live
> Where meditation was. . . .   (ll. 510–24)

Poetically magnificent as this statement is, one cannot but view it at first with some suspicion: one cannot help seeing it as a '*retreat*' from "uneasy thoughts" '[4] and from the stern reality of Margaret's anguish within an oblivious, at times hostile, universe. Certainly, the emphases of the passage run counter to those of the tale itself. The Pedlar's description earlier of how 'nettles rot and adders sun themselves' on the spot where Margaret 'nursed / Her infant at her breast' (ll. 109–11) has already established very different impressions in respect of death, nature and 'the forms of things'—impressions of loss and decay, sinister invasion and humanity's defeat, a return to primeval desolation. Or, turning specifically to the human drama, there is the stunning poignancy of Margaret's helplessness at Robert's

4. David Perkins, *Wordsworth and the Poetry of Sincerity* (Cambridge, Mass., 1964), p. 116. Italics mine.

freakish treatment of their children, his mind deranged and
affections blighted by circumstances which are the result of
famine and war and which remind us of Hardy's malign Fate.
Her own bare utterance is adduced to mark the depth of her
torment:

> One while he would speak lightly of his babes
> And with a cruel tongue, and other times
> He played with them . . .
> . . . 'Every smile',
> Said Margaret to me here beneath these trees,
> 'Made my heart bleed.'   (ll. 179–81, 183–5)

It is here that the narrative is interrupted at the end of the First
Part.

The story of Margaret after Robert has left to enlist is still
more haunting, and compelling in its strenuous authenticity of
detail and psychological insight. On one level, her persistent
hope that Robert will return arouses our sympathy and awe at
the mystery of undying attachment to person and place: waiting
for Robert,

> in that broken arbor she would sit
> The idle length of half a summer's day; . . .
> And when a dog passed by she still would quit
> The shade and look abroad. (ll. 450–1, 453–4)

Our spirit clings to Margaret in an embrace of pity and respect.
She attains something of the stature of a tragic heroine, refusing
to be crushed by disappointment.[5] It is a fact, however, that her
life is a study much less in grandeur than in futility and long
affliction. What makes the tale so profoundly disconcerting, and
so Wordsworthian, is its relentless admission of the dreadful
paradox that in the very greatness of the heart lies man's most
serious point of vulnerability. In Margaret the finest feelings
become an irresistible, unmanageable, 'weakness'. Although
she is never judged, we see in her a fatal absence of that quality
of patience which brings Emily in 'The White Doe of Rylestone'
(1807) 'firm repose' (Dedication, l. 50), that 'strength of
Reason' which makes the later heroine 'lofty, calm and stable'
(ll. 1625–8). Whereas Emily is a 'bright, encouraging example'
(Dedication, l. 52), her history inspirational, Margaret's fate

5. See *Humanity*, pp. 151–2.

is, at least implicitly, a terrible warning, her love and hope leading to an atrophy of spirit, curiously restless, that spreads outwards to affect her surroundings and her child. In spite of self-rebuke she is powerless to stay the gradual negation of her worthier self:

'And so I waste my time: for I am changed,
And to myself,' she said, 'have done much wrong,
And to this helpless infant . . .'   (ll. 352–4)

                    In every act
Pertaining to her house affairs appeared
The careless stillness which a thinking mind
Gives to an idle matter.   (ll. 380–3)

All 'Bespoke a sleepy hand of negligence' (ll. 399–401). Even the detail of Robert's garments hanging on 'the self-same nail' (ll. 431–4), in which Jonathan Wordsworth identifies 'the greatness of Margaret's hope',[6] speaks, equally and with telling irony, of human frailty: the living hope which drives Margaret on also arrests life by placing her in the grip of the past and an illusory future, so constricting her wider sensibilities and powers of action. Her brooding infects the babe, who 'from its mother caught the trick of grief' (ll. 409–11), her longing hardens to a disease evermore 'in the distance shaping things / Which made her heart beat quick' (ll. 454–7).

There is for Margaret no enrichment of purpose, no final redemption, but rather an inexorable 'heart-wasting' (l. 449) which ends in a deadlock of passive agony:

                    the nightly damps
Did chill her breast, and in the stormy day
Her tattered clothes were ruffled by the wind
Even at the side of her own fire. . . .
      . . . and still that length of road,
And this rude bench, one torturing hope endeared,
Fast rooted at her heart.   (ll. 483–6, 488–90)

There is a sort of beauty in Margaret's continuing devotion to this 'wretched spot'; but there is also horror. It is noticeable that hope is now expressly a torture and takes all nourishment to itself from the heart's fertile ground. The word 'endeared' is so used as to suggest that the affections have themselves become

6. *Humanity*, p. 142.

agents of hope's tyranny, helping to fix Margaret to the place in lingering sickness of body and mind.

It is true that the subsequent image of Margaret at peace in the bosom of Nature and the translation of her history into abstractions ('ruin and . . . change') seem no more or less than a rhetorical manoeuvre aimed at distancing dark realities, a manoeuvre by which, if we believe Edward Bostetter, 'Wordsworth has . . . denied the truth of his artistic experience'.[7] But this view of the Pedlar's speech will not quite do. For one thing, the speech is in some ways true to what has gone before. At no stage is the poem pessimistic, this possibility being forestalled by the Pedlar's (and thus Wordsworth's) refusal ever to yield to despair. And despite the idea of antagonism in words like 'chill' (l. 484) there is at the same time a suggestion that Nature, in its ambiguous workings, is reducing Margaret in preparation for the release of death: Nature which sharpens her suffering also frees her from it by opposing due processes of decay to the unnatural hope that denies her rest. Seen from this angle the Pedlar's speech represents, not an unsatisfactory change of emphasis, but a careful shifting of viewpoint to bring in a welcome note of comfort. In any case, we can hardly accuse Wordsworth of facile optimism or unwarranted simplification. We are witnessing a moment in a drama rather than a preacherly intervention by the poet. The measured intentness of the verse and the way in which the speaker appeals to a special occasion in the past to endorse his attitude of superior wisdom reveal a mind under strain, having actively to summon its own resources even as it gives a lead to the Poet. The Pedlar is spokesman for a 'wise and chearful' faith upon which the poem places highest value; but he and his 'philosophy' are shown in a light that fully acknowledges the truths and complexities of life and experience, that rejects alike not only the inevitability of despair but also the notion of easy or conclusive consolations. The wisdom of the poetry is greater than the wisdom offered by the Pedlar. After all, although the speech—to adapt words of Coventry Patmore's—introduces a 'focus radiating . . . calm . . . throughout . . . the difficulties and disasters of surrounding fate',[8]

7. *The Romantic Ventriloquists* (Seattle, 1963), p. 65.
8. 'The Point of Rest in Art', *Principle in Art etc.* (London, 1890) [*Principle*], p. 41.

it only throws into further relief those brutal facts of suffering, desolation, and grief which it would so patently smooth and generalize by its procedures.

The effectiveness of 'The Ruined Cottage', typically of Wordsworth, derives from the inclusiveness of its vision, a vision which expresses necessary steadying perspectives without surrendering the thrust or distorting the insights of intuitive perception. To the end these insights, essentially tragic, are allowed, or rather claim, their proper weight. However, it is not enough to make the obvious point that 'The Ruined Cottage' is a supreme achievement in the narrative-dramatic mode. Its confessional dimension must be taken into account. In so far as the young Poet is Wordsworth himself the poem embodies an undertaking in self-appraisal. Simultaneously, via the Pedlar, Wordsworth is putting his own resilience to the test, until in the final speech he formulates an outlook which balances and lightens, but by no means banishes or defeats, that tense preoccupation with suffering, emotional instability and the seeming lack of just order in the universe which is concentrated at the centre of his reading of Margaret's life and character.

This outlook does in fact consist of two elements that often recur as sources of stability in Wordsworth's poetry: the first is a 'cheerful faith' ('Tintern Abbey', l. 133) in his personal wholeness and the harmony of all Nature, the second an appeal to past occasions on the grounds that 'diversity of strength / Attends us, if but once we have been strong' (*Prelude*, xi. 327–8). The poem points, therefore, in the direction of continuing effort and resourcefulness in which faith and memory play a commanding part; and it suggests an important link between Wordsworth and Puritan meditation, though for the moment we must be content to refer to a single episode in Bunyan's *Pilgrim's Progress*, where Christian, struck by 'horror' at the River of Death, is supported by Hopeful's urging of faith ('Be of good chear') and the encouragements of former experience ('... call to mind that which heretofore you have received ...').[9]

9. R. Sharrock (ed.), Bunyan, *Grace Abounding and The Pilgrim's Progress* (Oxford, 1966) [Sharrock], pp. 266–7. Cf. Hopeful to Christian at Doubting Castle, Sharrock, p. 233, and Richard Baxter to the wavering convert, *The Saints Everlasting Rest*, 4th edn (London, 1653), Pt 4, pp. 187 ff. For detailed discussion of this subject, see my 'Wordsworth, Bunyan and the Puritan mind', *ELH*, xli (1974), pp. 212–32.

Beyond this, the Pedlar's closing speech also plainly betrays an emergent desire in Wordsworth for some fixed religio-philosophic stance sufficient to make all disagreeables evaporate, which was to take him eventually to 'the breast of [dogmatic] Faith' (*Excursion*, i. 955) and cause him to interpolate into the story of Margaret a developed statement of orthodox Christian solace.[10]

One feels, then, that the residue of 'uncertainties', Mysteries, doubts' left at the end of 'The Ruined Cottage' is due not to a willing and sustained 'Negative Capability',[11] but to an inability, fundamental to Wordsworth's greatness, to dismiss those apprehensions and leanings which stubbornly refuse him the peace of secure and definitive understanding. The result is a poetry that is both assertive and deeply honest, that stores the riddles it would solve. Although 'The Ruined Cottage' concludes in tranquillity, all that Wordsworth has gained is a strategic point of rest:

> . . . other melodies
> At distance heard, peopled the milder air.
> The old man rose, and hoisted up his load.
> Together casting then a farewell look
> Upon those silent walls, we left the shade;
> And, ere the stars were visible, attained
> A rustic inn, our evening resting place.
> (ll. 325-8)

The echo of Milton's *Lycidas* is significant.[12] As the declaration of King's apotheosis provides a way from worried speculation upon death and the ironies of Fate to feelings of quiet resignation, so here the evocation of Peace and Harmony in the Pedlar's speech gives access to a mood of passing calm. As psychological terminus the stillness is, like the actual evening landscape and 'resting place', transient and temporary. We have a moment of poise, incorporating a sense of the unknown future and hinting further difficulties and trials. Winning a species of repose Wordsworth yet remains a poet of on-looking self-sufficiency.

That these questions of repose and self-sufficiency, and of

10. 1845 *Excursion*, i. 934–40, 952–5 in *Poetical Works*, v. 39.

11. M. B. Forman (ed.), *The Letters of John Keats*, 2nd edn (Oxford, 1935) [Keats, *Letters*], p. 72.

12. See *Humanity*, pp. 150–1.

restlessness and instability, loom large in Wordsworth's poetry undoubtedly arises from his surviving awareness, indeed in part from a survival, of that 'self-haunting spirit' which had erupted into mental crisis in the aftermath of the French Revolution,[13] that tendency to gloomy introspectiveness, even solipsism, which he had once admitted in 'Lines, left upon a Seat in a Yew Tree' (?1795) in the (self-)portrait of one who 'would sigh, / Inly disturbed' (ll. 42–43). Geoffrey Hartman, discussing the crisis of 1793–6, has said that the poems of the 'great decade', 1797–1807, 'reflect the triumph of an outgoing sensibility over a brooding, self-centred mind'.[14] This is eminently true. The experience of 1793–6 proved a broadening and sensitizing factor in the poet's development. No writer goes out more keenly or generously to Man (and Nature) than Wordsworth in the period from 'The Ruined Cottage' through *Lyrical Ballads* ('Simon Lee', 'The Idiot Boy', 'Michael') to 'The White Doe', raising himself above the abstract humanitarianism of eighteenth-century poets like Thomson to a vigorous celebration of 'the great and simple affections of our nature'.[15] It should also be stressed, however, that the poems of the 'great decade' are often as much trials as triumphs, trials of an integrated personality withstanding the pressures of doubt and inner turmoil and sometimes the spectre of a being 'sick' and 'wearied out' (*Prelude*, x. 900). Wordsworth never tires of proclaiming 'The calm existence that is mine when I / Am worthy of myself' (*Prelude*, i. 360–1), but what this proclamation makes clear is that the 'Paradise within' (as Milton calls it) could never simply be taken for granted.

Wordsworth can, of course, be described as a celebrant of joy and serenity. Among his most memorable passages is the one in 'Tintern Abbey' depicting 'that serene and blessed mood' in which the weight of this 'unintelligible world' falls away (ll. 35 ff.). Yet this is, exactly, a particular mood, a treasured gift to which the poet turns as, in 'somewhat of a sad perplexity' (l. 60), he seeks to confirm the wholeness and privileges

13. See *Prelude*, x. 54–82, 890–905; cf. xiii. 226–32 and 1850 text, xiv. 282–90.

14. G. H. Hartman, Introduction to *Selected Poetry and Prose of Wordsworth* (New York, 1970) [*Selected Poetry*], pp. xxvii–viii.

15. Preface to *Lyrical Ballads* in *Poetical Works*, ii. 388.

of his identity by tracing significant continuities and influences
in his life. Even in 'Tintern Abbey' his 'genial spirits' are shown
to be at risk: the point is that he will not 'suffer' them to
'decay' (l. 113). 'Resolution and Independence' reveals just
how susceptible Wordsworth could be to thoughts of their complete destruction. In an atmosphere of embattled strain he
comes face to face with himself, the 'happy child of earth'
(l. 31), plunged suddenly into despondency—a reversal which
is an acutely personalized version of the Pedlar's position at the
end of the First Part of 'The Ruined Cottage'. Before moving to
'Resolution and Independence', however, it is worth noting
that a number of Wordsworth's 'characters'—Robert and
Margaret, Martha Ray, the shepherd in 'The Last of the Flock',
James in 'The Brothers'—fall victim to either frenzy or enerva-
tion. (The shepherd's all-consuming love for the flock he must
slaughter brings crazed weariness and the death of his human
affections, while James is led to a kind of suicide by habitual
disquiet.) Wordsworth's relation to these figures is not unlike
that of Bunyan/Christian to those that crowd the landscape of
The Pilgrim's Progress—to the man in the Iron Cage, for example, whose death-in-life of endless soul-trouble serves,
through Interpreter, as 'an everlasting caution'.[16]

'Resolution and Independence' is an outstanding instance of
Wordsworth rewriting experience as remedial *logos*, a procedure
for which Puritan 'occasional' meditation is the only real precedent. (There are remarkable similarities between the poem and
the recollection of an encounter with an aged beggar by
Abiezer Coppe, a seventeenth-century Ranter.)[17] A parabolic
drama of renewal from fears of 'madness' and death (ll. 22 ff.),
the poem ends with the poet admonished by the example of
the leech-gatherer's cheerful resolution:

> I could have laughed myself to scorn to find
> In that decrepit man so firm a mind.
>
> (ll. 137–8)

As in 'The Ruined Cottage', despondency is corrected, a point
of rest attained.

On considering 'Resolution and Independence' beside 'The

16. Sharrock, pp. 166–7.
17. Abïezer Coppe, *A Second Fiery Flying Roll* (London, 1649), chap. 3.

'Ruined Cottage' one is struck first of all by the fact that the subjective elements of the earlier poem have been laid bare and intensified. Wordsworth is engaged directly in two roles corresponding to two selves in confrontation. He is at once both Poet-Traveller (in the present as in the recorded past), exposed to the perils of a distraught imagination, and Poet-Interpreter who must effect a way into the light of self-possession. The outcome is less a victory than a desperate holding operation. The final stanza, apprehensive in itself, is pressed upon by a conception of the leech-gatherer which, in its aura of nightmarish supernaturalism and suggestions of isolation and ceaseless wandering, all but corroborates the Poet-Traveller's mood of downcast bewilderment:

> the lonely place,
> The old Man's shape, and speech—all troubled me:
> In my mind's eye I seemed to see him pace
> About the weary moors continually,
> Wandering about alone and silently. (ll. 127–31)

Wordsworth breaks through to a clear presence of mind, but we leave the poem with the impression that he remains a potential prey to the sickness described in 'Incipient Madness' as 'fastening on all things / That promise food' (ll. 9–10), and to the pessimism which had fixed compulsively upon the spectacle of the hanged man at the end of one draft of 'Salisbury Plain'[18] and had taken the initiative within 'The Thorn' by way of his fascination with the searing agony of Martha Ray and the landscape of numinous terror.

Bunyan again provides an apt comparison. The situation at the end of 'Resolution and Independence' is akin to Christian's escape from the vicious circle of deadly forebodings at Doubting Castle by producing a key from his bosom, an effort of mind over imagination in the cause of self-preservation.[19] Nothing is solved but the immediate crisis. This episode from *The Pilgrim's Progress* is what we sometimes feel Wordsworth's poems to be— one of a series of tests from each of which the worthier self emerges whole but still vulnerable.

While 'Resolution and Independence' is the most troubled of Wordsworth's poems, 'Michael' is his most disciplined. The

18. MS 2, ll. 658–66 in *Poetical Works*, i. 127 note.
19. Sharrock, pp. 234–5.

description of Michael after his only son Luke has fled abroad in
disgrace is well known:

> His bodily frame had been from youth to age
> Of an unusual strength. Among the rocks
> He went, and still looked up to sun and cloud,
> And listened to the wind; and, as before,
> Performed all kinds of labour for his sheep,
> And for the land, his small inheritance.
> And to that hollow dell from time to time
> Did he repair, to build the Fold of which
> His flock had need. 'Tis not forgotten yet
> The pity which was then in every heart
> For the old Man—and 'tis believed by all
> That many and many a day he thither went,
> And never lifted up a single stone.
>
> (ll. 454–66)

We are returned deliberately to the opening portrait of
Michael:

> stout of heart and strong of limb.
> His bodily frame had been from youth to age
> Of an unusual strength: his mind was keen,
> Intense, and frugal . . .   (ll. 42 ff.)

The effect of this 'recall' is above all to accentuate the radical
transformation at the centre of Michael's being. The shepherd's
relationship with his work and environment has become purely
practical, automatic: plain verbs ('went', 'looked up' . . .) and
the virtual exclusion of adjectives (which earlier—'keen',
'intense', 'frugal'—had rung out to signify a rich if austere
existence) tell of emptiness where there had been fullness and
passionate commitment. 'The pleasure which there is in life
itself' (l. 77) has gone from Michael.

Wordsworth shirks none of the pathos of Michael's predica-
ment. It is impossible to read the passage simply in terms of the
consoling statement that 'There is a comfort in the strength of
love' (l. 448). The fact is that the very continuance, or the
bereavement, of love and hope—for the continuance seems
inextricably one with bereavement—renders Michael's life
eternally burdensome. Visiting the spot which had been a
'covenant' between father and son (ll. 413–17) he is helpless
though unbroken, 'And never lifted up a single stone'. We rejoice in Michael's endurance, but it is this picture of the whole

man arrested under the influence of emotion that finds primary focus and most stays with us.

This concentration upon loss and change surely connects with Wordsworth's interest in problems of loss and change in his personal life. In 'Tintern Abbey' and the 'Immortality Ode' by evolving compensations for the passing of pure unselfconscious joy, by finding 'recompense' in the lasting integrity of the heart and in 'the philosophic mind', he shapes a way beyond the impasse, the doom, of mere instinctive survival such as is represented in Michael's final state. But Wordsworth's relation to the themes of 'Michael' can be approached less obliquely than this. In this poem he looks squarely at those same disturbing aspects of the human condition which he had grappled with in 'The Ruined Cottage': privation and stress, the hostility of Fate, Nature's disregard for Man, the paradoxes of powerful feeling and attachment. It is as if he were determined to prove in himself once and for all the 'just equipoise' of a mind 'tuned . . . / To sympathy with man' yet 'Serene . . . unclouded by the cares / Of ordinary life' ('The Pedlar', ll. 265 ff.). In the induction, moreover, he purposely presents himself in the Pedlar's function of Interpreter of 'human life', schooled like the Pedlar by the agency of Nature.[20] As on a much larger scale in *The Prelude*, he is bent both upon offering his credentials as poet and making personal trial of his inner power and harmony, qualities upon which these credentials do in fact depend. Within the bounds of the poem his success is emphatic, Michael's history being registered and communicated as moving yet bearable and even mysteriously satisfying, as, indeed, a 'still, sad music', 'Nor harsh nor grating, though of ample power / To chasten and subdue'.

In the final analysis, however, 'Michael' implies that, simply, whatever is is. Life is seen as an inexplicable, and inexhaustible, kaleidoscope of joy and sorrow, infinite strength and infinite vulnerability, long suffering and long endurance. Such a vision was not one Wordsworth could in the long run accept, however magnificently he had encompassed it here. Certainly it is not a vision which the individual might abide easily, or with which he might rest in peace of mind: he must constantly regulate its

20. See 'Michael', ll. 27–39; 'The Pedlar', ll. 261–8; 'The Ruined Cottage', ll. 221–36.

pressure—which is equivalent to holding the wavering balance of his inner self—lest he be crushed by feeling too much, as Keats puts it, 'the giant agony of the world'.[21] One senses even in 'Michael' a danger, though fainter than in 'The Ruined Cottage' or 'Resolution and Independence', of an overwhelming tragic intensity; in the last part of the poem Wordsworth is clearly working to temper and control the tragedy, even as he acknowledges it, by viewing it indirectly through the memory of others (ll. 462–6), by sustaining an assured and lucid style and by bringing in, finally, a generalized elegiac perspective (ll. 470 ff.). Wordsworth's subsequent poetry reveals a growing and understandable desire for the safe refuge of some dogmatic tradition by which the goings-on of the universe can be viewed from a distance. Hence his appeal to Protestant ideology with its premise that whatever is is both right and 'good', our 'fate, howe'er / Sad or disturbed' directed

> by a Being
> Of infinite benevolence and power;
> Whose everlasting purposes embrace
> All accidents . . .
>   (*Excursion*, iv. 14–17)

The movement in Wordsworth's poetry to tenet and precept represents on the one hand a reversal of strategy at the level of public authorship. *The Excursion* and the elevation of the institutions and philosophy of the English Church in *Ecclesiastical Sonnets* (1822) show that he came genuinely to feel that the Poet's mission of binding together the 'vast empire of human society' could best be achieved by teaching an inviolable wisdom based in 'laws and customs', rather than, as he had argued in the Preface to *Lyrical Ballads*, by upholding the principle of 'relationship and love' through contemplation of life's 'complexity of pain and pleasure'.[22] Yet the personal motive behind the change is equally conspicuous. Already in 'Ode to Duty' (1804) we find Wordsworth praying for splendid isolation from the 'weary strife of frail humanity' (l. 8), and in surrendering himself to Duty's sway he is by a massive effort of self-abnegation and self-discipline attempting a farewell to the fluctuating self-consciousness that for the moment still presides and in the

21. *The Fall of Hyperion*, l. 157.   22. *Poetical Works*, ii. 395–96.

past had made his poetry one of contention in 'The Vale of Soul-making', the 'World of Pains and troubles'.[23] Later, by a step into the realm of Faith and Tradition he sought the haven of external discipline and objective truth. In *The Fall of Hyperion* Keats makes a definite connection, which in Wordsworth is operative but unspoken, between public responsibility and the personal need for 'a repose that ever is the same': how can one who is, as Moneta says, 'a fever of thyself' pour out 'a balm upon the World' (ll. 169, 201)? Wordsworth's 'Lines composed upon an Evening of Extraordinary Splendour and Beauty' (1817) enacts this same dilemma, egocentric bearings having to be corrected in order to preserve a vocational course, stirrings within harnessed to a doctrinal reading of the effulgent landscape as a Jacob's ladder sent to lift men's thoughts heavenwards. At one point these stirrings provoke open resentment: 'This glimpse of glory, why renewed?' (l. 65). It is impossible here to distinguish a commitment to the role of teacher from the defensive reactions of a man for whom all uncalled feelings, including ones of joy, are now a painful pressure threatening a settled dependency upon sublime conceptions of Immortality and Divine Power.

For all the preachiness of Wordsworth's later poetry he did not sink into cosy complacency, all passion spent. His sense of mission aside, he remained to the end locked in combat with the deep-seated and fierce energies within him. As he neared 70, Isabella Fenwick, his confidante, could say of him:

How fearfully strong are all his feelings and affections! If his intellect had been less powerful they must have destroyed him long ago.[24]

Faith and Tradition did not bring him peace. The way taken in *The Excursion* and given embodiment in the Wanderer (a development of the Pedlar) is more cerebral than that of the earlier poems but it is still the way of the steadfast self striving beneath and against the 'calamities of mortal life', supplicating for obedient passions and 'an ability to seek / Repose and hope among eternal things' (*Excursion*, iv. 62–63). Wordsworth

23. Keats, *Letters*, p. 336.
24. Quoted in *Selected Poetry*, p. xxvii. Cf. the material marshalled in the last two chapters of G. McLean Harper's *William Wordsworth; His Life, Works and Influence* (London, 1916).

continued to be acutely conscious of the 'weakness of humanity': although Emily's patience earns her the protection of Heaven's loving-kindness, Laodamia perishes for earthly love, 'all too weak / In reason, in self-government too slow' (1814, ll. 139–40), and is doomed to a place apart from the 'blissful quiet' of 'happy Ghosts' (ll. 158–63). Wordsworth's awareness of such alternatives reminds us of Bunyan's uncertainty at the end of *The Pilgrim's Progress* where beside the sight of Christian's entry into the Celestial City is that of Ignorance being cast down to Hell.[25]

All the same, Wordsworth's later work is, most of it, comparatively flat and irrelevant. The religious and humanistic concepts and ideals presented in it are not a living heritage with which the 'modern' personality, writ large in Wordsworth himself, can instinctively connect, in which it can discover or fulfil itself. To Wordsworth they were historical, something to be revived, artificial; to us, his readership, the more so. Among the poet's contemporaries Francis Jeffrey foreshadowed the inevitable reaction of later generations when complaining that *The Excursion* repeats too much the 'verbiage of the pulpit'.[26] By the end of the century Matthew Arnold had categorically demoted the Wordsworth of a 'systematical philosophy' to the rank of a museum-piece.[27] At the beginning of the next John Davidson reflected the spirit of his times when he announced the absolute centrality of the Wordsworth who 'had to think and imagine the world and universe for himself' and bewailed his decline into a 'meaningless pedantry'.[28]

Ironically, Wordsworth's later poetry, originating in a desire to carry out a 'comprehensive mandate' (Dedication to 'White Doe', l. 60), has proved limited in its appeal. It survives only as a sublime monument to its author's grand designs and intellectual stamina. On the other hand, his earlier poetry (including *The Prelude*, which he never thought suitable for publication) was perfectly in tune with the emergent bias of the Age. At its centre lies a vivid realization of the crisis of modern man who,

25. *Sharrock*, p. 271.

26. *Edinburgh Review*, xlvii (November 1814), p. 4.

27. Preface to *Poems of Wordsworth* (1879), *Arnold's Essays in Criticism* (Everyman Library, London, 1964), pp. 304–5.

28. 'Wordsworth's Immorality and Mine', *The Theatrocrat* (London, 1905), pp. 10, 12.

in the absence of a coherent civilization and culture within which he might unselfconsciously exist and which, as artist, he might reflect and minister to, is left to forge his own identity, stability, and balanced relations with his environment and mankind. Wordsworth's cherished idea of the Poet bringing all men together was in fact a fond illusion. His greatest poetry achieves not this but, on the contrary, a vision in which each man stands single, in which the perils of selfhood and isolation are at once substantiated and heroically mastered, turned to aspiration and triumph, and the primal sympathies between man and Nature and man and man affirmed against all the evidences of dislocation. This vision might heal and inspire, as it did J. S. Mill, but it cannot foster a spirit of Community or redeem nations sunk to 'ignominy and shame' (*Prelude*, xii. 421 ff.). And the ideology of the later poetry itself, however much Wordsworth sought to establish its status as a time-honoured Orthodoxy under whose dispensation man could securely dwell,[29] has as its ultimate truth a sense of the individual soul, able through perseverance and the light of Hope to overcome the 'weakness and disease' to which it is forever open.[30]

This 'crisis of modern man' is evoked alike by Patmore's consternation at the lack of serenity across the life and literature of his century[31] and Davidson's delight in what he felt to be a purifying turbulence. It is the crisis which T. S. Eliot in *The Waste Land*, in still more difficult times, concedes in near despair, conjuring Peace, 'Shantih', in terms that deny its feasibility in relation to the Western Mind; and that for which Yeats framed a rhetoric to sing the glories of 'walking naked' and the inevitability of returning only to the drab chaos of subjectivity, the 'foul rag-and-bone shop of the heart'. Bunyan seems odd in such company, but he had given early and noteworthy expression to this crisis, his Puritanism, which cut him off from society and made salvation a matter for each man alone, producing a dynamic of uneasy selfconsciousness which precludes repose and throws stress upon the individual's capacity for

29. Especially in *Ecclesiastical Sonnets* and the address to the State and Church of England at the opening of Book VI of *The Excursion*.

30. For instance, the examples preached by the Pastor at *Excursion*, vi. 95–261.

31. 'Cheerfulness in Life and Art', *Principle*, p. 31.

steadfastness, for discovering steadying recognitions in personal history and in doctrine, for maintaining intercourse with his true self whether amidst the plausible corruptions of Vanity Fair or amidst the snares of disillusionment at Doubting Castle. Although *The Prelude* offers the best comparisons both with *The Pilgrim's Progress* and Bunyan's spiritual autobiography, *Grace Abounding*, the shorter poems are also fruitful, as we have seen, for Wordsworth's great epic of the individual soul is in important respects an expansion of them, not least in its being a hazardous but necessary psychological journey in which the traveller must meet with the weaker and darker aspects of his personality, directly or in projection, and make trial of the stronger and worthier.

In Wordsworth's day the tendency to introspection and alienation from Community and Tradition was no longer selective, as it had been in Bunyan's. The problems demonstrated in these two authors—call them problems of identity or existence, of 'How . . . are Souls to be made?', how won 'a bliss peculiar to each one's individual existence'[32]—were becoming the un-avoidable theme. It was of course in the later eighteenth and earlier nineteenth centuries that subjectivism, and individualism both positive and uncertain, assumed a central place in English poetry, in the wake of that growing disenchantment with the cultural possibilities of Augustanism which can be seen in Pope's move from the celebratory outlook of *Windsor Forest* to the almost despairing one of *The Dunciad*. We find this subjectivism emerging in the later Pope and in Gray, and in Cowper's *The Task* where feelings of spiritual and emotional infirmity, mirrored in such characters as Crazy Kate (i. 534 ff.)—a definite anticipation of Wordsworth's Margaret—and the Paralytic living in 'slavish dread of solitude' (i. 472 ff.), are answered by a going-out to the stimuli and composing influences of nature. Dr Johnson's writings, too, are pervaded by a sense of the individual's need to square up vigilantly to the ills and frailties to which humanity is heir. Johnson's rearguard Augustanism is, somewhat like his submission to the 'perpetual superintendence' of Providence, a defiant reaction to 'this state of universal uncertainty, where a thousand dangers hover about

32. Keats, *Letters*, p. 336.

us' and the phantoms of delusion and melancholy within.[33] His argument is man having 'to strive with difficulties and to conquer them', a life without repose and in which 'all may suffer . . . such maladies of the mind' as befall the astronomer in whom solitude and the 'power of fancy over reason' conspire to create insanity.[34]

Wordsworth seems at times to have as much in common with the so-called 'Augustan' Johnson as with his fellow Romantics; but perhaps this is to say no more than that they all reflect something of the same general *milieu*, for the trials and triumphs of the steadfast self in Wordsworth have their counterpart in the indefinite questings of the idealistic self in Shelley and in the struggles of the authorial and sometimes (as in 'Ode to a Nightingale') perplexed, sole, and unquiet, self in Keats. Certainly by the time of 'The Triumph of Life' (1822) Shelley was sensible of the obligation his generation had to take account of 'the mystery within', making Rousseau describe the great as failing because their lore 'Taught them not this, to know themselves' (ll. 208–15). In Byron's *Childe Harold* we have an incessant movement back and forth from ardent and melancholy inward-turning to consideration of the coherence and value, and the lack of them, in civilization and history. Nevertheless, Wordsworth does stand out by the rare clarity with which he recognizes a 'fall' into an industrialized world, a chaos and a travesty of civilization, where the mind is reduced to 'almost savage torpor', and by the naked urgency with which he champions, and sustains within himself, 'certain indestructible qualities of the human mind' which are rooted in the elemental life of the universe.[35] That the championing and sustaining involve an incumbent sense of man's insecurity within this universe and within himself lends them a peculiar authority.

33. *Rambler*, no. 184; cf. also *Rambler*, no. 32; *Adventurer*, no. 111; *The Vanity of Human Wishes*, ll. 135–64, 343–68.
34. *Rasselas*, chaps. 43–44.
35. Preface to *Lyrical Ballads* in *Poetical Works*, ii. 389.

Narrative modes in the
Waverley novels

BRIAN NELLIST

To his contemporaries in Britain and abroad, Scott was the
epitome of a Romantic writer. Hazlitt couples his name and
Byron's as the very types of the 'Spirit of the Age'. Yet, like
Byron himself, Scott was profoundly critical of phenomena we
think of as characteristically Romantic. Let us, for example,
take his use of the word itself in a passage from *Waverley*.[1] Flora
MacIvor leads the hero to a favourite retreat close to the castle
of Glennaquoich in the Highlands. There we find a 'romantic
waterfall' falling into a 'romantic reservoir' amid the 'romantic
wildness' of the surroundings. The insistent use of the word
carries a double irony, I think. Shortly before, the enthusiastic
Waverley has been compared to 'a knight of romance'. The
phrase makes explicit those slightly absurd, quixotic fancies of
the hero that Scott attributes to his nostalgic upbringing and
the wanderings of his undisciplined imagination through the
pages of Ariosto, Tasso, and Spenser. The author is turning to
good-natured and discreet parody a civilized delight in savage
scenery, which on another occasion, he, and we with him, would
be prepared to indulge. Here, however, the epithet signifies the
distortions characteristic of tourist vocabulary.

Yet there is a further irony to be observed. Waverley is an
alien, introducing with that word 'romantic' the values of an
alien culture. But it is alien precisely because what is to the
Englishman a charming picture after Salvator Rosa is to the
inhabitants of the castle their everyday reality. The feudal
loyalties of Glennaquoich that we have just read about, the immediate incorporation of the present by song into a legendary

1. *Waverley* (Edinburgh, 1883), chap. 22, p. 153. I have quoted the novels
throughout from this impression of the so-called Centenary Edition.

past, the great feast in the hall with the vaunts of the retainers, the ardent devotion, revealed later in the book, to the Chevalier, all signify the continued existence of a chivalric society, the proper subject of literary romance. What happens in the novel is that romance revival meets romance survival, is temporarily confused into thinking it can step inside a world it has hitherto known through literature and pictures, but ultimately recognizes its cultural estrangement. Waverley's 'romancing' represents an understandable but slightly absurd holiday from his real citizenship of an everyday reality of peace, prosperity, family life, and sound philanthropy. The romance, which is a dream to Waverley, is to Fergus and Flora a reality, often brutal, in which, for example, they are quite prepared to use the hero's misconceptions, as in this passage, to the advantage of their Cause. These romantic characters display Scott's characteristically ambiguous estimate of the romance imagination. The passionate energy with which they attempt to submit fluid reality to the demands of a noble image of life, rooted in the past, finds at once its apotheosis and fit judgement in their death or exile.

This conflict between figures obedient to great images and other characters, who apparently seek to live without images and disengage themselves from their demands, is a more fundamental fact of Scott's fictional world than the historical settings in which the conflict is usually worked out. History presented Scott with substantial, particularized images, out of which he could create significant pictures. But the pictures themselves display a struggle inherent in contemporary sensibility.

What we hear continually in the Waverley novels, I would suggest, is a dialogue between the claims of two literary modes. These modes, proposed by eighteenth-century criticism, are the romance and the novel. Though we are accustomed to think of them as literary terms, to Scott and his contemporaries they also involved cultural distinctions and it is in this sense I intend to use them here. In the 'Essay on Romance', written in 1824, Scott defined romance not as a medieval and Renaissance literary form, but as one with a distinctive point of view. Its interest depends, he says, upon 'marvellous and uncommon incidents'. This curt description is amplified by the contrasting definition of the novel:

a fictitious narrative, differing from the Romance, because the events are accommodated to the ordinary train of human events, and the modern state of society.[2]

The terms Scott uses imply a mingled sense of disappointment and resigned acceptance of the inevitable 'ordinary train'. In these terms, the 'romancing' of Waverley himself represents an excusable but misguided failure of 'accommodation'.

Scott's belief that the novel was the voice of modern society was a commonplace. Isaac Disraeli, who was scarcely an original critic, says:

romances went out of fashion with our square-cocked hats . . . The name of romance, including imaginary heroes and extravagant passions, disgusted; and [novels] substituted scenes of domestic life, and touched our common feelings by pictures of real nature.[3]

Yet that easy use of the word 'real' had disturbed other critics besides Scott. A sense that the novel had restricted reality by identifying it too easily with the socially representative is persistent in later eighteenth-century criticism. Even the austere Hugh Blair could write of 'the magnificent heroic romance, dwindled down to the familiar novel'.[4]

By representing in the same fiction the points of view of novel and romance, Scott deliberately rescued the novel from its cul-de-sac of realism. By showing the way in which the novelist's preference for the 'ordinary train of human events' is a matter of choice rather than simple acceptance and that it excludes other possibilities inherent in romance, Scott declares the relativity of our notions of historical reality. Romance, by the absoluteness of its claims, maybe seeks its own death, yet it also in the Waverley novels summons the partial allegiance of the reader. By exposing the present to the past, Scott can thus reopen a question which for most of his readers had already been complacently settled. As in *Old Mortality*, he can show the process by which social right becomes social wrong and rebellion becomes establishment. The Waverley novels were, and are, dis-

2. *Miscellaneous Prose Works* (Edinburgh, 1852), vi. 129. The debate about the place of the marvellous in the novel and Scott's part in it is discussed by Miriam Allott in *Novelists on the Novel* (London, 1959), pp. 3–20.

3. Isaac Disraeli, *Curiosities of Literature* (London, 1824), ii. 272.

4. Quoted from *Lectures on Rhetoric and Poetry* (1762) by Ioan Williams in *Novel and Romance, 1700–1800* (London, 1970) [Williams, *Novel*], p. 250.

turbing. In their subversion of moral certainties and a fixed
ground for the reader, Scott anticipates, like many Romantic
writers, the experiments of modernism. Unlike some modernists,
however, he does not dissolve the substantial realities of the phenomenal world into a purely personal viewpoint. Through the
historical medium, the viewpoints of romance and novel become images of rival cultures which have themselves created the
consciousness of the artist. Scott, like his wavering heroes, is a
solitary who knows he does not belong in the romance and feels
he does not want to belong in the novel. It is in confronting this
quandary that Scott stands most obviously beside the great
Romantic poets.

In restoring to prose fiction its inheritance of both narrative
viewpoints, Scott might seem to be merely repeating a standard
formula. Clara Reeve hoped in *The Old English Baron* to emulate
Horace Walpole in 'an attempt to unite the various merits and
graces of the ancient Romance and modern Novel'[5] and Dunlop
thought the 'romantic novel' almost an English invention.[6] Yet
Scott's departures from the method of the romance-tale signify
a deeper understanding of the fictional tradition. He himself
wrote about *The Castle of Otranto* as though it were a historical
novel. Its Gothic descriptions were a means of detaching the
reader from the assumptions of his own time until he could
recognize in the tale's portents an expression of the beliefs and
sensibility of 'a ruder age'.[7] The contrast with Scott's own
practice is clear enough and extends the critique.

Otranto is a holiday from the present of moral rationalization
that the author customarily observes. The result of trying to
substantiate the romance form by incorporating the methods of
psychological naturalism, appropriate to the novel, is simply to
render absurd the feelings he hoped to make real. Scott, on the
other hand, recognized that the viewpoint of the novel had
become primary and could not simply be ignored. His own
fragment of a Gothic tale, 'Thomas the Rhymer', he later included as a ludicrous and admonitory appendix to *Waverley*.
Where Walpole excludes the novelistic present, contemporary

5. Williams, *Novel*, p. 299.
6. John Dunlop, *The History of Fiction*, 3rd edn (London, 1845), p. 413.
7. Ioan Williams, *Sir Walter Scott on Novelists and Fiction* (London, 1968),
p. 89.

life always speaks in Scott's novels in the person of the narrator. 'The Author of Waverley' is a vital presence in his own works, as Francis Hart has so brilliantly demonstrated.[8] Scott describes situations where the novel is compelled to formulate itself as a distinct viewpoint within the total fiction. Walpole ignores the novel; Scott recreates it. In the sense in which Mr Beatty has elsewhere in this volume made the distinction, Walpole raids the past for false precedents; true precedent commands the respect and creative attention of Scott as much as of Byron. Walpole severs past from present in order to enjoy a change of scenery; Scott restores the present to the past, in order to recover all the possibilities inherent in that present.

The essay on romance of 1824 and the earlier discussion of chivalry, both written as articles for the *Encyclopaedia Britannica*, describe most clearly the nature of romance culture. Scott ascribes to it a quasi-religious seriousness:

that devotion to duty, and that disinterested desire to sacrifice all to faith and honour; that noble spirit of achievement which laboured for others more than itself.[9]

Such values give to Scott's novels the religious centre which they are often said to lack. Scott partly restores to currency what the irony of, for example, Cervantes had apparently occluded for ever. When in *Redgauntlet* Latimer hears Wandering Willie playing in the courtyard outside his gaol, his memory recalls the Lionheart and Blondel.[10] The instance seems absurd, to him as well as to us, yet irony does not destroy the exactness of the parallel. The reader is moved despite himself. More importantly, the dreams inspired by romance culture remain as a positive force within history through the agency of the romance heroes from Flora MacIvor to the Highland Widow.

Scott describes at the end of the essay on chivalry the reasons for the downfall of that romance culture and, again, the analysis helps the reader to understand certain emphases in the Waverley series.[11] The breakdown of feudal organization had released, he argues, a violence which the romance image was no

8. *Scott's Novels: The Plotting of Historical Survival* (Charlottesville, 1966). The first chapter is specifically relevant.   9. Ed. cit., p. 171.

10. *Redgauntlet*, ed. cit., chap. 9, p. 245.

11. *Miscellaneous Prose Works* (Edinburgh, 1852), vi. 111–25. The essay was written as early as 1815.

longer able to contain. In many of the tales, the highly struc-
tured formalities of romance stand as alien facts amidst a mess
of violence and subterfuge. The courtesy and irreducible superiority of Claverhouse in *Old Mortality* seem a disturbingly dis-
connected response to the brutalities to which his archaic
loyalties commit him. That novel also displays another major
cause of chivalric decline as presented in the essay, namely,
Protestantism's claim to a logic as exclusive as that of chivalry
itself. The language of guilt and sin in many of the Scottish
novels proves as bloodily resentful of the confusion inherent in
history as does the romance point of view. But the most crucial
of the reasons offered for the decay of the old image was the
growth of a new rationalism which insisted on firm boundaries
between imagination and fact. In this impulse lies for most
eighteenth-century critics the foundations of the novel. James
Beattie, for example, praised Cervantes for 'banishing the wild
dreams of chivalry and reviving the taste for the simplicity of
nature'.[12] Such confidence, however, provided the basis of
Scott's anxiety about the novel as a viewpoint.

All Scott's novels awaken the anxieties of the reader by facing
him with the equal yet irreconcilable claims of novel and romance. Some great crisis in which figures from, as it were, a set
of romance characters, active, imaginative, moved by great
legendary and literary prototypes, engage with figures who belong to the novel in their preference for peace, prosperity, the
continuity of family life, and freedom of personal choice, recurs
in tale after tale of the *Waverley* series. Even where the conflict
is most tenuous it still gives the primary vitality to such books
as *Ivanhoe* and *The Talisman*. In the novel concerned with the
remotest period that Scott described, *Count Robert of Paris*, he
ironically reverses his usual perspective. Byzantium during the
First Crusade appears a society corrupted by wealth, achieving
its ends by guile and subduing its people by spectacular shows
and appeals to their sense of cultural superiority. Western
chivalry, by contrast, with its plain violence regulated by codes
of honour, displays a moral superiority over the covert cruelties
of the more civilized Eastern Empire. Romance for once takes
its revenge on the culture of the novel. On the other hand, in
much greater books, *Rob Roy*, *The Heart of Midlothian*, and *The*

12. Quoted from *On Fable and Romance* (1783) in Williams, *Novel*, p. 319.

Fair Maid of Perth, Scott's imaginative and moral sympathies sustain the novelistic point of view. He tries to make the prudent heroes seize, by a still available decisiveness and imagination, the prerogatives usually reserved for romance.

Scott writes best of that period when the culture of the novel historically triumphs, partly because then romance attains its true tragic identity in its fight against inevitable odds. In tales of earlier periods, Scott seeks out moments when the middle-class culture of the novel sharply discloses itself amid the signs of romance decay. Before Louis XI in *Quentin Durward* and the independent Swiss republics in its sequel, *Anne of Geierstein*, Burgundian chivalry is defeated by its own archaic conceptions of politics and warfare. Not that Charles the Bold is any more honest than Louis, for example, but he has not learned to make systematic deceit the basis for action. In *Kenilworth*, the major characters have learned this lesson, but cannot surrender the magnificent claims of the chivalric image. The novel unfolds in a brilliant sequence of self-consciously theatrical characters and emblematically opposed descriptions. In order to reflect such shifts of sensibility the Waverley heroes are customarily passive victims of mischance. Henry Morton in *Old Mortality* departs from this norm, because he is almost the single exponent of the novelistic point of view in a fiction dominated by the rivalry of two image-ridden and exclusive cultures, chivalric and Puritan.

There is then, throughout the Waverley series, a constant dialogue to be heard between groups of characters who belong to different narrative designs, the novel and the romance. And it might seem at first as though the novel has, as it must have historically, always the last word. But many of Scott's more recent critics, quite properly reacting against the Victorian emphasis upon the glamour of ancient ways in Scott's narrations, have too readily made him simply the spokesman of prudence and property, of the outlook of the novel as he understood it. Yet the structure of the books often approximates more closely to that of romance. The unity of plot, on which some neo-classical criticism based its claims for the superiority of novel to romance, was overtaken in Scott's mind, as he wrote, by a rich improvization. Characters are created with exuberant fertility under the demands of theme and idea. The design of his novels, as of much Romantic poetry, is spatial, dependent on parallels and contrasts which the reader must observe for himself. Though brilliantly individualized, his characters are also images, just as the images of landscape and house are also protagonists. The explicit voice of the narrator may, on occasion, utter the wisdom of the novel but the design is that of the romance and design is an important measure of significance.

The books themselves, in fact, possess an insight beyond that of any part of them. Moreover, the presence of the narrator throughout, detached, ironical, generous, is absolutely crucial. We need, I think, a third term, other than that of romance and novel to describe this arbitrating presence. I would propose the epithet, fictional. After all, if the books are simply confirming the value of the novel, one wonders why the author takes the trouble to repeat what all his readers take for granted. No, it is the fictional voice which urges Scott to end his novels with a balance of comic and tragic resolutions, in which equal justice is shown to the other viewpoints. It is the fictional voice which distances the reader from the novelistic present as from the romance past. It is the fictional voice which gives expression to residual myths that unite romance and novel in the realistic worlds of *Guy Mannering*, *The Antiquary*, and *St Ronan's Well*. It is the fictional voice which creates hybrid characters. The 'romancing' Darsie Latimer in *Redgauntlet* becomes the spokesman for good sense, and Alan Fairford, the model of prudence, undertakes a dangerous quest on behalf of his romantic friendship for Latimer. Throughout the books one feels the urgency with which the novelist himself attempts to embrace both novel and romance and guarantee continuities. This transformation of what would otherwise only be a language of resigned acceptance is the true source of Scott's creative energy.

He has to fight for this inclusive vision, of course. The corrupt magnificence of the romance outlook achieves its most cogent utterance at the moment of its demise. Tragedy confirms the sort of success of which the romance world is capable and Scott cannot always afford to maintain a countervailing comic weighting against such tragic images. Thus, the *Bride of Lammermoor*, written in sickness, ends with pure disaster and its intensity is bought at the cost of the imaginative breadth that the fictional voice usually contributes to Scott's novels.

The means by which this lucid tragic image—and it is often

most precisely an image, like the single feather at the end of *Lammermoor*—is diverted to the purposes of the fictional viewpoint is through an act of memory. Memory, the act of fidelity to the past, of which the introduction to *Old Mortality* with its memory within a memory within a memory is only the best example, is the real basis of the fictional viewpoint in Scott. Memory is the basis of the prophetic utterances of Edie Ochiltree, Meg Merrilies, Wandering Willie, and the Norna, who are at once the exponents and conscience of the romance world. They are extensions of the narrator's own presence in the books. The comic characters, also, with their fluid identities, serve a similar function. Their way of life, compared with that of the time-ridden protagonists, is immemorial.

The heroes themselves are often agents of memory. At the end of *Waverley* the hero is left with his memories, as he was at the beginning, but the combined abnegation and loyalties of which memory is composed have now been tested and memory distinguished from dream. Waverley has become, as Fergus suggests and Donald Davie points out, the new hero of sensibility.[13] The memories at the end are associated with Fergus, the romance hero, and they belong to different categories, both of them present to the mind of Waverley himself. The first is proper to romance. For Flora, Fergus will become, as he himself ironically prophesies, saint and hero. The distortion is suited to the ideal and deathly realm to which Flora now belongs. White 'as the purest statuary marble',[14] she is destined for the stillness and asceticism of the religious life. The second memory is proper to the viewpoint of the novel, and is comic. The Bradwardine manor throughout the book is a sort of *locus mnemonicus* of the chivalric past and it now carries on its walls a painting of Fergus and Waverley in highland dress. Unlike the art of funeral effigy, this art has a decorative function, incorporating memory into the sense of ongoing life. It is significant, also, that, in one of those transitions comparable both in diction and meaning with moments in *Don Juan*, the paragraph that follows the act of piety before the portrait, should begin, 'Men must, however, eat, in spite both of sentiment and virtu'.[15]

13. *The Heyday of Sir Walter Scott* (London, 1961), p. 37.
14. *Waverley*, ed. cit., chap. 68, p. 425.
15. Ibid., chap. 71, p. 445.

Novel, romance, fiction: these then are the several viewpoints that Scott maintains, constantly questioning each other, assuming each other's guise, gaining temporary precedence, though usually in the end yielding priority to the fictional voice. If there is one book where they operate more openly than any other in the series and where we can see most clearly this fusion of literary mode with cultural viewpoint, it is *Redgauntlet*. I wish, therefore, to show in conclusion how these viewpoints collide and ironically expose each other's pretensions in this most complex and subtle of Scott's narrations. In expressing the triumph of viewpoint over fact here, Scott goes to extreme lengths. In one sense the book describes clearly the transfer of power from romance to the novel. To this end Scott invents as its centre a fictitious visit to England by Charles Edward, claimant to the throne after his father's death in 1766. This most tenuous of romance survivals carries extraordinary conviction in the book and convinces because of the capacity of Redgauntlet himself to create possibility where objectively none exists. As a structure, also, the book triumphantly vindicates Scott's episodic narrative procedures. Beginning as a series of letters, a third of the way through, it arbitrarily switches to narration, complete with a first chapter, because there are 'some things the reader could not otherwise know'. Twenty pages later, we return to first person narrative with Latimer's journal, and the rest of the book breaks off at quite accidental moments to interweave the activities of the other of the young friends, Alan Fairford. We are constantly guessing at what is really happening through the half-insights or the outraged reactions of figures not in the know. As in comparable works, *The Antiquary* and *Guy Mannering*, the centre of the book is not the narrative, though (locally) that is brilliantly compelling, but the way in which narrative is built up of multifarious hints, coincidences, chance discoveries, and above all conflicting interpretations of Redgauntlet himself. The novel is full of deliberate repetitions of events which assume quite different significances in their respective contexts. Lady Louisa Stuart found *Redgauntlet* absorbing but difficult.

there is no story in it, no love, no hero—unless Redgauntlet himself, who would be such a one as the Devil in Milton.[16]

16. D. Douglas (ed.), *Familiar Letters of Sir Walter Scott* (Edinburgh, 1894), ii. 208.

Event is absorbed into interpretation, then. The term, historical novel, implies an interpretation of the past. But in *Redgauntlet* it is the act of interpretation itself which is the fundamental subject of the book. The process is apparent at the start. Latimer's rescue from the sands of Solway by the Laird of the Lochs becomes for the reader himself an event of great significance through the art of Latimer's own 'rage of narrative', as he later calls it. In the following letter, however, the claim that anything has really happened is convincingly challenged by the ironical good sense of Alan Fairford. However, within the true romance perspective of the book's inner structure it does indeed have a significance beyond what is seen by either of them. The Redgauntlets are fated always to fail politically because an ancestor, Alberic, had trampled his son to death beneath his horse's hoof, in pursuit of his nation's advantage. The book's Redgauntlet, however, saves from death, and on horseback, a nephew who is his political enemy, once in ignorance, and later with full knowledge of the circumstances. The mysterious, haunting parallel, itself like something out of legend, is left to the reader's discovery. It is in such details that we hear the fictional voice. It records how a romance character contributes to the triumph of the novelistic commonsense of his nephew, and hence to the undoing of the family blight. Yet the detail itself ironically confirms the romance point of view.

The book develops through an increasing discovery of what is involved in novelistic and romance viewpoints. Latimer as novelistic hero nostalgic for romance, is submitted, like the reader, to a journey into the territory of true romance. He is simultaneously appalled and excited, until gradually both he and we with him are led to recognize the integrity and logic of a totally alien viewpoint, which he of course rejects, but which survives for the reader with a peculiar power. Events that begin as a simple adventure tale end by achieving the power to transform history itself. The Proteus-Archimago of this magic, by turns Laird of the Lochs, Herries of Birrenswerk, Squire Ingoldsby, and always Redgauntlet, seems capable of turning himself into the legal guardian of a young man who is apparently no connection, making the king's writ disappear, leading riots, being simultaneously in Edinburgh, Solway, and Cumberland, and finally reversing the direction of fifty years of the nation's life.

But the alternative, novelistic viewpoint has also grown in authority through the book, as it gradually comes to understand the opposition. It finds utterance through the mouths of Fairford, Latimer, and his unrecognized sister, Redgauntlet's niece, Lilias. Romance and novel are subtly associated. Latimer has turned the mysterious Greenmantle into a figure of devotion for his dreams. These are shattered when she displays remarkable forwardness in claiming his affection since he does not yet realize that she is his sister. Scott's generalization at this point, for all its sly disclaimer of relevancy, expresses a general novelistic disapproval of romance extravagance. Romantic passion creates what it sees, says the narrator, and wakes from its dream with disgust, where mutual esteeem, founded upon reason and contiguity of sentiment, is built to last.[17] The good sense is cognate with the comic resolution of this, as of so many other of the Waverley series. They end in a union of lovers which, far from being an acknowledgement of love's force, is associated rather with rest, loyalty to the family rather than to the beloved, and with the inheritance of property rather than the gaining of honour. Yet, as here with the miasmal Greenmantle, the hero's past is as often haunted by the ghost of a more fulfilling passion, denied by the novelistic present.

We have in the book, then, a dialectic of opposed images with an almost Blakean clarity, though a more than Blakean substance. The basis of the images is partly sexual and sexual relationships elucidate the moral expectations of romance and novel in *Redgauntlet*. There is no family life in romance. Private life had always been subordinate to public ends in the legendary history of the Redgauntlets. Latimer, as the child of his mother, has to undergo a ritual purgation of the timidity he inherits from her by wearing female disguise. His uncle hopes he 'will lay aside all effeminate thoughts', when it is discarded at the moment of decision.[18] The hope is empty since the romance Cause itself is to founder on the Chevalier's unwillingness to subordinate his own domestic arrangements to its demands. And at that very moment, Alan Fairford takes his first steps to woo Lilias behind the screen of Latimer's discarded female garments.

17. *Redgauntlet*, ed. cit., chap. 17, p. 353.
18. Ibid., chap. 22, pp. 410–11.

Yet if the energy of Redgauntlet's version of romance is de-
monic in its restlessness, Scott's critique of the culture of the
novel approaches satire in its vehemence. Joshua Geddes, the
Quaker, is obviously the primary spokesman for hearth and
home. An implicit parallel within the work clarifies the issue.
In Redgauntlet's wretched cottage only the coat-of-arms on the
silver acknowledges his identity. In the prosperous house at
Mount Sharon the scutcheon of honour over the fireplace has
been deliberately obliterated. Yet the peaceful paradise proves
maddeningly tedious to Latimer. Its prosperity is supported by
a form of fishery as socially destructive as the open robberies of
Geddes's rejected Border ancestors. His self-consciously plain
language, moreover, with its claim to absolute truth, falsifies
even his own nature, to comic ends, denying even such innocent
liberties as the right to change one's mind. It is an assault upon
the rich and ironical language of fiction itself (there is no literature at Mount Sharon) and makes impossible the full compre-
hension of human impulses.

Similarly, the apparently sane world of property and the law,
whose spokesman is Fairford Senior, has a dark basis which its
rationalist language cannot accommodate. Peter Peebles's complex suit about a disputed property, which started in 1745,
obviously comments sourly as a sub-plot on the follies and ruin
attending Jacobite intrigue. Yet Peebles is the victim of the
novelistic world, himself crazed with respect for the law and
money which are its objects of devotion. The apparently clear
language of legal process can serve self-destructive delusion as
readily as the claims of romance honour. It remains, at root,
madly egotistical and without the ennobling disinterestedness
which elevates Redgauntlet himself.

Peebles is one outcast from the novel; there are others. The
unforgettable Trumbull compounds for his smuggling with a
pious cant which earns him a place in the respectable world.
Hypocrisy is the covert recognition of what the novel cannot
formally acknowledge. Nanty Ewart, for anticipating his marriage to the girl he loves, is driven to the streets and eventually
into piracy and smuggling. Yet Ewart is consciously at home
only in the country of the novel. He is, like Peebles, a parody of
romance created by a novelistic culture which can find no
room for the vitalities he represents.

No wonder then that Louisa Stuart was puzzled by the book. The book simultaneously undermines the satisfactions of both romance and novelistic viewpoints yet takes continual pleasure in all the phenomena that both attitudes produce. In the work of no other Romantic writer is the idea of 'negative capability' more completely realized. Yet the book has a unity which triumphantly transcends this dilemma. Its true centre is the narrator's own consciousness, admitting all, ironical, tragic, humorous, always observant—the fictional viewpoint. Through this consciousness the romance that dies lives to the memory, and the novel that triumphs is reminded of its partial blindness. Indeed that triumph only becomes possible when George III and his emissary, Black Colin Campbell, discover a political language, comparable in the imaginative boldness of its clemency to the claims of romance. The clearest representative of the authorial voice in the work is Wandering Willie, another master of narrative. Wandering Willie's tale, coming as it does early in the book, provides, as a story within a story, a model for the reader's attitude to the whole work. The legend-creating faculty at work in that tale is a source of fictional truth.

It is in Willie's tale that we first hear of the Redgauntlets, and what he offers is an interpretation rather than a plain history. In the violence and cruelty of the romance world Steenie, Willie's grandfather and the story's hero, has been haplessly involved by his master ('He saw muckle mischief and maybe did some, that he couldna avoid').[19] The placing of that master in Hell leaves apparently no doubt of the moral judgement involved. The group of legendary Cavaliers among whom he roisters clearly represents a society forbidden by the values of the present and always condemned by the awakened conscience. Yet Steenie's Hell is also as ambiguous as Tam o'Shanter's witches. It is a place which excites sympathy for what the moral sense knows is forbidden. Its inhabitants are not without loyalty to their own people; Steenie gets his receipt. None of the company seems exactly to suffer. The life they lived above is preserved with all its contents and discontents in a permanent Scottish Elysian Fields. Only Steenie's new master, a Redgauntlet afflicted with the twinges of the novel, is dismayed to learn of his father's whereabouts.

19. *Redgauntlet*, ed. cit., Letter 11, p. 114.

Steenie and Willie himself accept the vision with equanimity.

Willie, as substitute for the narrator, is kin to those prophetic figures in all the books who preside over the transfer of loyalties and possess insight into the nature of historical process. Meg Merrilies, Edie Ochiltree, the Norna, even Flora herself, are literary figures who understand the intuitions of literature because they are themselves the repositories of popular song and legend or Old Testament prophecy. They are often figures who survive social change. They are as often social outcasts, professional observers. Like Wordsworth's pedlar they are filled with unshakeable imperturbability as they watch the changes of the dance. Willie may wander, but he never wanders from his home: he is 'of every country in broad Scotland'.[20] That ideal country for which all Redgauntlet's activities are undertaken, exists at the end only in the consciousness of the old ballad-monger and fiddler, and, of course, Scott himself.

In the face of such an extraordinary original work as *Redgauntlet*, then, with its fundamental extensions of the language of the novel, yet its loyalty to the form, Scott still seems, for all the recent distinguished criticism, a neglected writer, locked away in a special cupboard, rather than standing where he should beside his peers, the other major novelists. More than any other novelist of his time he was fundamentally concerned with the nature of fictional reality and with challenging the claim of the novel to work within a fixed standard of reality. He achieves this by restoring to currency within the framework of the novel itself, the outlook of romance, not as the register of some private nightmare or the symbol of some new conception of human nature, let alone a jaunt into the Gothic past, but as an alternative world, seeing the same phenomena in different ways from the novel, and ruled by different laws. Romance exists in his novels as a dangerous possibility, dangerous not simply because it exhibits to the present possibilities it has excluded but because it subverts the claims of the present to any simple-minded moral progression. The viewpoint of the novel is, of course, always accepted finally by Scott, but that it is accepted only acknowledges its relativity. Scott is a long way from Conrad, yet romance in the Waverley novels has something of the unnerving quality of the alienating viewpoint in Conrad's novels. The

20. *Redgauntlet*, ed. cit., Letter 10, p. 105.

return to normality can only be accomplished by an irony. The peace and apparent concord at the end of a Waverley novel involve a calculated act of self-blinding. Scott apparently accepts that, in some ways, civilized life is superior to the romance past. But this is a difficult thing for him to assert; he does it on personal grounds allowing that 'civilized life' itself is only a possibility existing for a time within historical flux. Redgauntlet admits his nephew's loyalty to the current establishment: 'I am convinced he will not change it, should it in turn become the losing [side].'[21] In this subverting of the viewpoint of novel by romance and of romance by novel, Scott does create a new fictional design.

The historical form, which was his individual solution of this problem, proved capable of easy imitation and produced misreading. The historical novel became either a masquerade of contemporary ideas in old clothes, as in *John Inglesant* or even *Romola*, or antiquarian inquiry made palatable to the inquisitive reader, as in the entertaining work of Mr Alfred Duggan. Scott's attitude to history is closer to that of Byron in *Childe Harold*, or, with obvious differences, of Yeats. His novels embody a state of cultural shock. Of course, Scott cannot, like the great European novelists of the nineteenth century, go on to formulate or explore new possibilities. As in *Redgauntlet*, he continues loyal to the time-honoured patterns of survival and renewal, marriage, inheritance, the transfer of loyalties, the remembering and forgetting of the past. In this, curiously, he seems closest to Byron, one of his most assiduous readers. The structure of the novels as it is described here is rather like that encapsulating of romance adventure within sceptical narration in *Don Juan*, though of course the tone of the Waverley novels differs from that of the poem. Yet, like Byron, Scott appears to see further precisely because he refuses to commit himself philosophically. For both of them the comment made by the economist, Nassau Senior, in 1821 in reviewing Scott's novels seems apt. He ascribes the popularity of the Waverley novels, not to their historical form, but to the union in them of 'the most irreconcilable forms and the most opposite materials . . . tragedy and the romance, comedy and the novel'.[22]

21. Ibid., chap. 23, p. 446.
22. Quoted in J. T. Hillhouse, *The Waverley Novels and their Critics* (Minneapolis, 1936), p. 51.

Coleridge's poetic language

N.F.BLAKE

Although Coleridge stands with Wordsworth at the threshold of the Romantic revolution, it is on the basis of his development of the theory of Romanticism that his contribution to the change which took place in English poetry at that time is more usually assessed. Similarly his poetry is investigated for its visionary or mystical qualities, whereas, so far, little has been done to examine his language or to evaluate how the Romantic attitude towards poetry affected his vocabulary. This may be partly because Lowes's *The Road to Xanadu* has suggested to many that Coleridge's vocabulary is part and parcel of his reading in obscure geographical and scientific books and partly because it is Wordsworth who has always been regarded as the innovator in poetic diction. However, the concentration on Wordsworth may give a false impression of how changes in poetic fashion affected the development of poetic language, since he is unique in many ways. A consideration of Coleridge's language provides a necessary corrective.

The importance of the Romantic period lies in the changing attitude to the poet and his language. In the Augustan period the poet was regarded as a cultivated man whose work was consciously fashioned and constructed in accordance with certain modes and accepted patterns. His language observed the necessary decorum and was, in its turn, regarded as the norm by which elegant usage could be judged. This privileged position was undermined by two processes. The first was the development of writings on rhetoric and syntax by people who may be called professional grammarians. Language and usage were increasingly regulated by such grammarians rather than by the practice of the poets. Indeed, since the grammarians frequently found fault with the language of the poets, the latter could no longer be regarded as models of good English. Thus a novelist like Jane Austen can get Miss Tilney to say in chapter 14 of *Northanger Abbey*:

'He is for ever finding fault with me for some incorrectness of language, and now he is taking the same liberty with you. The word "nicest", as you used it, did not suit him; and you had better change it as soon as you can, or we shall be overpowered with Johnson and Blair all the rest of the way.'

(Blair is Hugh Blair the rhetorician, and no doubt the Johnson invoked here was the dictionary-maker rather than the stylist.) The second was the changing attitude to poetic inspiration. A poem ceased to be an object made out of patient toil and in accordance with accepted rules, for the poets were seers and visionaries whose work must necessarily reflect their inspiration. Fruman has shown how deeply Coleridge was affected by this idea of the poet in so far as he falsified the evidence about the composition of his poems which were made to seem like the creation of a night rather than works which were constantly revised and improved.[1]

The new attitude to poetry will inevitably mean that each poet will have to set about creating his own language. No longer can he simply take over the literary language of the day and develop it within limits to his own ends, for there can no longer be an accepted tradition of poetic language. That uniformity which is such a hallmark of the literary language of earlier periods cannot be maintained. Those with plenty of self-confidence, like Byron, or who work with unshakeable principles of poetic composition, like Wordsworth, will survive readily enough in the new conditions, for either they will ignore the new tendencies or they will use them to support their own departures from the past. Inevitably the crisis will be most severe for those with the least confidence: in the Romantic period that means people like Coleridge and Keats. They will not have that support which an established literary language could have given them. Increasingly the struggle of poetic creation will become associated with the finding of a suitable language and medium. Naturally, such a period, in which the past has ceased to be respectable and in which every poet is supposed to have his own God-given language, will create tensions for individual

1. N. Fruman, *Coleridge the Damaged Archangel* (New York, 1971) [*Archangel*], pp. 3 ff.

poets, for a poet's sense of tradition is normally so strong that the past cannot be so readily neglected.

In the first flush of Romanticism it may have seemed that there was a straightforward choice between the traditional language of English poetry and the real language of men. For Coleridge the latter was never a serious possibility. Thus, although he was born in Devon and spent much of his life in Somerset, he was apparently not influenced by the local dialects of south-west England. It is rare to find dialect words in his poems and the status of some of those recorded is doubtful. In 'The Three Graves' the line which originally read 'Still swung the spikes of corn' was altered in *Sibylline Leaves*, 1817, to 'Still swung the strikes of corn'. According to E. H. Coleridge's note, *strikes* is a Somerset word which was deliberately substituted for *spikes* because it made better sense.[2] But *strike* is a common word from the time of Chaucer onwards in the sense of a 'bundle of straw, etc.'[3] While in Coleridge's poem the necessary sense is 'a small handful', it may be a sense he developed from the literary word rather than one which he borrowed from a regional dialect. For though in his Notebooks Coleridge did make lists of words and images which might be of use to him in his poetry, there is no evidence of any interest in colloquial or dialectal forms and there are certainly no lists of them. Lowes has pointed to one Somerset word used in his Notebooks,[4] but it is doubtful whether there are many more. The reason for this absence of interest in speech is clearly that Coleridge was too much imbued with the standard eighteenth-century attitude to books and nature. His imagination was inspired by his reading and not by his experience, and even nature was something he saw through others' eyes rather than through his own.

It is usual to divide Coleridge's poetic output into three major sections: the early poems prior to the Annus Mirabilis, the works written in that famous year, and the writings which follow it. Fruman has tried to characterize these periods. In his early work Coleridge is an imitator who is using the late eighteenth century as a model. He borrows and copies freely.

2. E. H. Coleridge, *The Poems of Samuel Taylor Coleridge* (London, 1912), i. 276.

3. See *OED*, s.v. *Strike*.

4. J. L. Lowes, *The Road to Xanadu*, 2nd edn (London, 1951), p. 456.

In his major poems written in the Annus Mirabilis there is a particular inspiration from Wordsworth, who was able to direct Coleridge's language into new channels. Finally, the last period was one in which he was forced to turn to foreign or classical works for inspiration.[5] Fruman has suggested that in each period Coleridge was acted upon by some exterior agency: he lacked inner inspiration. As a young poet he would naturally imitate those poets who were writing immediately before or at the same time as he. Even his experiments, such as his imitations of Spenser, are not uncharacteristic of the late eighteenth century. Yet a noteworthy feature of his 'Lines in the manner of Spenser', for example, is that this poem is hardly more Spenserian than many of his other poems written about the same time. One or two archaic features are included, such as the use of initial *y*- in past participles, but otherwise the diction and style are very much in an eighteenth-century mould. Imitation was an acceptable mode then, though it did not imply an attempt to recreate the language of an earlier period. More often it involved a rewriting of some earlier piece or the superimposition of a linguistic veneer on an eighteenth-century poem. This is how we should consider Coleridge's imitations at this time: at this stage in his career there is little to distinguish him from other minor late eighteenth-century poets.

It will now be easier to leave aside the poems of the Annus Mirabilis to concentrate on the period immediately following, for, if Coleridge may be said to have found his own style in the major poems, one naturally wishes to investigate what style he used in his later poems. According to Fruman, Coleridge had no personal initiative: he was influenced by others, so that, when he and Wordsworth parted, he was forced to rely upon different forms of inspiration, in this case, particularly the works of German poets. The importance of these poems lies in their language. Unless he translated them so literally that their diction was more German than English, he would be forced to look for some English model. If he no longer had Wordsworth to guide him and if he had grown out of his eighteenth-century background, what language was he to use? At the same time we must realize that Fruman's curt dismissal of these poems as mere translations is the result of regarding Coleridge as an

5. *Archangel*, pp. 221–81.

out-and-out Romantic. Whether the poems are good or bad is a separate point. But what we should not forget is that translation was an accepted tradition in English poetry to which many of our famous poets had contributed over the last several hundred years. It is only when such a high premium is placed on originality that poetic translation will be regarded as inferior.

In order to consider the language of Coleridge's later period I would like to consider his 'On a Cataract':

> Unperishing youth!
> Thou leapest from forth
> The cell of thy hidden nativity;
> Never mortal saw
> The cradle of the strong one;
> Never mortal heard
> The gathering of his voices;
> The deep-murmured charm of the son of the rock,
> That is lisp'd evermore at his slumberless fountain.
> There's a cloud at the portal, a spray-woven veil
> At the shrine of his ceaseless renewing;
> It embosoms the roses of dawn,
> It entangles the shafts of the noon,
> And into the bed of its stillness
> The moonshine sinks down as in slumber,
> That the son of the rock, the nursling of heaven
> May be born in a holy twilight!
>
> The wild goat in awe
> Looks up and beholds
> Above thee the cliff inaccessible;—
> Thou at once full-born
> Madd'nest in thy joyance,
> Whirlest, shatter'st, splitt'st,
> Life invulnerable.

This is a poem based on 'Der Felsenstrom' by Friedrich Leopold Stolberg, a minor poet of the Gottingen school.[6] In fact Stolberg's poem is forty-six lines long, though only the first seven were used by Coleridge and it is not worth reprinting more than that here.

> Unsterblicher Jüngling!
> Du strömest hervor
> Aus der Felsenkluft!

6. Stolberg's poem is edited in A. Sauer, *Der Göttinger Dichterbund, Dritter Teil* (Stuttgart, 1895), pp. 75–76.

> Kein Sterblicher sah
> Die Wiege des Starken!
> Es hörte kein Ohr
> Das lallende Rieseln im werdenden Quell!

It is perhaps worth emphasizing that Coleridge translated only those first lines; otherwise his poem is very different from Stolberg's. It is possible that he may have needed inspiration to set his poetic faculty in motion, but once engaged it produced a poem which was his own. Stolberg's poem is sentimental and descriptive, where Coleridge's is abstract and ambiguous. In these opening lines there are few usages which could be described as un-English, even though Coleridge follows the pattern of the German sentences. Only his *leapest from forth* strikes one as clumsy, for we would expect *leapest forth from* and the construction may have imitated *strömest hervor*. An important readjustment of the strophe is the balance provided by the repetition in

> Never mortal saw . . .
> Never mortal heard . . .

While the first line is a direct translation of *kein Sterblicher sah*, the second has imitated the same pattern instead of following the German *es hörte kein Ohr*. This has given the stanza more rhetorical strength and directness in a way frequent in Coleridge. He either repeated key words at the beginning of parallel sentences or linked clauses together by using a negative at the beginning of each. The use of *nor . . . nor . . .*, for example, might almost be described as a distinguishing feature of the 'Ancient Mariner' and it is also found in the writings of the eighteenth-century poets like Gray, whose 'Elegy' has an example at lines 111–12. Although both Stolberg and Coleridge are using a free verse form, Coleridge's lines seem more disciplined as a result of this rhetorical alignment.

What occurs in the German poem may be altered or supplemented by Coleridge. A good example is *Felsenkluft*, 'a rocky cleft', which is changed to 'the cell of thy hidden nativity'. The use of *cell* and *nativity* gives these lines a greater sense of anthropomorphism, which is found in the original principally in the opening line. Both words were in fact used by Milton and the eighteenth-century poets, from whose work Coleridge presumably took them. One of them is a typical part of the

Augustan poetic diction and the other an abstract Latin word. Likewise the last line of the German extract is expanded by Coleridge into three lines, none of which reflects what is in the original. Again this addition contains much that is typical of his diction. The two adjectives are firstly a compound adjective made up of an adjective and a participle, and secondly what I may call a negative adjective, that is a word defining a quality which is said to be absent by the use of a negative suffix or prefix. As we shall see, both types were commonly used by Coleridge and eighteenth-century poets. Other parts of the diction show the same affinities. *Charm* in the sense 'sound' is found in *Paradise Lost* and the verb *lisp* was a favourite with some Augustan poets. At the same time the use of 'his voices' and 'the son of the rock' continues that feeling of anthropomorphism already noted. The effect of these changes is to create a more abstract and generalized picture. Definite descriptive features are omitted so that it is no longer possible to tell from Coleridge's English version alone that it is a cataract which is being described. What anthropomorphic qualities there were in the German have been greatly enhanced so that the mysterious quality and general applicability of the poem are increased.

Of particular interest are the adjectives in these lines and, indeed, in the whole poem. As I have already mentioned, Coleridge frequently uses what I have called negative adjectives. In his opening line the use of *unperishing* may have been influenced by Stolberg's *unsterblicher*, but it was a common enough word in late eighteenth-century poetry and is found in Cowper's 'Annus Memorabilis'. A negative prefix occurs also in *inaccessible* and *invulnerable*, and the negative suffix in *slumberless* and *ceaseless*. The suffix is particularly frequent in Coleridge's writings and may be said to be one of the elements which provide the sibilant music of 'Kubla Khan', as in

> Through caverns measureless to man
> Down to a sunless sea.

Similar forms occur throughout his poems, as the following examples show: *toothless*, *leafless* ('Christabel'), *numberless* ('Frost at Midnight'), *footless* ('Eolian Harp'), *viewless* ('Reflections'), *branchless* ('Lime Tree Bower'), and frequently they are the adjectives which linger longest in the mind as they are among the more striking. Adjectives with negative prefixes are almost as common, as for example *unsandal'd*, *unsettled* ('Christabel'), *unvarying* ('Lines at Brockley Coomb'), *unfeathered* ('To a Nightingale'). It is significant that such adjectives are found as frequently in eighteenth-century poetry, and a cursory look through Gray's 'Elegy' produced the following: *unfathom'd*, *unseen*, *dauntless*, *inglorious*, *guiltless*, *noiseless*, *uncouth*, *shapeless*, *unletter'd*, *unhonour'd*, *artless*, *listless*, *hopeless*. It is not difficult to appreciate the attraction of such words. They are more generalized and also imply a contrast. A positive word, such as *barefoot*, for example, may be too strong and definite, and it does not of itself force the reader to imagine its opposite, a foot with a shoe on. But the negative adjective *unsandal'd* conjures up the picture of a missing sandal, of something which ought to be there but is not. The word impels us to think of the contrast between a foot with and a foot without a sandal. Hence such words help to create a tension between what is and what might be, and this is why Gray used them in his 'Elegy'. Coleridge found them useful for the same reason, for his poems often create a mood which is built round a contrast.

The other type of adjective is the compound consisting of a noun or adjective and a participle. In 'On a Cataract' there are only two examples, *deep-murmured* and *spray-woven*; but many examples occur elsewhere in his poems. In 'Christabel' they include *broad-breasted*, *blue-veined*, and *grey-haired*, and, in the 'Ancient Mariner', *bright-eyed* and *star-dogged*. Apart from the bisyllabic adjective in *-y*, this is the type which we associate particularly with the Augustans. Thus in Gray's 'Elegy' we find such instances as *ivy-mantl'd*, *incense-breathing*, *straw-built*, *long-drawn*, and *hoary-headed*. Such compounds may well have arisen because the couplet compelled compression in language, and may then have remained because of their usefulness. Compound adjectives of this type remained the most frequently used by Coleridge, who does not seem to have experimented with compounds in the way that Keats and Shelley were to do.[7]

In the rest of this poem the diction has the same qualities that we have already noted. There are new words like *joyance*, a Romantic word reintroduced by Coleridge, but otherwise the

7. See J. H. Neumann, 'Coleridge on the English language', *PMLA*, lxiii (1948), p. 642.

vocabulary reminds us of the typical words used by either Milton or Gray, *portal, embosoms, shafts, stillness*. Many words are Latinate or abstract. Many in *-ing* occur, usually verbal nouns. Indeed, as so often in eighteenth-century diction, there is more vigour in the verbs than in the nouns, as in the final lines of the poem:

> Madd'nest in thy joyance,
> Whirlest, shatter'st, splitt'st,
> Life invulnerable.

Repetition and a rhetorical arrangement are found. The two lines

> It embosoms the roses of dawn,
> It entangles the shafts of the noon,

are identical in their structure, and the two final nouns, though not rhyme words, are similar in sound. They form what is virtually a balanced couplet. A balance within a single line is found in the line, 'That the son of the rock, that the nursling of heaven'. Careful attention was clearly given to the choice of the words so that the poem had a soft musical charm, which is perhaps not altogether in keeping with the subject of the poem. Thus the *r* and *m* sounds of *deep-murmured charm* provide a sonority which is in pleasing contrast to the *l* sound of the *lisp'd . . . slumberless* of the following line. There is perhaps less alliteration than usual in many of Coleridge's poems, but the nasals and sibilants are dominant in 'The moonshine sinks down as in slumber'. Finally one may remark on the use of periphrasis in such phrases as *roses of dawn, shafts of the noon*, and *nursling of heaven*.

All these features go together to make 'On a Cataract' a late eighteenth-century poem. Its language is abstract rather than concrete, and when it is concrete it is never sensuous. Though the subject is one of grandeur and possible forcefulness, everything is kept quiet and urbane. There is little particularization and there is no striking imagery. All fits into an established tradition. Even the tendency to anthropomorphize the cataract makes the over-all effect general, since there is a widespead applicability of this one natural phenomenon. There are attempts at innovation in the vocabulary, for *joyance, slumberless*, and *spray-woven* are new creations or re-creations by Coleridge. But these are insufficient to suggest that he is a linguistic innovator since they are all formed after accepted patterns. Even the use of a freer metre and the striving for a different musical effect are not uncommon in the late eighteenth century: one need look no further than Gray's poems to find parallels.

It would be dangerous to draw many general conclusions from a brief investigation of a single poem. Yet it is clear that even after the Annus Mirabilis Coleridge was still writing poems with a late eighteenth-century diction and approach. The use of a German source could have freed him from that tradition if he had wished to escape. The evidence of this poem suggests that he never ceased to be a late eighteenth-century poet, though his major poems and his association with Wordsworth have encouraged us to regard him as primarily a Romantic. We have seen in passing that the major poems themselves contain many of the linguistic features which we can regard as typical of Coleridge and the late eighteenth century, though they are less evident because they are overlaid with other styles. But in 'Kubla Khan' the eighteenth-century diction is very evident, though in the 'Ancient Mariner' and 'Christabel' it has been modified by the influence of the ballads and Walter Scott respectively. But I think these influences should be considered as temporary diversions rather than as permanent changes of direction, for we know that Coleridge was readily influenced by immediate external influences. Basically he remained an eighteenth-century poet in diction and approach, though that basis can be overlaid by other temporary influences. It is probably this underlying eighteenth-century sympathy which led him to be so critical of Wordsworth's approach to language in that famous chapter 17 of the *Biographia Literaria*. For, after all, much that Wordsworth in his preface had complained of in Gray could with equal validity be laid at Coleridge's door. Wordsworth by his example and his preface had undercut Coleridge's position, and it was natural for him to react somewhat vigorously. We have perhaps been so infatuated with Coleridge's philosophy and visionary qualities that we have overlooked the affinities of his diction with the eighteenth century. The problem of trying to work within a convention which was becoming theoretically untenable and outmoded may have been an important factor in his life and poetic output. It can only have increased his feeling of insecurity, and hence contributed to that deviousness which Fruman found so characteristic of his life.

'Taste' and 'tenderness' as moral values in the novels of Jane Austen

HERMIONE LEE

I

In using aesthetic sensibilities as indications of morality, Jane Austen was doing nothing new. She was following the eighteenth-century doctrine that good taste is a mark of virtue. From Shaftesbury's theory that 'the man of virtue . . . is the man who recognizes what is good by its beauty'[1] to Burke's description of how delicate sensibilities arise from strong, pure feelings,[2] throughout the century the appreciation of nature and art was felt to imply a certain standard of morality. The idealization of nature, in Platonic terms, as the material form of even greater heavenly beauty, and the corresponding idealization of taste as the expression of good character, led to various interrelated fashions and habits of thought of which Jane Austen was both aware and wary. Firmly accepting the fundamental idea of a relationship between taste and morality, she was thoroughly satirical of the excesses to which that idea could lead.

It was felt that taste for art, taste for literature, and taste for nature, were related, and were all three suggestive of one's moral worth—and of one's social standing. Hume's statement in his *Essays* of 1741, that

One obvious cause why many feel not the proper sentiment of Beauty, is the want of that delicacy of the imagination which is requisite to convey a sensibility of the finer emotions[3]

1. See Basil Willey, *The Eighteenth-Century Background* (London, 1962), p. 72.
2. See Edmund Burke, 'On Taste', Introduction to the 'Essay on the Sublime and the Beautiful', *Works* (Oxford, 1906), i. 78 (first published 1756).
3. David Hume, 'Of the Standard of Taste', *Works* (London, 1903), p. 239 (first published 1741).

led, by way of Shaftesbury and Burke, to the idea that taste was
the privilege of those few whose 'natural sensibility to Beauty',
as Hugh Blair put it, had been added to by a 'good understanding' resulting from education and culture.[4] 'The power of receiving pleasure from the beauties of nature and of art' (Blair's
definition of taste) was only open to a certain class of mind:

He whose heart is indelicate or hard, he who has no admiration of
what is truly noble and praiseworthy, nor the proper sympathetic
sense of what is soft and tender, must have a very imperfect relish
of the highest beauties of eloquence and poetry.[5]

Archibald Alison, in his popular lectures *On Taste*, of 1790, developed the association between aesthetic awareness and moral
sensibility:

There is not one of these features of scenery which is not fitted to
awaken us to moral emotion . . . to make our bosoms either glow
with conceptions of mental excellence, or melt in dreams of moral
good.[6]

Blair and Alison, the theorists, were in accord with the prac-
titioners of the picturesque, men like Knight, Uvedale Price,
and Humphrey Repton:

The man of good taste . . . knows that the same principles which
direct taste in the polite arts direct the judgement in morality; in
short, that a knowledge of what is good, what is bad, and what is
indifferent, whether in actions, in manners, in language, in arts, or
science, constitutes the basis of good taste and marks the distinction
between the higher ranks of polished society and the inferior orders
of mankind.[7]

During the second half of the century, the fashions in taste
which arose from the accepted relationship between virtue and
perception became commonplace, the more so as they were incorporated into the novels of sensibility. The love for seventeenth-century French landscape painters such as Claude, and

4. H. F. Harding (ed.), Hugh Blair, *Lectures on Rhetoric and Belles Lettres*
(Southern Illinois, 1965) [Blair], i. 16, 21 (first published 1783).
5. Blair, p. 23.
6. Archibald Alison, 'On Taste', *Works* (Edinburgh, 1811), i. 436. First
published 1790.
7. J. Nolen (ed.), Humphrey Repton, *The Art of Landscape Gardening*
(Cambridge, Mass., 1907), p. 67 (first published 1795 and 1803).

for landscape poets such as Thomson, Dyer, and Cowper; the artificially wild landscapes, packed with grottoes, waterfalls, ruins, solitary hermits, and irregularly positioned cows, which wealthy land-owners created in imitation of popular paintings and poems; the elaborate quarrels between the definers of the picturesque; the habitual, invariable poetic raptures over landscape expressed by the heroines of Mrs Radcliffe, Maria Edgeworth, Fanny Burney, and Charlotte Smith: all these ramifications from the initial alignment between taste and virtue became susceptible of ridicule. Jane Austen followed a tradition of satirizing such fashions in taste as much as she reacted against those fashions. By her time, the pretentions and affectations linked with the cult of the picturesque were already under fire. (One example out of very many is Richard Graves's *Columella, or the Distres't Anchoret* (1779), referred to in *Sense and Sensibility* (p. 88),[8] with its anecdote of the professional hermit, who, hired to decorate some picturesque grounds, was sacked for being found drunk. Peacock's *Headlong Hall* (1816), has, in the character of the absurd 'improver', Mr Milestone, a late example of satire on the picturesque.) Similarly, the dangerous effects of the cult of sensibility had for some time been the subject of satire and attack; this character sketch from Fanny Burney's *Camilla* shows the tradition of which *Sense and Sensibility* was part:

To all that was most fascinating to others, she joined unhappily all that was most dangerous for herself; an heart the most susceptible, sentiments the most romantic, and an imagination the most exalted . . . Whatever was most beautifully picturesque in poetry, she saw verified in the charming landscape presented to her view in the part of Wales she inhabited; whatever was most noble or tender in romance, she felt promptly in her heart, and conceived to be general; and whatever was enthusiastic in theology, formed the whole of her idea and belief with regard to religion.[9]

Evidently Catherine Morland's excessive susceptibility and Marianne's excessive sensibility and 'enthusiasm' arise from this tradition of satirizing hackneyed contemporary fashions in

8. Page references to the novels are to the edition by John Davis and James Kinsley (Oxford, 1971), based on the 1923 edition of R. W. Chapman, and to Chapman's edition of Jane Austen's *Minor Works* (Oxford, 1954).

9. Fanny Burney, *Camilla* (Oxford, 1972), p. 487 (first published 1796).

taste. Marianne's unbalanced emotionalism is frequently identified with her attitude to literature and landscape, as when she
convinces herself, in spite of Elinor's admonitions, that, 'among
the objects in the scene', the gentleman on horseback riding towards them is Willoughby (p. 74). Like a picturesque land-
scape-gardener, she fakes the prospect to make it suit her
emotions. The real figure on horseback in Marianne's landscape, Edward, will soon be teasing her about her romantic
taste for the picturesque.

But it is not only in Jane Austen's early work that affectations
and excesses arising from standard fashions in taste are ridi-
culed. Mrs Elton's plan for an alfresco picnic in *Emma* (p. 320)
—'a sort of gipsy party'—is close in spirit to the delightful
juvenile satire, in *Evelyn*, on Gilpin's theories about the picturesque grouping of animals (p. 181). The caricature of the
Man of Feeling, Sir Edward, in *Sanditon*, with his pretentious
tastes for the 'new' writers, Wordsworth, Scott, and Burns, and
his immoral behaviour, is characteristic of the point of view
which had earlier, in Marianne, linked intolerance and im-
patience of social restraints with a love of the picturesque. John
Dashwood's acquisitive, unimaginative taste for 'improvements'
in *Sense and Sensibility* will be followed by the portrayal of Henry
Crawford, a destructive 'improver'. Emma's admiration for the
unimproved Donwell Abbey, with 'all the old neglect of prospect' (p. 323), again rejects the fashion (rather as Wordsworth
rejects the taste for the picturesque).[10]

But, though Jane Austen criticizes the affectations in the
contemporary fashions of taste, she accepts the principles from
which those affectations arose. Pretentions to 'taste' and 'tenderness' are exposed, but true 'taste' and 'tenderness' are shown,
always, to be signs of moral virtue. No clearer indication of this
can be found than the passage in *Persuasion* in which Anne Elliot
consoles herself, during an unhappy autumnal walk, by

repeating to herself some few of the thousand poetical descriptions
extant of autumn, that season of peculiar and inexhaustible influence on the mind of taste and tenderness, (p. 300)

10. See Wordsworth, *The Prelude* (1805), xi. 150–84. For an account of
Jane Austen's response to the cult of the picturesque, see Martin Price, 'The
Picturesque Moment' in Frederick W. Hilles and Harold Bloom (eds),
From Sensibility to Romanticism (Oxford, 1965).

but finds that a clear perception of the landscape itself corrects any tendency towards self-indulgence:

the ploughs at work, and the fresh-made path spoke the farmer, counteracting the sweets of poetical despondence, and meaning to have spring again. (p. 301)

II

Jane Austen's consistent alignment of 'taste' and 'tenderness' with morality is evident from the way in which she employs the two words. In delineating character, she uses a collection of words which suggest her moral outlook. These words fall into two groups: there are words for parts of the character, such as sense, temper, understanding, disposition, mind, feeling, and judgement, and words for qualities in the character, such as taste, tenderness, elegance, enthusiasm, and delicacy. She inherits the habit of grouping such words together from the literature with which she was familiar:

> God gives to every man
> The virtue, temper, understanding, taste,
> That lifts him into life.
> (Cowper, *The Task*, iv. 789–91)

Johnson's *Lives of the Poets* are full of such groupings, as are Blair's *Sermons*.[11] By balancing these words, Jane Austen is able to convey with great care and precision the constant underlying themes of her work, which are that virtues and vices are the

---

11. For examples in Johnson, see G. B. Hill (ed.), *Lives of the Poets* (Oxford, 1905), i. 481–7 and iii. 82–276. For examples in Blair, see Sermon 32, 'On Sensibility', *Works* (London, 1820), iii. 127–39. For Jane Austen's constant use of such vocabulary, see, for instance, 'To the Memory of Mrs Lefroy' in R. W. Chapman (ed.), James Austen-Leigh, *Memoir of Jane Austen* (Oxford, 1926), p. 58:

> Listen! it is not sound alone, 'tis sense,
> Tis genius, taste, and tenderness of soul;
> Tis genuine warmth of heart without pretence,
> And purity of mind that crowns the whole.

Mary Lascelles, in *Jane Austen and her Art* (1939; reprinted Oxford, 1968), has a valuable comment: 'To us Jane Austen appears like one who inherits a prosperous and well-ordered estate—the heritage of a prose style in which neither generalizationn or abstraction need signify vagueness, because there was enough close agreement as to the scope and significance of such terms' (p. 107).

result of innate disposition as well as of acquired understanding, that the head and the heart must work together, and that external accomplishments should reflect inner integrity.

'Taste' is one of the most important of these words. In *Sense and Sensibility*, which is concerned with the detrimental effect of false or indulgent taste on the personality, the word is used as a key to most of the characters. For instance, in chapter 4, Elinor and Marianne argue about Edward's 'taste'. Elinor finds it 'delicate and pure' (p. 16). To Marianne, Edward's lack of 'rapturous delight' for drawing means that he has no taste. It is she, in the discussion, who uses the word in the plural, in its more superficial sense (one rarely used by Jane Austen) to mean 'preferences':

I have not had so many opportunities of estimating . . . his inclinations and tastes.

Later, she applies the phrase 'natural taste' (p. 18) solely to Edward's drawing. Elinor uses the word more profoundly (ironically, since it is Marianne who is convinced that she alone puts a proper value on taste) to indicate Edward's moral perceptions, rather than his enthusiasms or talents. In this she anticipates Mr Knightley, who automatically links 'sense and taste' (*Emma*, p. 298) (where Marianne would link 'sensibility' and 'taste').

In *Mansfield Park* the distinction is frequently drawn between superficial 'tastes' (most obviously, that of the Crawfords for the theatricals) and genuine, moral taste:

She [Mary Crawford] had none of Fanny's delicacy of taste, of mind, of feeling. (p. 73)

Sir Thomas regrets, in the end, that he has concentrated on giving his daughters superficial tastes rather than moral values, or genuine 'taste'. The extent to which the Bertram girls have learned to link outward accomplishments with moral stature is well expressed by Maria's remark:

I cannot but think that good horsemanship has a great deal to do with the mind. (p. 62)

Those who possess genuine 'taste' also feel deeply and observe clearly. False 'taste' is merely a heartless elegance. The characters who are 'deep in hardened villainy' (*Sense and Sensibility*,

p. 159)—Willoughby, Wickham, Mr Elliot, Lady Susan, the
Crawfords—or who are vain and proud—the Bingley sisters, the
Bertram sisters, Sir Walter and Elizabeth Elliot—all have, or
pride themselves on having, good taste, and are also elegant in
their manners and their appearance. In the contrast between
these characters and characters such as Fanny or Anne, a
moral distinction is being drawn between those who want to
be seen, and those who want to see, to the best advantage.

Without feeling, no taste can be genuine. But just as taste, for
it to be an indication of true moral worth, requires a foundation
of tenderness, so tenderness must be disciplined by accurate perception, if it is not to be mere self-indulgence or affectation.
When it is not so disciplined, it is satirized.

In *Northanger Abbey*, 'tender' is one of the words used to burlesque the novel of sensibility, as when the Morlands's composed leave-taking of their daughter

seemed rather consistent with the common feelings of common life,
than with the refined susceptibilities, the tender emotions which
the first separation of a heroine from her family ought always to
excite, (p. 16)

or when Isabella and Catherine are said to pass 'so rapidly
through every gradation of increasing tenderness' (p. 32). Satirical uses of the word are found elsewhere: Elinor is cynical
about the extent of Lucy's 'tender regard' for Edward (*Sense
and Sensibility*, p. 121); Emma runs off to laugh in secret at Mr
Elton, 'leaving the tender and the sublime of pleasure to
Harriet's share' (p. 75).

But tenderness comes to be seen as a great virtue in *Emma*:

Warmth and tenderness of heart, with an affectionate, open manner,
will beat all the clearness of head in the world, for attraction.
(pp. 241–2)

Emma is accusing herself here of having a clear head rather
than a warm heart. But at this very moment her lack of clear-
headedness is apparent, in her mistaken belief that Frank
Churchill is transferring his affections from herself to Harriet.
And the impetuous, emotional decision she now makes—that
Harriet is worth a hundred cold Jane Fairfaxes or Emmas—is
equally mistaken. Emma, in fact, possesses both a warm heart
and a clear head, but is using them both misguidedly and ir-

responsibly. She will come to realize, through acquiring a sense of responsibility, that tenderness and perception cannot be rivals, but must be joined, and so reaches a mental state comparable to Fanny's or Anne's, where 'her judgment was as strong as her feelings' (*Emma*, p. 391).

In *Persuasion*, where the heroine is both tender and responsible from the start, the word is used with increasing resonance, so that, by the end, Anne Elliot comes to be seen as the personification of tenderness:

All, all declared that he had a heart returning to her at least; that anger, resentment, avoidance . . . were succeeded . . . by the tenderness of the past; yes, some share of the tenderness of the past. (p. 393)

'Your feelings may be the strongest', replied Anne, '. . . but . . . ours are the most tender.' (p. 438)

There they returned again into the past, more exquisitely happy, perhaps, in their re-union, than when it had been first projected; more tender, more tried, more fixed in a knowledge of each other's character, truth, and attachment. (p. 445)

In all three excerpts tenderness is linked with suffering, waiting, and endurance. The idea of pain as a necessary part of tenderness is found even in the last paragraph of the book:

Anne was tenderness itself, and she had the full worth of it in Captain Wentworth's affection. His profession was all that could ever make her friends wish that tenderness less. (p. 455)

Although the word has such powerful moral stature by the end of the book, it has also been used ironically. Mrs Musgrove's lamentations for 'poor Dick', her 'tenderness and sentiment' (p. 285), are ludicrous, we are told, when her 'comfortable substantial size' is considered. Since *Persuasion* shows the reawakening of the tenderness of the past from memory to actuality, the satire on Mrs Musgrove is more than an incidental piece of harsh wit: it acts as a burlesque on the book's main theme. Similarly, the romantic offstage love between Louisa and Captain Benwick—not one of the most convincing relationships in the novels—serves as a mild satire on sensibility, set against the more fullblooded sensibility of the hero and heroine. Captain Benwick's abandonment of his heartfelt romantic pose, that of fidelity to a lost object, proves Anne's point in her speech to

Captain Harville and acts as a useful humorous alternative to the serious passion of the main plot. Louisa's nerves, 'susceptible to the highest extreme of tenderness' (p. 340), and her relationship with Benwick, lead, when described by the matter-of-fact Charles Musgrove, to a parody on 'taste and tenderness':

If one happens only to shut the door a little hard, she starts and wriggles like a young dab-chick in the water; and Benwick sits at her elbow, reading verses, or whispering to her, all day long. (p. 424)

III

In *Mansfield Park*, 'taste' and 'tenderness' are linked as expressions of moral strength. They sanctify places and relationships with a sense of the past, and are given the force of religious principles. Many of the enthusiasms and tastes which, in *Sense and Sensibility*, were satirized as excessive, are here reinstated, in Fanny's character, as moral standards opposed to the careless, destructive romanticism of the Crawfords. In no other novel of Jane Austen's are aesthetic tastes so strongly indicative of moral worth. The book contains no irrelevancies: landscape gardening, architectural improvements, card games, choice of reading, theatricals—all its details contribute to the expression of a rigid moral scheme. Through Fanny's perceptions we are forced to reject what, undirected, we might regard as charming (Mary Crawford), as harmless (the theatricals), or as attractive (Henry Crawford's proposal).

In the opposition between Mary and Fanny we are in the peculiar position of having to admire and sympathize with the limiting, restrictive character rather than with the volatile, energetic one. The moral difference between them is clearly revealed in the scene where they are sitting in Mrs Grant's shrubbery: a pastime which often gives rise to

some tender ejaculation of Fanny's on the sweets of so protracted an autumn. (p. 187)

Fanny's reflective outdoor mood (very like Anne Elliot's in language and tone), links aesthetic appreciation, practical awareness, and tenderness for the past. She speaks of the shrubbery, admiring its adaptation from a 'rough hedgerow' (and thereby indicating that she is not irrationally rigid in the dislike of improvements she showed in the conversation about Sotherton). She moves on to a reflection on the wonderful power of man's memory. Then, noticing that Mary is 'untouched and inattentive' (lacking, that is, in Fanny's tenderness and taste) she returns to the evergreens, apologizing for her 'wondering strain', whereupon Mary comments:

To say the truth . . . I am something like the famous Doge at the court of Lewis XIV, and may declare that I see no wonder in this shrubbery equal to seeing myself in it. (p. 188)

Cynicism of the court and of the city are closely related. Inasmuch as Mary notices the pastoral setting at all, she brings to bear on it a corrupt cosmopolitanism. Her indifference to the shrubbery, except in so far as it leads her to think about herself, is characteristic of all her offhand dealings with the visible world, which she alters to suit her own ends. Though she has a cynical view of life, her playfulness with reality sometimes resembles the romantic Marianne's creation of private landscapes. By contrast, Fanny's romanticism, though it can be fanciful and naive, is also practical and precise. Where Fanny, on the journey to Sotherton, is happily engaged in

observing the difference of soil, the state of the harvest, the cottages, the cattle, the children,

Mary is described as having

none of Fanny's delicacy of taste, of mind, of feeling; she saw nature, inanimate nature, with little observation; her attention was all for men and women, her talents for the light and lively. (p. 73)

In fact her perceptions about character are extremely fallible. In her attempts to manipulate people, she very often has little idea of what kind of mind she is dealing with: with Fanny and Edmund she makes many mistakes. It is Fanny, in the shrubbery, who notices that her conversation is not interesting to Mary, and alters it accordingly. Throughout, Fanny's clarity of perception about people is linked to her appreciation of, and tenderness for, 'inanimate nature'.

Mary's playfulness with reality (which, like her brother's, finds a satisfying outlet in play-acting), is attractive; but in spite of its attractiveness, it is always shown to be ruthless, an attempt to impose her will on things as they are. Whether she is trying to get a horse and cart for her harp during the harvest, or refusing to be dictated to by a watch, or using the weather for her own ends ('South or north, I know a black cloud when I see it; and you must not set forth while it is so threatening' (p. 188)) her self-interested carelessness is always in contrast to Fanny's tender appreciation of reality. This is humorously implied by the way in which Fanny always particularizes:

'Poor William! He has met with great kindness from the chaplain of the Antwerp,' was a tender apostrophe of Fanny's, very much to the purpose of her own feelings, if not of the conversation, (p. 100)

whereas Mary always generalizes: 'One scarcely sees a clergy-man out of his pulpit' (p. 83).

Fanny's humanizing of the landscape around her stems from her strong feelings for tradition and security, for the sanctity of place and past. (These feelings are contrasted not only with Mary's insensitivity to landscape, but also with Maria Bertram's cold-hearted, pretentious attitude to the Sotherton estate, and with Henry's ruthless, rootless talents for 'improvements'.) The association Fanny makes in the shrubbery scene between the beauties of nature and the wonderful activity of the human memory is the key to her emotional life, to the union she makes between taste and tenderness. Her moral aestheticism is one which thrives on association. She is not a lover of the new. (Like her aunt Bertram, Fanny is a creature of habit and sets her face against change; the difference between them is that Fanny never takes anything for granted.) The preservation of child-hood emotions in Fanny, signified by William's cross and Ed-mund's chain, is at the moral, and indeed religious, centre of the book. It is the lack of such feeling for tradition which damns the Crawfords and Maria Bertram.

The scene in the chapel indicates how much religious prin-ciple and a taste for tradition are linked together. Fanny is saddened to learn that the custom of family prayers has been discontinued:

A whole family, assembling for the purpose of prayer, is fine! (p. 77)

There is a mixture of literary fancifulness and practical sense in Fanny. Her feelings about the chapel are secular and domestic rather than 'enthusiastic'. She is praising the value of family unity and family tradition as much as the value of prayer itself. But, at the same time, her romantic anticipations of a Gothic chapel have been disappointed:

No signs that a 'Scottish monarch sleeps below'. (p. 77)

Here, and elsewhere, her romantic tastes are presented humorously, though sympathetically. Fanny's love for the medieval, which leads her to relish the 'spirit of chivalry' in Edmund's name (p. 190) and to look for banners in the chapel at Sotherton, is a comic indication of a serious morality. A similarly comic tone is found in the description of Fanny's room, that 'nest of comforts', where Fanny's respect for the minutiae of her past, her feeling for inanimate objects, and her romantic enthusiasms, are linked together. Fanny's purpose in visiting her room,

to see if by . . . giving air to her geraniums, she might inhale a breath of mental strength herself, (p. 137)

is touching and funny, but to be taken seriously. The associations with Wordsworth, Mrs Radcliffe, and William Gilpin which the transparencies of Tintern Abbey, a cave in Italy, and 'a moonlight lake in Cumberland' call up, are humorously made.[12] But such humorous treatment of Fanny's 'taste and tenderness' is very different from the satire of which it reminds us, the satire on hackneyed novelistic fashions found in *Northanger Abbey* and *Sense and Sensibility*. The difference in the treatment of Fanny's and Marianne's tastes is especially important. Fanny and Marianne have the same tastes. Both are laughed at for them. Both remain sympathetic in spite of this satire. But their enthusiasms bear different relations to reality. Fanny's 'sensible' romanticism, her taste for Cowper and Scott and stars and geraniums, is the fanciful side of the tenderness which also enables her to see clearly and judge rightly. She puts principle before taste: her love of Cowper arises out of her attitude to existence. Marianne's excessive sensibility is topsy-turvy:

As for Marianne, I know her greatness of soul . . . Thomson, Cowper, Scott—she would buy them all over and over again; she would buy up every copy, I believe, to prevent their falling into unworthy hands; and she would have every book that tells her how to admire an old twisted tree. (p. 79)

12. See F. W. Bradbrook, 'Sources for Jane Austen's Ideas about Nature in *Mansfield Park*', *Notes and Queries*, ccvi, NS viii (1961), pp. 222–4.

Marianne feels that virtue is the result of taste, and the prerogative of those who have taste. She thus attempts to act out a literary existence, grounded on taste, which is incompatible with the realities of social, moral, and emotional life. Fanny (who cannot act) sometimes appears to be satirized for her literary enthusiasms in a similar way. But in *Mansfield Park* the irony is there, not to warn against such sensibilities, but to make them more endearing and hence more acceptable.

Fanny's tastes and sensibilities are not merely ornaments in a private landscape: they reflect the moral structure of the whole book. This is particularly apparent in her preference for Cowper, a preference which we know Jane Austen shared[13] and which, like Mary Crawford's taste for Pope, is an indication of Fanny's level of morality.

Fanny's liking for Cowper reinforces her whole outlook. Her character incorporates many of the values expressed in his poetry. It is easy to see why Fanny admires and quotes from *The Task*. Her reflections at night on 'the sublimity of Nature', which has a power greater than that of painting, music, and poetry to 'carry people more out of themselves' (p. 102), her interest in the details of the landscape during the journey to Sotherton, and her bliss on returning to Mansfield and finding 'the change . . . from winter to summer'

when farther beauty is known to be at hand, and when, while much is actually given to the sight, more yet remains for the imagination; (p. 407)

these passages echo Cowper's heartfelt, religious appreciation of the sanctified, familiar, domestic, rural scene:

> Scenes must be beautiful which, daily view'd,
> Please daily, and whose novelty survives
> Long knowledge and the scrutiny of years.
> (*The Task*, i. 177–9)

The moral certainty in the familiar statement that 'God made the country, and man made the town' (i. 749) is also found in the strong opposition between the decorum of the country and the corruption of the town in *Mansfield Park*, and in Fanny's conviction that 'the influence of London' was 'very much at war with all respectable attachments' (p. 394). Cowper repeatedly

13. R. A. and W. Austen-Leigh, *Jane Austen: Her Life and Letters* (1913), p. 178.

emphasizes the peace and tranquillity embodied in rural life:

> Our groves were planted to console at noon
> The pensive wand'rer in their shades. (i. 759)

Nature is, above all, soothing (i. 141, 199). Fanny's ideal life, too, is one lived in rural calm and lack of bustle. She alone appreciates Sir Thomas's liking for the quiet family circle; she resists the chaos of the theatricals; her weakness and immobility are symptoms of her love of peace, as are her unshakeable affections, what Edmund calls the hold of her heart 'upon things animate and inanimate' (p. 316). Cowper's ideal existence, portrayed in *The Task* with growing religious intensity, is similarly moral, domestic, and peaceful. He, like Fanny, asks for

> Fire-side enjoyments, home-born happiness, (iv. 140)

and for 'friendship' and 'peace' (iii. 691). The desire for tranquil stability is not indolence, but a need to go on living in a place which has become sanctified by memory, association, and a personal sense of tradition. Love of the country is an indication of a mind 'Cultured and capable of sober thought' (i. 322), of one who 'attends to his interior self' (i. 373), according to both Cowper and Jane Austen. Love of nature is not merely an indication of virtue, but a religious experience, when nature is seen through eyes aware that their perception is an act of worship. This is implied in the continuation of the passage which is in Fanny's mind, during the conversation about improvements for Sotherton:

> Ye fallen avenues! once more I mourn
> Your fate unmerited, once more rejoice
> That yet a remnant of your race survives.
> How airy and how light the graceful arch,
> Yet awful as the consecrated roof
> Re-echoing pious anthems!   (i. 338–43)

The analogy between the avenue and the church, is, one may suppose, in Fanny's mind when she quotes this passage. The only one of Jane Austen's heroines to have explicitly Christian virtues, she also embodies most fully the author's identification of sensibility with morality. In *Mansfield Park*, Jane Austen seems to go beyond the traditional eighteenth-century use of 'taste' and 'tenderness' to indicate virtue, and to suggest that they also imply salvation.

The revival of Elizabethan drama and the crisis of Romantic drama

N.W.BAWCUTT

William Hazlitt began an article on 'The Periodical Press', published in 1823, with a question often asked at the time, 'Whether Periodical Criticism is, upon the whole, beneficial to the cause of literature?'[1] Strictly speaking, the point at issue was whether or not writers were encouraged by vigorous contemporary criticism of their work, but the question can reasonably be made to bear a wider significance. The periodicals published in the first quarter of the nineteenth century contained a great deal of literary criticism, ranging widely through English, foreign, and classical literature, and, though much of the interest was simply a matter of curiosity or antiquarianism, we can often detect a concern for the health of contemporary literature. For one anonymous critic Ben Jonson's plays could serve as a corrective for certain mistaken tendencies of the time:

Were the tribes of creeping rhymesters and would-be dramatists of the present day to explore his works—if we should not be delivered from their tediousness, we might from their absurdity. If the great men, which this age has undoubtedly produced, would profit by his example, they might learn that severity of style is the concomitant of severity of manners, and that the rock-based edifice of Jonson is firm from its simplicity, and reverend because unpolluted.[2]

The past is presented as a model and a stimulus for the present. But the rediscovery of the past had its drawbacks. If it could

1. *The Edinburgh Review*, xxxviii (1823), p. 349; reprinted in A. R. Waller and A. Glover (eds), *Collected Works of William Hazlitt* (London, 1902–4) [*Collected Works*], x. 202.
2. 'Ben Jonson's Works', *The Retrospective Review*, i (1820), p. 199.

be shown that the great writers of the Elizabethan period had
infinitely greater powers of creativity than eighteenth-century
poets and dramatists, the effect might be to set an impossibly
high standard, and to make the young author of the early
nineteenth century feel that his abilities were totally inadequate
to his ambition. This theme of the past as simultaneously an
inspiration and a burden has been handled brilliantly by W. J.
Bate.[3] Professor Bate has, however, relatively little to say about
drama, so that I would like to concentrate on one aspect of the
Romantic revaluation of the past, its attitude towards the Elizabethan dramatists apart from Shakespeare, considered in relation
to the Romantic attitude towards the drama of its own time.
Most of the evidence will be taken from early nineteenth-
century periodicals.

The problem of the relation between past and present was
particularly acute in drama. Poetry in England had undergone
many mutations, but had had a relatively continuous tradition,
and there were several poets of the late eighteenth and early
nineteenth centuries who could sensibly be put forward to prove
that poetry was healthy and flourishing. The position was completely different for drama, and Hazlitt was one of many who
expressed a decided sense of inferiority:

The age we live in is critical, didactic, paradoxical, romantic, but it is
not dramatic. This, if any, is its weak side: it is there that modern
literature does not run on all fours. . . . Our ancestors could write a
tragedy two hundred years ago; they could write a comedy one
hundred years ago; why cannot we do the same now?[4]

Tragedy was often regarded as the supreme literary genre,
combining magnificent poetry with a profound insight into
human character and emotions, and it was humiliating to an
age that felt it had recovered the true standards of greatness not
to be able to offer something of its own in the form that most
clearly illustrated those standards. As a writer in *The Retrospective Review* put it,

We long to see a stately subject for tragedy chosen by some living
aspirant—the sublime struggle of high passions for the mastery,
displayed—the sufferings relieved by glorious imaginations, yet

3. *The Burden of the Past and the English Poet* (London, 1971).
4. Drama review in *The London Magazine*, i (1820), p. 432; reprinted in
Collected Works, viii. 415.

brought tenderly home to our souls—and the whole conveying one grand and harmonious impression to the general heart. Let us hope that this triumph will not long be wanting, to complete the intellectual glories of our age.[5]

Of course, in discussions of this kind Shakespeare himself was a major presence—if there had been no Shakespeare in Elizabethan drama the position would have been very different— but it can, I think, be shown that the revaluation of the contemporaries of Shakespeare did much to sharpen the debate.

One question that must be discussed at the outset is whether Romantic criticism of non-Shakespearian drama is merely an extension of eighteenth-century attitudes, with nothing distinctively new. It is true that the revival of interest in plays by Shakespeare's contemporaries started in the eighteenth century. Between 1700 and 1800 there were two editions of Ben Jonson's complete plays, three of Beaumont and Fletcher's, and two of Massinger's, and their better-known plays were occasionally revived on the stage. There were also various separate reprints and anthologies, the most important of which was Dodsley's *A Select Collection of Old Plays*, first published in 1744 and reprinted in 1780. Collectors and scholars like Garrick, Capell, and Malone built up splendid collections of play-texts which found their way into the British Museum and other great libraries.

If we look more closely, however, at critical attitudes towards non-Shakespearian drama, we find very little of the enthusiastic response that the Romantics were to show. In the eighteenth century Shakespeare was commonly regarded as the Great Exception, the untaught Genius thrown up by chance in an otherwise barbarous age; according to Rowe, 'We are to consider him as a Man that liv'd in a State of almost universal License and Ignorance',[6] and Lord Lyttelton, speaking in the persona of Pope, exclaimed, 'Consider from how thick a Darkness of Barbarism the Genius of Shakespeare broke forth!'[7] Even opponents of this attitude, like John Upton, who argued that the age of Queen Elizabeth, and the Queen herself, were

5. 'Rymer on Tragedy', *The Retrospective Review*, i (1820), p. 15.

6. *Some Account of the Life &c. of Mr William Shakespeare* (1709), reprinted in D. Nichol Smith, *Eighteenth Century Essays on Shakespeare*, 2nd edn (Oxford, 1963) [Nichol Smith], p. 15.

7. George Lyttelton, *Dialogues of the Dead*, 4th edn (London, 1765), p. 126.

deeply learned,[8] did little to excite interest in Shakespeare's dramatic contemporaries, though Upton obviously had a mild admiration for Ben Jonson, and published *Remarks* on three of his plays in 1749.

Indeed, some of the scholars who were most widely read in Elizabethan literature were almost as dismissive as Lyttelton. The third volume of Capell's *Notes and Various Readings to Shakespeare*, published under the title of *The School of Shakespeare*, was an anthology from a very wide range of Elizabethan and Jacobean plays, but the extracts were chosen simply because they contained an interesting word or phrase, not for their poetic or dramatic value, and Capell made it clear that one purpose of his work was to demonstrate how immeasurably superior Shakespeare was to the other dramatists of his time:

Nothing can raise the wonder we hold him in to a pitch exceeding what it has stood-at and stands at this time, sooner than would a knowledge which is pointed-to here,—that of the English stage's condition when this star rose on it, or shall we call it this sun: Mysteries, and Moralities, with here and there a translation, make up something the better half of what had then been produc'd on it; and the few attempts at original in the comic and tragic line, fall beneath a couple of pieces the world is acquainted with—'Gorboduc' and '*Gammer* Gurton's *Needle*', which is saying all that is necessary relating to his preceders. But would he be loser, were his successors look'd into? much the contrary . . .[9]

Richard Farmer stressed that we must turn to Shakespeare's contemporaries, not to the classics, in order to understand him:

Nothing but an intimate acquaintance with the Writers of the time, *who are frequently of no other value*, can point out his allusions, and ascertain his Phraseology,[10]

but the phrase I have italicized is a revealing indication of his attitude, and Thomas Denman, in a review of Lamb's *Specimens of English Dramatic Poets*, was justified in regretting that Elizabethan writers had too often been regarded as 'mere repositories of forgotten facts and obsolete phrases'.[11]

8. John Upton, *Critical Observations on Shakespeare*, 2nd edn (London, 1748), p. 5.
9. Preface to 'Notitia Dramatica, or, Tables of Ancient Plays', *The School of Shakespeare* (London, 1783), without pagination.
10. *An Essay on the Learning of Shakespeare* (1767), in Nichol Smith, p. 201.
11. *The Monthly Review*, lviii (1809), p. 349.

We can occasionally find attempts in the eighteenth century at more positive assertions, but they tend to be half-hearted and ineffectual. William Guthrie, a hack writer from the middle of the century, put forward the stock argument that Shakespeare had single-handedly ennobled a drama hitherto crude and ignorant, but then went on, rather less conventionally, to suggest with considerable diffidence that by the time of James I the English theatre was at its greatest:

The strength of Shakespeare, the regularity of Johnson, the genteel manner of Fletcher, were all encouraged, and each had his just proportion of applause; nor am I sure whether this was not the period in which, take it all in all, England did not see her stage in its highest perfection.[12]

George Colman wrote his little pamphlet, *Critical Reflections on the Old English Dramatick Writers*, in 1760, and addressed it to Garrick, pleading with him to revive the best plays of Massinger, Fletcher, and Jonson (the only dramatists Colman named). Colman was well aware that these plays were commonly thought to be full of absurdities, and tried to defend them, not by any fundamental revaluation, but by arguing that audiences willingly tolerated similar absurdities in certain plays of Shakespeare. Richard Farmer noted that in *MacFlecknoe* Dryden had spoken of James Shirley with contempt, but clearly felt that Shirley had been undervalued: as he put it, 'his Imagination is sometimes fine to an extraordinary degree'.[13] But when all the evidence of this kind is put together (and there may well be more of it waiting to be discovered), it hardly equals the chorus of enthusiastic praise during the twenty years following the publication of Lamb's *Specimens* in 1808.

There was certainly no steady rise in appreciation of Shakespeare's contemporaries in the later eighteenth century. Veneration for the Bard himself became increasingly fervent, but had an unfortunate effect on his fellow-dramatists, if we may trust a single witness, Monck Mason, writing in 1798:

he now shines forth, with a blaze of splendor, which has cast into the shade every other ancient dramatic writer, even those who were formerly his rivals in excellence.[14]

12. *An Essay upon English Tragedy* (London, 1757), p. 13.
13. Nichol Smith, p. 170.
14. J. Monck Mason, *Comments on the Plays of Beaumont and Fletcher* (London, 1798), Preface, p. iii.

Even Beaumont and Fletcher had been pushed into oblivion:

. . . these elegant writers are now so totally neglected, that many copies of the last edition of their plays still remain unsold, though published near twenty years ago.[15]

If this is the case, it follows that Lamb was more of a pioneer than some recent scholars have been willing to allow.

Up to this point I have used the term 'Romantics' as a convenient abbreviation for 'the writers of the first quarter of the nineteenth century', but it would be seriously misleading to give the impression that enthusiasm for Elizabethan drama was confined to the poets and essayists we normally think of as 'the Romantics'. Lamb's *Specimens* was the most influential single work, and Hazlitt's *Lectures on the Dramatic Writers of the Age of Elizabeth*, delivered as lectures in 1819 and published in 1820, were favourably noticed in a number of reviews. Yet William Gifford, editor of the *Quarterly Review* and arch-enemy of many Romantic writers, was himself a scholar and editor of some distinction in the field of Elizabethan drama, and Francis Jeffrey, editor of the *Edinburgh Review*, was also an enthusiast. At the same time as *Blackwood's Edinburgh Magazine* was publishing the notorious attacks on Hunt, Hazlitt, and Keats as the 'Cockney School of Poetry', one of the contributors to these attacks, John Wilson, published in the same magazine, under the initials 'H.M.', a series of 'Analytical Essays on the Early English Dramatists' which includes the first attempt at extended discussion of Marlowe and Webster. Wilson was in fact more adventurous than Coleridge, who usually confined himself to the conventional trio of Jonson, Fletcher, and Massinger, and often belittled them in order to exalt Shakespeare.

The full range of the material available needs to be stressed. To the books of Lamb and Hazlitt may be added works like Nathan Drake's *Shakespeare and his Times* (1817), which gave a full and often sympathetic, though rather pedestrian, discussion of Elizabethan drama. Thomas Campbell's *Specimens of the British Poets* (1819) contained a number of short criticisms of individual dramatists, and provoked a thoughtful review from John Wilson.[16]

15. Ibid., pp. iii–iv.
16. *Blackwood's Edinburgh Magazine*, v (1819), pp. 217–31. The second half of this review was reprinted, as 'A Few Words on Shakespeare', in Wilson's *Works* (Edinburgh, 1857), vii. 420–31.

Wilson himself was not the only author to embark on a series of discussions: John Hamilton Reynolds published two articles, 'On the Early Dramatic Poets', in *The Champion* for January and March 1816, and promised a third which never materialized; in 1820 and 1821 *The European Magazine* published four articles on 'English Dramatists' (mainly on Webster and Chapman) and a two-part article 'On the Life and Principal Writings of Marlo [*sic*]' signed with the initials 'J.T.M.'; and from 1820 onwards *The Retrospective Review*, founded with the deliberate intention of reviving interest in unjustly neglected works of English literature, chiefly from the sixteenth and seventeenth centuries, published long discussions of nearly all the major Elizabethan and Jacobean dramatists. Their author may have been C. W. Dilke, who is known to have contributed to *The Retrospective Review*, and who edited an important anthology of *Old English Plays* in six volumes, published in 1814–15.

A large amount of miscellaneous material also exists which can often be found only by patiently going through the bound volumes of periodicals. Reviews of books frequently began with a general discussion, so that it is not surprising that Francis Jeffrey started a review of Weber's edition of Ford's plays for the *Edinburgh Review* in August 1811, with a broad survey of Elizabethan and Jacobean drama. It is much less inevitable that B. W. Procter, who wrote several plays and dramatic fragments in a diluted Elizabethan style under the pen-name 'Barry Cornwall', should have begun a review of plays by Sheridan Knowles and T. L. Beddoes with a general history of English tragedy that places most of its emphasis on the great Elizabethans.[17] And there is nothing whatever to indicate to the casual reader that the first twenty pages of what seems to be a long account of Paltock's *Peter Wilkins*, in *The Retrospective Review*, vii (1823), in fact deal intelligently with several of the issues raised in this paper, and include illustrative references to the history of English drama.

The pioneering work, Lamb's *Specimens*, not only helped to make the plays more easily available but also had a powerful influence in moulding critical attitudes. It may be true that the book was not a best seller, and was ignored by the leading periodicals of the time (though the reviews it did get were

17. 'English Tragedy', *The Edinburgh Review*, xxxviii (1823), pp. 177–208.

mostly favourable), but there are enough brief allusions to it to suggest that all the enthusiasts for Elizabethan drama in the early nineteenth century (including John Wilson) had read Lamb and usually regarded him as an accepted authority. Lamb broke away from the antiquarian approach of Capell and Farmer, and concentrated on plays that vividly presented 'human life and manners'.[18] The charge sometimes brought against Lamb that he taught his readers to regard the plays as 'poetry' rather than 'drama' is unjust: he wanted to illustrate 'the moral sense of our ancestors' as shown in 'the conflicts of duty and passion, or the strife of contending duties', and in order to do this he tended to choose complete scenes, or sections of scenes, rather than isolated passages, as he justifiably claimed in his preface. It is perhaps a pity that the edition of 1835 reprinted the 'Extracts from the Garrick Plays', which are mostly short; modern editions frequently conflate the two series of selections into one, and thus give a misleading impression of the original edition of 1808.

Lamb's critical remarks were brief and unsystematic, but forcibly expressed, and many contemporaries were struck by the occasional extravagance of his enthusiasm. The most daring example was his comment on the final scene of Ford's *The Broken Heart*. Princess Calantha's stoical endurance of the sufferings which lead to her death so impressed Lamb that he went to the extreme of comparing it with Christ's agony on the cross.[19] Some reviewers nervously deplored what they felt to be irreverent, and Gifford was stung into his notorious description of Lamb's comments as the 'blasphemies of a poor maniac'.[20] Hazlitt was less impressed by the play, and in his *Lectures* courteously disagreed with Lamb,[21] but T. N. Talfourd, reviewing Hazlitt, sprang to Lamb's defence.[22] Lamb's influence is clearly at work in a remark on the same scene in *The Retrospective Review*:

18. All quotations in this paragraph are from Lamb's 'Preface', as given in E. V. Lucas (ed.), *The Works of Charles and Mary Lamb* (London, 1904) [Lucas], iv. xi–xii.

19. Lucas, p. 218.

20. Review of Weber's edition of Ford, *The Quarterly Review*, vi (1811), p. 485.

21. *Lectures on the Dramatic Literature of the Age of Elizabeth*, in *Collected Works* [Hazlitt, *Lectures*], v. 273.

22. *The Edinburgh Review*, xxxiv (1820), pp. 445–6.

The last scene unites beauty, tenderness, and grandeur, in one harmonious and stately picture—as sublime as any single scene in the tragedies of Aeschylus or of Shakespeare.[23]

Hitherto 'bardolatry' had been confined to Shakespeare himself; Lamb extended it to some of his contemporaries, and aided the process by which the Elizabethan dramatists in general became 'a race of giants',[24] and not merely a foil to Shakespeare.

Lamb was also one of the earliest critics to use Elizabethan drama as a standard by which to condemn the drama of his own time, and in his notes on Middleton and Rowley's *A Fair Quarrel* and Rowley's *A New Wonder, A Woman Never Vext* he attacked 'the insipid levelling morality to which the modern stage is tied down' and the reluctance of modern dramatists to portray human passions honestly and truthfully.[25] Some of his comments moved beyond drama to suggest that the progress of civilization had rendered modern life more uniform and abstract, in such a way that the creative imagination found less material to work on. In Elizabethan days different types of clothing could indicate the class, profession, and character of the wearer, but in modern times these external distinctions were gradually disappearing:

The blank uniformity to which all professional distinctions in apparel have been long hastening, is one instance of the Decay of Symbols among us, which whether it has contributed or not to make us a more intellectual, has certainly made us a less imaginative people.[26]

And in a wryly humorous note to Jonson's *The Case is Altered* he suggested that it was easier to portray the raptures of a miser in an age when wealth consisted of tangible gold and jewels than in the age of the bank-note.[27]

Discussion of Elizabethan drama became increasingly popular in the dozen or so years following Lamb's *Specimens*, and reached its peak in the years 1818–21. No later critic established

---

23. 'Rymer on Tragedy', *The Retrospective Review*, i (1820), p. 14.
24. Hazlitt, *Lectures*, p. 180.
25. Lamb, *Specimens*, pp. 114–15 and 126. (For further discussion of this topic see R. C. Bald, 'Charles Lamb and the Elizabethans', in C. T. Prouty (ed.), *Studies in Honour of A. H. R. Fairchild* (Columbia, Miss., 1946), pp. 169–74.)
26. Lamb, *Specimens*, p. 71.   27. Ibid., p. 245.

himself with the authority of Lamb, and it is, I think, more profitable to consider this body of criticism as a whole than to look at critics individually, especially as there was often a remarkable unanimity of opinion, even among those who disagreed violently when they turned to politics or other areas of literature. The defects of their criticism are obvious enough, and there would be little point in approaching it in purely critical terms. The treatments of individual dramatists were frequently sketchy and superficial, and even when separate plays were handled at greater length there was always a tendency towards elaborate plot-summary and extensive quotation. They showed no awareness of the complex background to the drama of theatrical and literary conventions as analysed by modern critics like M. C. Bradbrook and Madeleine Doran. Yet if the nineteenth-century critics were amateurs in this sense, they were also amateurs in the sense that they loved their subject, and showed a missionary fervour to communicate their enthusiasm to others in a way which is not always apparent in the highly sophisticated world of modern scholarship.

The shift in taste radically revised the accepted historical pattern of English drama. Until quite late in the eighteenth century it was possible to regard modern drama as beginning at the Restoration, with Shakespeare as an isolated genius from an earlier age. By 1820 the emphasis had become very different. Repeatedly we find a perspective in which Shakespeare and his fellow-dramatists together formed the great national school of drama—for many critics the greatest the world has ever known—from which there had been a gradual but apparently inevitable decline into the humiliating nullity of the contemporary stage. One anonymous drama reviewer began his work in 1820 with a 'Comparison between Ancient and Modern Dramatists' (with 'Ancient' standing for Elizabethan, not classical) in which he sadly noted this decline, and acknowledged that modern attempts at serious drama—Shiel's *Evadne*, Maturin's *Bertram*, Milman's *Fazio*, Bucke's *The Italians*—were hardly superior to Dryden, Lee, and Otway, let alone the Elizabethans.[28]

28. *The London Magazine; and Monthly Critical and Dramatic Review*, i (1820), pp. 86–89. (This periodical is given its full title to distinguish it from *The London Magazine* edited by John Scott, which also began publication in 1820.)

This revised pattern was not intended to degrade Shakespeare. He was no longer to be regarded as the solitary genius; as Hazlitt put it:

He was not something sacred and aloof from the vulgar herd of men, but shook hands with nature and the circumstances of the time, and is distinguished from his immediate contemporaries, not in kind, but in degree and greater variety of excellence. He did not form a class or species by himself, but belonged to a class or species.[29]

Yet Hazlitt was perfectly willing to concede Shakespeare's immense superiority, though not in such a way as to belittle his fellow-dramatists:

If we allow, for argument's sake (or for truth's, which is better), that he was in himself equal to all his competitors put together; yet there was more dramatic excellence in that age than in the whole of the period that has elapsed since.[30]

There were various attempts to describe the relationship between Shakespeare and the others. For John Wilson, Shakespeare was 'one of a great body—the chief of a mighty band'.[31] But Wilson's admiration for Marlowe and Webster did not blind him to the fact that Shakespeare alone had the shaping powers of a great artist:

Except in him, we look in vain for the entire fulness, the self-consistency, and self-completeness, of perfect art. All the rest of our drama may be regarded rather as a testimony of the state of genius—of the state of mind of the country, full of great poetical disposition, and great tragic capacity and power—than as a collection of the works of an art.[32]

B. W. Procter ('Barry Cornwall') considered that Shakespeare was supreme because he united excellencies that can only be found separately among his contemporaries.[33]

One result of setting Shakespeare among his fellows was to show that English admiration for him was not, as supercilious French critics asserted, a strange aberration of taste, but the natural result of the fact that he embodied and expressed the

29. Hazlitt, *Lectures*, p. 180.   30. Ibid., p. 181.
31. Review of Campbell's *Specimens*, *Blackwood's Edinburgh Magazine*, v (1819), p. 217 [Review of Campbell].
32. Ibid., p. 226.
33. 'English Tragedy', *The Edinburgh Review*, xxxviii (1823), pp. 190-1.

deepest qualities of the English temperament, not in isolation
but as part of a powerful national movement. For Francis
Jeffrey it was essential to establish that

there was a distinct, original, and independent school of literature in
England in the time of Shakespeare, to the general tone of whose
productions his works were sufficiently conformable,[34]

and C. W. Dilke put in his own italics to emphasize that Elizabethan drama was

a *national* and *original* drama, *regulated by its own laws, and of course only
to be estimated by them.*[35]

These two concepts, 'national' (sometimes 'native' was used
instead) and 'original', were for many critics the key to Elizabethan drama; it reflected the English character at its most
genuine, and owed nothing to outside influence. By reviving it
they were, as Jeffrey put it,

enlarging that foundation of native genius on which alone any lasting
superstructure can be raised, and invigorating that deep-rooted stock
upon which all the perennial blossoms of our literature must still be
engrafted.[36]

The modern English writer needed to turn to the past in order to
discover his deepest identity.

The character of the drama seemed to reflect the characters
of the dramatists themselves. With no great respect for the rules
of criticism, or stifling sense of literary decorum, they were free
to express themselves openly and honestly. It was self-evident
to John Wilson that they were not sedentary intellectuals, but
mingled freely with other men in all their various activities.[37]
Their social relationships were easier than those of modern
writers—or so J. H. Reynolds deduced from their habit of
collaboration:

There is something amiable in the partnership productions of these
authors: they freely joined their abilities, and contributed to one
work, boldly and unsparingly. . . . It does not appear that a selfish
avarice for solitary praise was common with them. We have no

34. 'Ford's Dramatic Works', *The Edinburgh Review*, xviii (1811), p. 284
['Ford's Dramatic Works'].
35. *Old English Plays* (London, 1814), i. x.
36. 'Ford's Dramatic Works', p. 285.
37. Review of Campbell, p. 219. Cf. Hazlitt, *Lectures*, p. 190.

example in later times of these friendly conjunctions of genius. A fondness for individuality has long been popular, and mankind, in literature as in life, seem to have ceased to be social.[38]

It was natural enough that in describing the general characteristics of plays written by men of this kind Jeffrey should speak of 'great force, boldness, and originality',[39] or Reynolds of 'naked simplicity and majestic strength',[40] or that for John Wilson the central theme of the drama was 'man as he appears to imaginative and impassioned thought'.[41]

Similar phrases were used to describe the dramatists' powers of style. John Wilson asserted that they gave expression to the best qualities of the English language:

In them, more than in any body of writers, is contained the richness and power of our English speech. . . . They wrote when the language was free and unfettered—when it was far more vivid, forcible, significant in the common uses of life.[42]

They had no false refinement, and were masters of a pregnant simplicity which was able to convey deep feeling in a colloquial phrase. As Hazlitt put it:

It is as if there were some fine art to chisel thought, and to embody the inmost movements of the mind in every-day actions and familiar speech.[43]

Thomas Doubleday said much the same thing, and gave examples from Shakespeare and Webster of effects of deep pathos produced by homely and domestic allusions which a French writer of tragedy would not have dared to use.[44]

What had formerly been regarded as artistic blemishes in the plays were now seen as indications of truth and reality. Wilson gave a list of the main characteristics of the drama as a whole— its rejection of the unities, its careless and disjointed plots, its mingling of comic and tragic effects—but presented them not

38. 'On the Early Dramatic Poets', *The Champion*, January 1816, reprinted in L. M. Jones (ed.), *Selected Prose of J. H. Reynolds* (Cambridge, Mass., 1966) [*Selected Prose*], pp. 29–30. Cf. Hazlitt, *Lectures*, p. 224.

39. 'Ford's Dramatic Works', p. 276.

40. *The Champion*, 1816, in *Selected Prose*, p. 28.

41. Review of Campbell, p. 217.   42. Ibid., p. 219.

43. Hazlitt, *Lectures*, p. 237.

44. 'The Causes of the Decline of the British Drama', *Blackwood's Edinburgh Magazine*, xxiii (1828), pp. 36–37.

as faults but as a means of conveying to an audience a sense of the spontaneous and unpredictable quality of human life.[45] Modern dramatists, according to Jeffrey, gave their characters elaborate set-speeches in which every ramification of the point under debate was systematically explored. Elizabethan dramatists, in comparison, were much more casual:

The persons of the drama are made to speak like men and women who meet without preparation in real life. Their reasonings are perpetually broken by passion, or left imperfect for want of skill. They wander from the point in hand, . . . and after hitting upon a topic that would afford a judicious playwright room for a magnificent see-saw of pompous declamation, they have always the awkwardness to let it slip, as if perfectly unconscious of its value.[46]

The result, of course, was that the early dramatists gave us 'nature', the later ones merely rhetoric and eloquence. Even the indecency of the early plays, whose existence had to be admitted, could be seen as a frank acknowledgement of human vices which were still as powerful as before, but which modern writers glossed over or alluded to in euphemisms.[47]

It was natural that Romantic critics should speculate on the underlying causes of this splendid outburst of creativity. The commonest theory was that the shock of the Reformation awoke dormant national energies, and it was sometimes suggested that the translation of the Bible into English helped the process.[48] (In striking contrast to modern attitudes, there was no hint of a 'Renaissance' spreading from Italy to England.) But no-one pointed out that the Reformation would never be repeated, and in view of the critics' desire to revive the qualities of Elizabethan writing it is perhaps a little strange—and perhaps an indication of an inherent pessimism—that they sometimes described the process which led to the great period of drama in terms which implied that it was by definition unique and impossible to recreate. The sudden flowering of drama, for Jeffrey,

can only be compared to what happens on the breaking up of a virgin soil,—where all indigenous plants spring up at once with a

45. Review of Campbell, p. 218.
46. 'Ford's Dramatic Works', p. 286.
47. Compare Dilke, Preface to *Old English Plays* [Dilke], pp. xv–xvi; Reynolds, *The Champion*, 1816, in *Selected Prose*, p. 29; and Hazlitt, *Lectures*, p. 229.
48. See Dilke, pp. xi–xii, and compare Hazlitt, *Lectures*, pp. 181–3.

rank and irrepressible fertility, and display whatever is peculiar or excellent in their nature, on a scale the most conspicuous and magnificent.[49]

Jeffrey recognized that a soil long-cultivated does not produce the same kind of crop, but did not draw out the implications of this analogy for his own time. Reynolds used a different metaphor:

We look back upon the early Dramatic Literature of our country, with that sort of delight, with which we reflect upon the pure and beautiful and solitary light of the morning . . . The Drama, at the time of Elizabeth and James, was the day-dawn of our Poetry, and had an openness and grandeur which have never, in succeeding times, been surpassed. In the present age, it is certainly in its eventide,—and all the light that beams, is but the reflected brightness of a Power that is gone.[50]

Hazlitt argued that Nature was as glorious now as it had ever been, but the Elizabethan poets, 'coming first', had 'gathered her fairest flowers'.[51] It would seem obvious enough that processes of this kind cannot be reversed by later generations.

When it came to accounting for the decline of drama in the later seventeenth century, one cause was unanimously put forward, the triumph of French neoclassical standards in all fields of English literature. Jeffrey provided the most thoughtful discussion of this topic; he realized that it might seem odd that a native tradition of such power and vitality should allow itself to be dominated by foreign attitudes, but explained that unfortunate historical accidents, such as the decay of drama and poetry during the civil war, and the restoration of a king and court accustomed to French fashions, made resistance impossible.[52]

Why were modern dramatists so patently inferior to their great ancestors? The easiest way of arriving at the answer was to impute to the moderns qualities exactly opposite to those of the ancients. The ancients were bold; the moderns were timid and too much in awe of criticism.[53] The ancients were original, and went straight to life for their inspiration, whereas the moderns copied art; as Hazlitt put it:

49. 'Ford's Dramatic Works', p. 276.
50. *The Champion*, 1816, in *Selected Prose*, pp. 27–28.
51. Hazlitt, *Lectures*, p. 191.
52. 'Ford's Dramatic Works', pp. 278–80.
53. 'Lord Byron's Tragedies', *The Edinburgh Review*, xxxvi (1822), pp. 417–19 ['Lord Byron's Tragedies'].

The poetry of former times might be directly taken from real life, as our poetry is taken from the poetry of former times.[54]

The ancients wrote great poetry but were not afraid to use colloquialisms; the moderns, as George Darley (writing under the pen-name of 'John Lacy') asserted in a pungent series of articles, made all their characters speak with a kind of thin, feeble 'poeticality' that was neither poetry nor prose.[55]

A few critics made a further distinction, that the ancient dramatists were mostly professional men of the theatre, whereas the modern dramatist was ashamed of his calling, or wrote closet plays not intended for performance. Jeffrey rebuked Byron for claiming in the preface to *Sardanapalus* that he had never wanted his plays to be acted:

If Lord Byron really does not wish to impregnate his elaborate scenes with the living spirit of the drama, if he has no hankering after stage effect, if he is not haunted with the visible presentment of the persons he has created, if, in setting down a vehement invective, he does not fancy the tone in which Mr Kean would deliver it, and anticipate the long applauses of the pit, then he may be sure that neither his feelings nor his genius are in unison with the stage at all. Why, then, should he affect the form, without the power of tragedy?[56]

And Jeffrey would have liked to see John Kemble and Mrs Siddons in a revival of Ford's *The Broken Heart*.[57] But Jeffrey, unfortunately, was in a minority; most of his fellow-critics—even Hazlitt, for all his interest in the theatre[58]—tended to treat the old drama as books to be read rather than as plays to be acted, and this hardly helped to recreate a live theatrical tradition.

Part of the blame for the inferiority of modern drama lay on

54. Hazlitt, *Lectures*, p. 191.
55. See 'Letters to the Dramatists of the Day', *The London Magazine*, viii (1823), pp. 81–86, 133–41, 275–83, 407–12, 530–8, and 646–52, and ix (1824), pp. 60–64, 272–6 (a reply by B. W. Procter), 469–73 (Darley's reply to Procter), and also 'Old English Drama—*The Second Maiden's Tragedy*', x (1824), pp. 133–9. A brief account of these letters is given in C. C. Abbott, *The Life and Letters of George Darley*, 2nd edn (Oxford, 1967), pp. 39–45.
56. 'Lord Byron's Tragedies', p. 422.
57. This is said in a footnote added to later reprints of 'Ford's Dramatic Works', such as *Contributions to The Edinburgh Review* by Francis Jeffrey (London, 1844), ii. 307.
58. See Hazlitt, *Lectures*, pp. 246–7.

the changed conditions of modern life. Hazlitt had much to say on this point; he agreed with Lamb concerning the 'Decay of Symbols'[59] and felt that the violent and unpredictable quality of Elizabethan life was more in keeping with the spirit of great tragedy than the relative security of his own time.[60] In the *London Magazine* review whose opening sentences are quoted above, he tried to explain the undramatic nature of his age by arguing that man increasingly spent his time thinking about political problems and philosophical issues at the expense of his private emotional life:

We participate in the general progress of intellect, and the large vicissitudes of human affairs; but the hugest private sorrow looks dwarfish and puerile . . . In a word, literature and civilization have abstracted man from himself so far, that his existence is no longer *dramatic*; and the press has been the ruin of the stage, unless we are greatly deceived.

This 'bias to abstraction' could not be reconciled with dramatic poetry, which is 'essentially individual and concrete'.[61]

Some of Hazlitt's contemporaries disagreed with him. T. N. Talfourd commented:

We can observe in these Lectures, and in other works of their author, a jealousy of the advances of civilization as lessening the dominion of fancy. But this is, we think, a dangerous error; tending to chill the earliest aspirations after excellence, and to roll its rising energies back on the kindling soul.[62]

Talfourd was convinced that nature would continue to produce great writers (he does not explicitly say dramatists), and that they would find a means to express themselves. Other critics steered cautiously between optimism and pessimism. John Wilson felt, rather like Hazlitt, that the poetry of his time had 'not dealt enough with life and reality', and that imagination showed a tendency 'to separate itself from real life, and to go over into works of art'. But 'life is still strong', and if life and imagination could be reunited the spirit of dramatic literature might still be revived.[63]

59. Ibid., pp. 190–1.   60. Ibid., p. 189.
61. *The London Magazine*, i (1820), p. 433; reprinted in *Collected Works*, viii. 417.
62. *The Edinburgh Review*, xxxiv (1820), p. 449. There are strikingly similar arguments in *The Retrospective Review*, ii (1820), pp. 194–5.
63. Review of Campbell, pp. 230–1.

One way of accepting the decline of the drama without being pessimistic about the future of literature in general was to argue that the 'dramatic' feelings of the age had found new channels to express themselves. A writer in *The Retrospective Review*, who had a fervent admiration for Jane Austen, claimed that the novel was now the dominant genre of the time:

A species of writing so long held in dubious estimation has thus obtained a high rank in the literature of our age; and, having absorbed the dramatic talent of the nation, vies, in interest and dignity, with the noblest productions of our most illustrious bards.[64]

Wordsworth was clearly the greatest poet of his age, but was too contemplative (as Wilson tactfully put it)[65] or self-centred (as Hazlitt bluntly put it)[66] to succeed as a dramatist, and despite the obvious limitations of his talent Sir Walter Scott was the only writer of the day whose range and variety was such that a critic like John Scott was prepared to give him the epithet 'Shakespearean'.[67]

Yet if we return to the beginning of our argument, and repeat Hazlitt's question about the effects of periodical criticism, the answer may be depressing. The Great Modern Tragedy so eagerly hoped for in the nineteenth century never materialized; the nearest that Victorian poets came to it was in the dramatic monologue, which had no connection with the theatre, while their attempts at actable poetic drama were unsuccessful. The only real and lasting effect of Romantic criticism of Elizabethan drama was in fact a purely critical one: it established Shakespeare's contemporaries as figures of permanent importance in the history of English literature.

64. 'Peter Wilkins', *The Retrospective Review*, vii (1823), p. 136.
65. Review of Campbell, pp. 230–1.
66. *The London Magazine*, i (1820), p. 436; reprinted in *Collected Works*, viii. 420–1.
67. 'The Author of the Scotch Novels', *The London Magazine*, i (1820), pp. 12–13.

Lord Byron:
poetry and precedent

BERNARD BEATTY

> *Thalaba*, Mr Southey's second poem, is written in open defiance of precedent and poetry. Mr S. wished to produce something novel, and succeeded to a miracle.[1]

Byron's comment of 1809 reveals his characteristic respect for precedent. How seriously can we take Byron's concern with precedent and the nature of poetry? To answer such a question will involve reopening the perennial literary problem of tradition and originality which peculiarly troubles modern minds. Byron's coinage of 'precedent and poetry' is helpful here in its freshness, pithiness, and precision. It invites thought. I want to adopt and adapt the formulation in order to throw some light on Byron's thought and practice which, in their turn, provoke exact inquiry into tradition in poetry.

Southey is often accused by Byron of submitting to political tyranny whereas his poems defy literary precedent. Byron, on the contrary, is in 'open defiance' of political repression but his poems openly submit to precedent. Byron's submission to precedent is offered not as some personal quirk but as a representative way of making poetry at a time when, so Byron thought, the natural intimacy of precedent and poetry was either rejected altogether as in *Thalaba* and the Preface to the *Lyrical Ballads*, or travestied by the faked use of the past in, say, Chatterton's poems. His own poetry is a polemic for precedent. We have to engage with that polemic if we are to understand Byron and his poetry accurately.

We are not accustomed to take his poetry in this way. Byron usually appears, when he appears at all, in accounts or anthologies of Romantic criticism, as a spirited if theatrical spokesman

1. E. H. Coleridge (ed.), *The Works of Lord Byron: Poetry* (London, 1898–1903) [*Poetry*], i. 313, n. 1.

for Romantic self-expression. Thus in M. H. Abrams's standard work *The Mirror and the Lamp* there are some dozen references to Byron all of which state or assume Byron's position to be satisfactorily represented in his much-quoted assertion, '[poetry] is the lava of the imagination whose eruption prevents an earthquake'.[2]

This statement does, of course, represent a position of Byron and it is one expressed often enough elsewhere in his prose and verse. It is a position which influences but does not govern his practice. How rarely, for example, do we find this standard quotation given in full:

I by no means rank poetry or poets high in the scale of intellect. This may look like affectation, but it is my real opinion. It is the lava of the imagination whose eruption prevents an earthquake.[3]

He goes on to stress that the writing of poetry may thus prevent poets from going mad but 'I prefer the talents of action'.[4]

The fact that Byron has so little regard for poetry when it is in accord with the theory confidently ascribed to him[5] may recommend caution. We should be cautious, too, about accepting other possibilities that the full quotation might appear to support. It is not true for example that Byron always treats, in the dismissive manner he adopts here, theories which explain poetry away as an overflow of feeling. It is not true that Byron always sees poetry as attempted catharsis. But neither is it true that Byron has another and opposite theory to that of exalted self-expression, such as neo-classicism, which is more properly his. Nor finally is it true, as these negatives perhaps suggest, that Byron has no consistent concern at all but oscillates uncertainly between critical stances. Most of these alternatives have been offered, at one time or another, as Byron's essential viewpoint. In poetry as in politics, however, Byron seems to be in touch with a number of contradictory viewpoints but, on the other hand, his own practice is coherent and not accidentally so. It is the hidden grounds of this real coherence that concern us here. Byron's marriage of poetry and precedent provides our starting-point and our conclusion: it is not a passing formulation confined to local use in 1809.

2. R. E. Prothero (ed.), *The Works of Lord Byron: Letters and Journals* (London, 1902–4) [*Letters*], iii. 405. Quoted by M. H. Abrams in *The Mirror and the Lamp* (Oxford, 1953) [Abrams], p. 139.   3. *Letters*, iii. 405.   4. *Letters*, iii. 405.   5. For example, Abrams, p. 146.

When, for example, Byron criticizes Southey's *A Vision of Judgement* twelve years after criticizing *Thalaba*, he mocks Southey's use of the bad precedent of hexameters, and his own poem, 'The Vision of Judgement', is offered as one grounded in true precedents. We need to distinguish here between stated and implicit precedents:

> But, for precedents upon such points, I must refer him to Fielding's *Journey from this World to the next*, and to the Visions of myself, the said Quevedo, in Spanish or translated ... The whole action passes on the outside of heaven; and Chaucer's *Wife of Bath*, Pulci's *Morgante Maggiore*, Swift's *Tale of a Tub*, and the other works above referred to, are cases in point of the freedom with which saints etc., may be permitted to converse in works not intended to be serious.[6]

These stated precedents are invoked to justify particular procedures within the poem. But they invite us to locate it in a general perspective too. After all, the author of this Vision is Quevedo Redevivus. As usual, Byron means what he says. But he wants us also to notice his tone. He uses devices of ironic detachment such as the persona of Quevedo Redevivus to gain, almost unnoticed, his reader's assent to far-reaching claims. So here, he states explicitly that his poem is not serious. He implies however that it is at least as serious as the three works he mentions and should be associated with their kind of seriousness. He makes a limited point, he makes a joke and he invites us to speculate upon the implications of a tradition. In the same way his poem criticizes George III and Southey in pointed ways, makes us laugh for laughter's sake, and reminds us that there is a central line of vision writing which is not solemn and single-toned but open to comedy, satire and the grotesque.

Byron's tone appears more plainly perhaps when compared with a similar passage in Dryden's Preface to 'Eleonora'. Dryden writes:

> And on all Occasions of Praise, if we take the Ancients for our Patterns, we are bound by Prescription to employ the magnificence of Words, and the forces of Figures, to adorn the sublimity of Thoughts. Isocrates amongst the Grecian Orators, and Cicero, and the younger Pliny, amongst the Romans, have left us their Precedents for our Security.[7]

6. *Poetry*, iv. 483–4.
7. J. Kennedy (ed.), *The Poems and Fables of John Dryden* (Oxford Standard Authors edn, Oxford, 1962) [*Poems of Dryden*], p. 467.

This reminds us that Byron's justifying reference to precedents in a Preface to a poem is itself precedented. Byron is making an identical acknowledgement but, because he lives in a different age, his reference, though apparently more casual than that of Dryden, is knowingly provocative in its conservatism where Dryden's is relaxed and assured. Byron, like Dryden, puts his precedents in a chronological line. At the beginning of this line doubtless is Seneca's *Apocolocyntosis*, a farcical account of the fate of the Emperor Claudius's soul after death. At the other end of the line, Byron's poem acknowledges not only Southey's particular Vision but implicitly the fashion for vision writing. Byron's vision is a rebuke to the fashion based upon a reminder of different precedents for vision writing, for Byron's poem is a true vision and Southey's is not. When Byron says,

> The spirits were in neutral space, before
> The gate of Heaven; (stanza xxxv)[8]

that is exactly where they are. The poem is full of references, usually comic, to immense distances and differing time-scales which, though used to deflate Southey's 'sublime' vision, also make us accept without question the location of Byron's poem. Southey's poem depends on solemn paraphernalia, Byron's vision is unearthly. Keats once wrote,

You speak of Lord Byron and me—There is this great difference between us. He describes what he sees—I describe what I imagine. Mine is the hardest task. You see the immense difference.[9]

Such a distinction can be posited but who has 'the hardest task' may be considered further. The trouble with Southey's *Vision* is that it is merely imagined. Byron's is seen. And, despite its 'felt' particulars, Keats's 'Hyperion' is flawed by a pervasive 'made-up' quality. At times it, too, is imagined rather than seen. Byron's 'The Vision of Judgement' reminds its readers that there are other routes (such as Quevedo's *Suenos*) to visionary insight, not less Dantean than those which, for example, H. F. Cary's early nineteenth-century translation of the *Divina Commedia* appeared to suggest. Byron's poem can afford to assimilate implicitly the immediate precedent of satirical tales,

8. *Poetry*, iv. 499.
9. Hyder Rollins (ed.), *The Letters of John Keats* (Cambridge, Mass., 1958), ii. 200.

such as those of Peter Pindar, based on the mannerisms and doings of George III. All this may be granted. It is such a standard critical procedure to relate a poem to its antecedents and Byron's manner is so casual that we may miss the careful calculation of his practice. For whilst the poem only comes to proper life when we see how it assimilates its precedents into its own life, it does not authorize any random or, as it were archaeological, use of the past, such as is active in Southey's hexameters and in much twentieth-century critical respect for 'tradition'. T. S. Eliot's comment of 1919 is still apposite:

You can hardly make the word [tradition] agreeable to English ears without this comfortable reference to the reassuring science of archaeology.[10]

We could after all relate Southey's *Vision* to its precedents and in the long discussion of previous attempts to anglicize the hexameter in his Preface Southey appears to the casual reader to be seriously thinking about style and tradition. If Byron is right, he is not. The readiness of the nineteenth and twentieth centuries to assume that any use of the past is essentially 'traditional' is one of Byron's targets.

Much Romantic literature is engaged in the deliberate use of the past. We think immediately of the use of the ballad by Scott, Coleridge, and Keats or the attempted revival of Elizabethan drama so conspicuously rejected by Byron. This recovery, or apparent recovery, of the past is at first sight opposed to the cults of novelty and introspection which we loosely associate with Romanticism. In fact the two are closely connected as Robert Langbaum has shown in his introduction to the *Poetry of Experience*.[11] In the twentieth as in the early nineteenth century, the cult of tradition is itself a means of breaking with the coherent past. For example the championing of 'metaphysical' poetry was (and still faint-heartedly is) a means of disengaging, or apparently disengaging, from late nineteenth-century practice. In this way it repeats the Romantic use of sixteenth- and seventeenth-century poems as models in order to disengage from the eighteenth century.

10. T. S. Eliot, *Selected Essays* (London, 1932), p. 13.
11. Robert Langbaum, 'Introduction: Romanticism as a Modern Tradition', *The Poetry of Experience* (London, 1957).

Byron's poetry is designed to suggest a different model of poetic continuity from the one to which we have become accustomed. This is why Byron dissociated himself from the widespread conviction that the time in which he lived was a good one for poetry. Not because he could not see that Wordsworth, Coleridge, and Keats were great poets but because they were bad precedents. He often felt that he himself was too much a part of his time to be a good precedent:

I called Crabbe and Sam [Rogers] the fathers of present Poesy, and said, that I thought—except for them—*all* of '*us youth*' were on a wrong tack. But I never said that we did not sail well. Our fame will be hurt by *admiration* and *imitation*. When I say *our*, I mean *all* (Lakers included), except the postscript of the Augustans. The next generation (from the quantity and facility of imitation) will tumble and break their necks off our Pegasus, who runs away with us; but we keep the *saddle*, because we broke the rascal and can ride. But though easy to mount he is the devil to guide; and the next fellows must go back to the riding-school and the manège, and learn to ride the 'great horse'.[12]

In making a claim, however, for the consistency of Byron's concern with poetic continuity which is evident in the deftness of the letter I have just quoted, I am not urging his revaluation as a critic. The minimal presence of Byron in critical anthologies and the like, though it has misled, is not, in itself, misleading: Byron, like Chaucer or Pope, is concerned not with critical theory but with poetic practice. On the other hand, despite his customary sense of inadequacy to the task as disclosed above, his own poetic practice is a calculated intervention in the taste of his time designed to set forth the right 'tack' for English poetry. His reply to Southey's 'open defiance of precedent and poetry' is in the careful relationship of precedent and poetry effortlessly brought to life in 'The Vision of Judgement'. Byron's most considered commentary on certain parts of the Preface to *Lyrical Ballads* is *Don Juan*. Byron's response to the Romantic demand for neo-Shakespearian drama is even more instructive. Neither Shakespeare's poetry nor his drama has ever formed a natural precedent in English. If they have not done so in the past, they cannot be made to do so at will by subsequent effort because any direct appropriation of an earlier author's

12. *Letters*, iv. 196.

language (and for an English poet, Shakespeare's style cannot be readily detached from his characteristic diction) without any intervening history of use must result in some kind of pastiche. It is not inappropriate that the first hero of *The Dunciad*, Theobald, had published 'The Cave of Poverty, A Poem. Written in Imitation of Shakespeare'.[13] Theobald has had his successors but convincing use of Shakespeare as a precedent takes advantage of the tone, both knowing and daring, which results from risking pastiche. This is Thom Gunn's engaging device in such poems as 'Carnal Knowledge' and 'The Beach Head'. Only by a new tradition of such use could Shakespeare's poetry ever become a natural precedent for future English poets.

The relation of Milton to Spenser, two major precedents for English poetry, is not immediately apparent but it is intimate and crucial. Dryden claimed that 'Milton has acknowledged to me that Spenser was his original'.[14] The relation of Ezra Pound to Anglo-Saxon, Chinese, or Provençal verse is immediately apparent but it is neither intimate nor necessary. Byron was after a relation to his immediate past like that of Milton's to Spenser. Essentially this meant an incorporation of Pope's achievement in a new style, for since Pope's death there had been no decisive shift in English poetry. Pope was Byron's 'original' as Spenser had been Milton's. Byron's contemporaries too often rejected what preceded them and, instead, ransacked the past with an early version of Pound's archaeological eclecticism. That is what Romantic neo-Shakespearian tragedy is. Byron opposed it for this reason, not by a critical preface but by what is, arguably, the most carefully pondered body of drama in English after that of Ben Jonson. Shelley, whose *The Cenci* is the most plausible of the neo-Jacobean dramas, saw clearly the different ambition of Byron. In a letter to Byron (21 October 1821) after reading the first five cantos of *Don Juan* he writes:

This sort of writing only on a great plan and perhaps in a more compact form is what I wished you to do when I made my vows for an epic. But I am content. You are building up a drama, such as

13. See J. Butt (ed.), *The Poems of Alexander Pope* (Twickenham edn in one vol. London, 1963) [*Poems of Pope*], p. 352.
14. *Poems of Dryden*, p. 521.

England has not yet seen, and the task is sufficiently noble and worthy of you.[15]

Drama is a special case because of the undigested precedent of Shakespeare and the absence of any central tradition of tragic theatre in English. The absence of actual precedents led Byron to write plays that might form good precedents for the future. One could say—it would, unfortunately, be a typical use of the word—that in this he formed part of the 'tradition' of Jonson, Milton, Dryden, and T. S. Eliot. But whilst there is a similarity of stance connecting these figures, they are not connected by any actual dramatic tradition.

English poetry is a different matter. Byron is not concerned here with consciously establishing new precedents but with creatively continuing a richly precedented life which involves both co-operation with what is received and considered redirection. Here the case of Romantic drama enables us to make a distinction which though simple is far-reaching in its implications and appears to be understood and vindicated by Byron's practice whilst being forgotten and covered up by his age.

Shakespeare's drama is, after all, a decisive precedent for continental Romantics, especially for the Germans. Why should Shakespeare quicken Goethe's *Götz von Berlichingen* and deaden Keats's 'Otho the Great'? There are, obviously, a number of factors which are relevant here. But the case is essentially simple. The English Romantics imitate Shakespeare's style and his language. The continental writers (perforce) imitate only his style.[16] They used Shakespeare as Byron used Alfieri for his dramas, Berni, Pulci, and Casti for *Beppo*, or as Yeats used Noh plays. Style and language form precedents in different ways. Good styles usually become international though often labelled 'French', 'Swedish', etc. They are consciously created and maintained. Language, on the other hand, is local and is transmitted constantly but obscurely. Poets, especially, cannot

15. F. L. Jones (ed.), *The Letters of Shelley* (Oxford, 1964), ii. 358.
16. Dr John Margetts of the German Department at Liverpool informs me that C. M. Wieland's prose translation of Shakespeare (1762-6) was the principal means by which the writers of the *Sturm und Drang* encountered Shakespeare. This translation can only convey a crude sense of style and structure and takes little account of Shakespeare's diction. Interestingly, it is the philosophical critics of the time such as J. G. Hamann and J. G. Herder who appear to have best understood Shakespeare in English.

choose or treat the one as they do the other. They can be eclectic about style but not about language. English poets must write English, but they can write in whatever style they please, if it also pleases others. Byron was alert to this primary distinction and his poetry respects it. For example, he writes to John Murray about the style of *Beppo*:

Croker's is a good guess; but the style is not English, it is Italian; Berni is the original of all. Whistlecraft was my immediate model . . . Berni is the father of that kind of writing, which, I think, suits our language, too, very well;—we shall see by the experiment.[17]

English poetry may incorporate an Italian style but not the Italian language. Thus, in a review of the English-Italian poems of W. R. Spencer, Byron comments,

It is very perceptible in Mr S.'s small pieces that he has suffered his English versification to be vitiated with Italian *concetti*; and we should have been better pleased with his compositions in a foreign language, had they not induced him to corrupt his mother-tongue.[18]

English poetry has constantly reverted to common European sources such as Greek tragedy, Horace's epistles or Petrarch's sonnets to form new precedents for style but, when successful, accomodated to native precedents of language. We can contrast, for example, Byron's *English Bards and Scotch Reviewers* which is written in Pope's language and style (mediated by Churchill and Gifford), with his 'The Vision of Judgement'. This is written in a language which comes, less obviously but unquestionably, from Pope and Dryden. The pointed satire on Southey's dullness or Junius's spectral elusiveness recalls the idiom of *The Dunciad*. There are a number of cadences in Byron's poem which recall Pope's manner and yet use a different currency. For example, Byron writes,

> The Cherubs and the Saints bowed down before
> That arch-angelic Hierarch [Michael] . . .
> He [Lucifer] merely bent his diabolic brow
> An instant . . .   (stanzas xxxi, xxxvii)[19]

This may be placed alongside a passage in Book IV of *The Dunciad*:

17. *Letters*, iv. 217.   18. *Letters*, ii. 419.   19. *Poetry*, iv. 497, 499.

> Before them march'd that awful Aristarch;
> Plow'd was his front with many a deep Remark: . . .
> Low bow'd the rest: He, kingly, did but nod.
>
> (ll. 203–4, 207)[20]

But the effect of Pope is felt more clearly in passages which cannot be directly paralleled in Byron's poem, such as lines 269–74, also from the fourth book of *The Dunciad*:

> Then take him to devellop, if you can,
> And hew the Block off, and get out the Man.
> But wherefore waste I words? I see advance
> Whore, Pupil, and lac'd Governor from France.
> Walker! our hat'—nor more he deign'd to say,
> But stern as Ajax' spectre rode away.[21]

Here it seems more precise to say that Pope anticipates Byron, rather than Byron recalls Pope, because of Byron's remarkable assimilation of his precedent. Similarly, the finely balanced portraits of Michael, Lucifer, Wilkes and George himself in 'The Vision of Judgement' recall the idiom of *Absalom and Achitophel*. Without these immediate precedents Byron's poem would be inconceivable. Yet the poem is not written in the style of Pope and Dryden but in a new style, a deliberately restricted version of the *Beppo* manner. We are aware too, despite the inescapably acknowledged derivation of the language, that it is incorporating as much as may be of the cultural idiom of Byron's society. Pope and Dryden provide Byron not only with a set of poetic formulations which can be reused or transposed but also with a model assimilation of current language into an assured poetic context. This is not always understood. We have often been asked to applaud Byron's poems in *ottava rima* as though they somehow proceeded directly from contemporary speech. Byron's letters are usually invoked at this point.

But C. O. Brink, challenging the customary view that Horace's hexameter poems are versified prose, argues that,

Horace accommodates a small, carefully controlled, amount of colloquial language. . . . The quantity may be small; but, I suspect, an optical illusion has made it look large.[22]

This comment can be used to point to something essentially

---

20. *Poems of Pope*, p. 777.   21. *Poems of Pope*, pp. 780–1.
22. C. O. Brink, *Horace on Poetry* (Cambridge, 1971), p. 445.

similar in Byron's 'colloquial' poetry, although of course the demarcation between poetic and prosaic words is different in Latin and in English. There is, for example, throughout *Don Juan*, a deliberate balancing of poetic usages, quotations and colloquial idiom. Each gives and takes life from the other. Pope is a master of this art, though Burns was a more immediate model for Byron. The discussion of poetry which frames 'The isles of Greece' section in *Don Juan* is a good example of Byron's relaxed use of received expressions supporting his critical argument. 'The isles of Greece' poet is presented as one of Byron's contemporaries who does not respect precedents,

> He praised the present, and abused the past,
> Reversing the good custom of old days,
> 　　　　　　　(canto III. lxxix)[23]

and is correspondingly eclectic,

> Thus, usually, when *he* was asked to sing,
> He gave the different nations something national; . . .
> His muse made increment of anything,
> From the high lyric down to the low rational.
> 　　　　　　　(canto III. lxxxv)[24]

The wonderful line 'His muse made increment of anything' which, superficially, seems to fit the author of *Don Juan*, in fact picks up, as E. H. Coleridge points out in his edition, a passage in S. T. Coleridge's *Biographia Literaria* which refers to Southey. It is a prophetic pillorying of that 'creative imagination', destructive of 'precedent and poetry', which has dominated the discussion of poetry from Byron's time to our own.

After 'The isles of Greece', Byron returns to his discussion and makes his well-known attack on Wordsworth. The immediate occasion for this was the publication in 1819 (the first for four years) of two new poems by Wordsworth, *Peter Bell* and *The Waggoner*. Shelley, normally impressed, responded with the satire of 'Peter Bell the Third'. He was stirred into satire by Wordsworth's pompous preface to *Peter Bell* dedicating the poem to Southey, and by the Christian toning of the poem which, Shelley thought, endorsed the insights of suffering and yet confirmed the horrors of hell. Byron, writing at almost exactly the same time as Shelley, incorporated his comment on

the same poems in the current stanzas of *Don Juan*.[25] But Byron,
unlike Shelley, does not talk about content so much as diction.
The diction of *The Waggoner* and the Prologue to *Peter Bell*
vacillates 'from the high lyric down to the low rational' with a
vengeance. Byron does not object to a mixed diction, as his own
practice in *Don Juan* shows, but he wants different dictions used
for different purposes or interrelated for specific effects. He
comments,

> If he [Wordsworth] must fain sweep o'er the ethereal plain,
> And Pegasus runs restive in his Waggon,
> Could he not beg the loan of Charles's Wain?
> Or pay Medea for a single dragon?
> . . .
> 'Pedlars,' and 'Boats,' and 'Waggons!' Oh ye shades
> Of Pope and Dryden, are we come to this?
>
> (canto III. xciv, c)[26]

This criticism works only in so far as Byron's perceptible stiffen-
ing of his verse's texture ('fain sweep', 'ethereal plain', 'Wain',
'ye shades') emphasizes the baldness of Wordsworth's idiom
whilst at the same time it in no way threatens the natural vigour
of Byron's manner. The remaining eleven stanzas of the canto
offer a representative *tour de force* of married idioms including
passages of translation, high lyric, and comic rational, juxta-
posed or blended for calculated effects. Of course the language
of *Don Juan* is often plainer or more idiosyncratic than my
argument suggests but *Don Juan* is always rooted in traditional
artifices rather as the freedom of Pope's final Horatian manner
is still perceptibly ballasted by verse habits acquired in poems
of a different character which are allowed to emerge where
appropriate for purposes of support or contrast.

In fact those poets who most successfully incorporate the
idioms of everyday speech into good poetry, such as Horace,
Dante, Chaucer, Dryden or, among more recent poets, Hardy,
Yeats and Hugh MacDiarmid, are also clearly committed at
other times (sometimes, confusingly, at the same time) to periphrasis, poetic diction and figures of all kinds. We may praise
such poets' competence in different idioms but we rarely ask

25. I say 'poems' rather than 'poem' because Shelley is presumably
referring to *The Waggoner* in Part 2, stanza v of his poem.
26. *Poetry*, vi. 177.

ourselves if their success in conveying the illusion of natural speech is directly related to their command of poetic diction because we have been brought up on on a different story. That story has only received wide acceptance in this century but it is founded on the Preface to *Lyrical Ballads*. I am going to extract, I hope not too unfairly, two simple emphases from that brilliant and complex piece of writing. Wordsworth, after relating the style of his poems to their language,[27] acknowledges that his attempt to bring his language 'near to the language of men' has

necessarily cut me off from a large portion of phrases and figures of speech which from father to son have long been regarded as the common inheritance of Poets. I have also thought it expedient to restrict myself still further, having abstained from the use of many expressions, in themselves proper and beautiful, but which have been foolishly repeated by bad Poets till such feelings of disgust are connected with them as it is scarcely possible by any art of associa-tion to overpower.[28]

Wordsworth here dissociates precedented idioms and living language. When he comes, therefore, in his next paragraph to discuss the language of Gray's sonnet, 'In vain to me the smiling mornings shine', he distinguishes between 'prose' lines and 'poetic diction' lines as though the poem would be better if it was written entirely in 'prose' lines. But Gray, like Byron, is using the one against the other for calculated effect. The life of the poem does not erupt in some lines and stagnate in others. The style of the poem contains and uses both registers as any reading of the poem, outside its appearance in Wordsworth's preface, shows.

The *Lyrical Ballads* include poems such as 'The Idiot Boy', which appears to avoid poetic diction, and 'The Ancient Mariner', which is full of deliberate archaisms—the stuff of a new poetic diction for the Victorians. Wordsworth was casting out natural precedents for poetic language and Coleridge was bringing in antique novelties. Both are the consequence of the theory in the Preface for, despite its advocacy of natural speech, it subverts that blend of recent and received usages which sus-tains the illusion of natural speech in poetry.

27. W. J. B. Owen and J. W. Smyser (eds), *The Prose Works of William Wordsworth* (Oxford, 1974), i. 130.
28. Ibid. i. 132.

This separation does not govern Wordsworth's practice in his best poems, for, even within *Lyrical Ballads*, the language of, say, 'Tintern Abbey' is both natural and precedented, nor does it govern Coleridge's in, for example, 'Dejection: an Ode'. But their better practice is not a deliberate advertisement for a better theory, nor do we judge the theory in the light of their practice. We lend to the theory something of the authority which derives from the practice as though the stature of the poems guaranteed the cogency of the theory. The Preface is, needless to say, not to be dismissed by my simplification of its argument but Wordsworth's intention is simplifying. His prose is polemical in the same way and about the same issues as Byron's poetry. I say poetry rather than *Don Juan*, because, though the latter is Byron's principal attempt to provide a successor to *The Dunciad* (not in order to continue Pope but to continue English poetry), nevertheless Byron is always concerned with the same kind of poetic problems and is constantly finding solutions to them.

Let us consider *Childe Harold's Pilgrimage*. This is a poem perhaps over-praised in the nineteenth century, certainly underpraised in the twentieth. It has however been given the serious reading it deserves in the last decade by such American critics as R. F. Gleckner[29] and J. J. McGann.[30] Their bias is to the interpretation of content via structure rather than to the criticism of style. It is not surprising, though still welcome, that the poem should impress when read in this way. The structure of *Childe Harold's Pilgrimage* is, in most respects, much more modern, less precedented, than that of *Don Juan*. As with *The Waste Land*, it is for the reader to make the connections between its parts whereas these are much more authorially controlled in *Don Juan*. For example, if St Peter's is compared to the Alps at the end of canto IV of *Childe Harold's Pilgrimage* and the Alps are discussed at the end of canto III, we may pause to interrelate the two passages and consider what the poem has to say about Nature and Art in the light of these and other references. But Byron does not specifically refer to the earlier part of the poem in the later reference, whereas, in the fifteenth canto of *Don Juan*, we are explicitly asked to compare Aurora Raby to

29. R. F. Gleckner, *Byron and the Ruins of Paradise* (Baltimore, 1967).
30. J. J. McGann, *Fiery Dust. Byron's Poetic Development* (Chicago, 1968).

Haidee in terms of the relation between Nature and Art though
Haidee is near the beginning of the poem and Aurora is at the
end. We have been slow to see, or recover, this 'modern' feature
of *Childe Harold's Pilgrimage* because its style is so obviously 'old-
fashioned' and it is difficult to find a modern critical language
which can cope here. In our century the style has customarily
been labelled 'fustian' when put alongside the 'colloquial mode'
of *Don Juan*. We have assumed that the structure is old-
fashioned too; now we discover that the structure of *Childe
Harold's Pilgrimage* is more interesting than we thought. It nearly
always is in Byron's poems. To our surprise, this most celebrated
of Romantic poems remains to be read. We are now in danger
of criticizing the style for failing to be as original as the
structure.

I do not want to mount a full-scale defence of the style of
Childe Harold's Pilgrimage here. But it is part of my larger argument to claim that the style of the poem contributes to its
greatness as well as sharing in its shortcomings. Byron's recognition of precedents is careful, independent, and essential to his
poem's procedure and originality. This may seem unlikely. Imitations of Spenser's stanza or manner were common in the
eighteenth century. James Beattie's celebrated poem, *The
Minstrel*, appeared in 1771. Wordsworth wrote eight Spenserian
stanzas in his copy of *The Castle of Indolence* in 1802. Thomas
Campbell's well-received tale, *Gertrude of Wyoming*, appeared in
1809, the year of Byron's departure on his 'Pilgrimage'. The
diction, versification, and rhetorical devices of Campbell's
poem, which Byron had read, are remarkably close to those of
Childe Harold's Pilgrimage. How then is Byron's idiom in his poem
precedented rather than merely fashionable, original rather
than predictable? Byron's Preface to the first two cantos gives
us some guidance. After specifically rebutting possible charges
of plagiarism in his subject matter, Byron goes on to invoke
the sanctions of precedent for his style:

The stanza of Spenser, according to one of our most successful poets,
admits of every variety. Dr Beattie makes the following observation:
'Not long ago I began a poem in the style and stanza of Spenser, in
which I propose to give full scope to my inclination, and be either
droll or pathetic, descriptive or sentimental, tender or satirical as
the humour strikes me; for if I mistake not, the measure which I

have adopted admits equally of all these kinds of composition.'
Strengthened in my opinion by such authority, and by the example
of some in the highest order of Italian poets, I shall make no
apology for attempts at similar variations in the following composition; satisfied that, if they are unsuccessful, their failure must be in
the execution, rather than in the design sanctioned by the practice
of Ariosto, Thomson and Beattie.[31]

It is clear from this that Byron considers his use of the Spenserian stanza to be in need of justification. Byron originally intended the poem to have more of a medley character than it
finally had. The Preface, nevertheless, remains appropriate.
Byron is saying that he is writing a substantial poem of a new
kind which will incorporate many different possibilities of relation to its many subjects. He has chosen the Spenserian stanza
which was associated (not unfairly despite Spenser's virtuosity)
with particular kinds of effect. These effects are marvellously
realized for example in Wordsworth's tribute in *The Prelude*:

> Sweet Spenser, moving through his clouded heaven
> With the moon's beauty and the moon's soft pace.
> (iii. 281–2)[32]

Byron wants to use the stanza in a different way and says that
this is a precedented possibility. Beattie and Thomson are ex-
emplars here but more in theory than in fact. *The Castle of Indolence* by its very title confirms the Spenserian stereotype. *The
Minstrel*, like *Gertrude of Wyoming*, is directed towards a simplifying pathos rather than to the dramatic juxtapositions which
Byron had in mind for *Childe Harold's Pilgrimage*. These poems
suggest possibilities but do not establish the voice of the author
in the stanza. More revealing is Byron's references to Ariosto
and 'the example of some in the highest order of Italian poets'.
To refer the Spenserian stanza to possibilities inherent in the
Italian octave is to refer back through Spenser to his precedents. The Spenserian stanza is, in its origins, an attempt to
provide an English equivalent for the stanza of *Orlando Furioso*
which, like the latter, can be adapted to a variety of purposes.
Spenser achieves this but he also imparts a particular and personal character to his stanza. In Thomson, Beattie, and others,

31. *Poetry*, ii. 4–5.
32. E. de Selincourt (ed.), *The Prelude (1805)* (Oxford Standard Authors
edn, Oxford, 1933), p. 42.

the attempt to realize the varied possibilities of the form persist as precedents for Byron. But Byron, though consciously indebted to these models and scrupulously acknowledging them, is the first to achieve a complete remodelling of the stanza in a major poem. Curiously, the effect is not quite the intended one. *Childe Harold's Pilgrimage* does not end up as a medley poem though it does centrally depend upon dramatic juxtapositions of tone and situation which exploit precisely those possibilities which Byron quotes from Beattie. Byron's version of the medley style is, of course, to come later in his direct appropriation of *ottava rima*. He uses the Spenserian stanza rather as Spenser does, displaying its variety but also imposing a character. Yet this, too, proves Byron's hypothesis. The stanza works as well for his dramatic eloquence as for Spenser's moral narrations. Indeed we ought to read *The Faerie Queen* in the same way as we must read *Childe Harold's Pilgrimage* rathre than in the manner appropriate to Beattie's *The Minstrel*. For Beattie presumably read his Spenser with ballad and late medieval narrative models in mind which are quite inappropriate to the teasing structures of both *The Faerie Queene* and *Childe Harold's Pilgrimage*. Byron's originality brings him very close to his distant precedent but at this stage the whole discussion of what is original and what is precedented becomes blurred, as it should, and it would require different kinds of inquiry to continue. We must acknowledge Byron's agility in areas not normally thought of as his by contrasting this history with Shelley's use, after Byron's, of the same stanza form.

In his Preface to *The Revolt of Islam*, Shelley writes:

> I do not presume to enter into competition with our greatest contemporary Poets. Yet I am unwilling to tread in the footsteps of any who have preceded me.[33]

Like Byron, he acknowledges his choice of Spenser's stanza, enticed by 'the brilliancy and magnificence of sound' which it can produce.[34] In Shelley's case, this unlikely, though typical boast to be free from precedent is true. The style of *The Revolt of Islam* is independent, brilliant, but colourless. It is instru-

---

33. T. Hutchinson (ed.), *The Complete Poetical Works of Percy Bysshe Shelley* (Oxford Standard Authors edn, Oxford, 1905), p. 34.
34. Ibid., p. 36.

mental, though not decisive, in the poem's failure to hold any reader's attention for long. Shelley's mastery of the difficult stanza is assured but it is clear that he has not thought out the possibilities of the form. Doubtless its use at all and its freedom from the tincture of Spenserian parody, so inescapable in eighteenth-century use, is owing to Byron's celebrated example. More to our purpose is Shelley's use of the same stanza four years later in *Adonais*, this time without any comment on the style. Shelley's use here is strongly influenced by Byron's in *Childe Harold's Pilgrimage*. Behind *Adonais*, partly because of the subject-matter, we often catch the echo of Byron's voice in the unusually slow movement, in many of the alexandrines and transitions and in some whole stanzas such as xxviii, xxix, xxxvii. But the poem is better written and more Shelley's (because more someone's) than *The Revolt of Islam*. Again, to catch someone else's voice behind a poem may seem common enough. But this must be the first time that we hear in any poem written in Spenserian stanzas anyone's voice other than that of the author or Spenser himself. This is not simply to be explained in terms of Byron's and Shelley's personalities. The voice, or voices, which Byron achieves in *Childe Harold's Pilgrimage* rise out of his preferred stanza form. It is this voice rather than some general Byronic mannerisms which reappear in *Adonais* as can be seen if comparison is made with Shelley's direct version of Byron's voice in 'Julian and Maddalo'. Byron freed the Spenserian stanza from Spenser and therefore from its liability for parodic purposes, whilst at the same time making it available for use in major poetry. Byron frees the stanza from its past by respecting its precedents. This is the standard paradox by which his poetry lives. We might as well say Poetry as 'his poetry' for even Wordsworth's practice witnesses more to Byron's theory than to his own.[35]

Byron's use of the Spenserian stanza, then, commands respect and attention. It is true that the poem opens with a good version of Spenserian parody before assuming the independence suggested in the Preface, but this initial acknowledgement of eighteenth-century precedent authorizes that independence. It is the developing practice based on intelligent intentions that

35. See, for example, G. Tillotson's Byron Foundation Lecture, *The Continuity of English Poetry from Dryden to Wordsworth* (Nottingham, 1967).

we must trust, rather than the abstract coherence which Byron disliked so much. Enough, I hope, has been said to make it seem unlikely that Byron's choice and use of the Spenserian stanza is simply some general early nineteenth-century fashion.[36] How different, for example, is his use from that of Keats in 'The Eve of St Agnes' who appears to seek out rather than transform the 'indolence' associations of the stanza. If this results in 'The Eve of St Agnes', it seems wrong to complain. But Keats's use of the stanza closes possibilities to his successors that Byron had opened. The stanza passes thence to a final 'dying glory' in Tennyson's 'The Lotos-Eaters', behind which we can hear the last echoes of Spenser's voice.

We must revert to the different continuities appropriate to style and to language. Burns, for instance, uses the Spenserian stanza fluently in 'The Cotter's Saturday Night'. The stanza appears, however, without its customary Spenserian diction. Instead it is ballasted with Scots words which in turn provoke, as usual with Burns, the diction of Augustan reflective commonplaces. Burns is following the Scots precedent of Fergusson rather than the anglicized practice of Thomson and Beattie. Spenser is thus ousted but nothing specific is done with this stanza and, unlike Byron, Burns does not acquire a voice in it which can be distinguished from that of his other poems. *Childe Harold's Pilgrimage*, though flawed, is largely successful, then, in transforming the practice of Thomson and Beattie and achieves a real recovery of lost possibilities in the Spenserian stanza. If we have not already done so, we must try to find a language to characterize this success as well as acclaiming the poem's structure. Indeed the discontinuities of the structure are offered to our interpretation by the stanza form itself which has been adopted because of its aptitude to form blocks of expression which can be dramatically linked or contrasted almost in the manner of a sonnet sequence.

Certain generalizations may now be hazarded which summarize my argument and, I hope, Byron's. The diction of immediately preceding poetry must form a part, preferably a

36. Cf. Graham Hough's dismissal: 'It must be confessed that the verse [of *Childe Harold's Pilgrimage*] is not very distinguished. The Spenserian stanza requires some approach to the Spenserian richness and dreamy music.' *The Romantic Poets* (London, 1953), p. 101.

recognized part, of any major poem even though it demands
incorporation with colloquialisms, new coinages, and in different styles. Immediately preceding styles are dangerous models
but any style, old or modern, may be tried provided that it
'suits' the language. Any diction other than that of immediately
preceding poetry cannot be directly recovered. The only route
to old dictions is via imitations which begin as pedantry, pastiche, or parody. Thus Byron's Spenserian stanzas do not derive
from Spenser, for then Byron would be acting like a Romantic
neo-Shakespearian tragedian. They derive from eighteenth-
century, parody-linked imitation, and are all the better for that
since parody may sustain an idiom for later generations to use
in quite a different way. All this should seem straightforward
enough. But we have constantly lost sight of these things as did
many of Byron's generation who were recommended to cut
themselves off from the diction of immediately preceding poetry
and, at the same time, were impelled to revive old idioms in
'open defiance of precedent and poetry'.

I have dwelt at some length on Spenserian stanzas as well as
ottava rima because the precedented originality of *Don Juan*'s
style is more readily granted and usually contrasted with the
derivative nature of *Childe Harold's Pilgrimage*. The larger point
however is that Byron in all his major achievements, *Childe
Harold's Pilgrimage*, *Don Juan*, and the dramas, always thinks
radically about a tradition and that his choice of style and diction (different in each case) itself embodies a critical theory in
action whose effect he calculates. In this he differs, by and
large, from his contemporaries whose work we so often interpret
via their own critical remarks: not always accurately. To make
these claims for Byron is either common sense or nonsense and
yet it appears to be so far from the former that Byron is rarely
credited with any capacity for thinking about the nature of
poetry. His well-known view is that poetry is 'the lava of the
imagination'. But then Byron's vision of the future of English
poetry and culture was percipient. He did not form an enduring
precedent for style though he has for sensibility. *Childe Harold*
had effects, of course, but increasingly overcome by the anti-
discursive tendencies of Keatsian diction. Byron's classical
dramas failed, as Eliot's have done, to provide a counter to the
helpless eclecticism of the English theatre. *Don Juan* is greater

than any English poem written since its publication but, though critically accepted and widely read now, it has not formed part of the historical development of English poetry. Instead it presented a decisive model to Pushkin and others, much as the Italians did for Byron. Byron's version of the past has not become ours. He is no more a real precedent for English poetry than Shakespeare is for English drama. He can be admired and imitated of course but that is a different matter. If W. H. Auden wanted to imitate the manner of *Don Juan*, he had to approach it through the history of light verse, not the history of English verse, for there is no other intervening route. So long as this is so, it is hazardous for an English reader to approach Byron's poetry as though some local critical attention will enable one to see what is central. Perhaps we have to see the precedents before we can see the poetry.

Shelley and 'Satire's scourge'

ANN THOMPSON

In his book *Portraits in Satire*, published in 1958, Kenneth Hopkins wrote that 'the satiric element' in Shelley comprises 'the least valuable, the least readable, of his work',[1] and this judgement would still appear to be representative of modern criticism in general; it is certainly strongly implied by the extraordinary lack of explicit comment on this aspect of the work of a poet who must be accounted one of the most deeply and self-consciously committed political writers we have ever had. Shelley is still treated as primarily a lyrical poet, although the philosophical and political content of such poems as *Prometheus Unbound* has of course been recognized. The satirical poems are a comparatively small proportion of his output and my aim is not to force them into a central position in the canon but to claim that they deserve better than total neglect. It seems to me that they are not only interesting and valuable in themselves but can also provide an especially interesting area in which to study some of the most important questions in Shelley criticism, in particular the intensity (and perhaps *naïveté*) of his moral attitudes, and the difficulty of expressing this intensity in acceptable poetic language.

Shelley's own attitude towards satire may have encouraged the neglect of his works in that genre. In his 'Fragment of a Satire on Satire', written in 1820 in response to a number of attacks in print on Robert Southey, he is extremely dubious about what he sees as the negative violence of the form, and heavily ironic about its claims to be constructive:

> . . . if Despair
> And Hate, the rapid bloodhounds with which Terror
> Hunts through the world the homeless steps of Error

1. Kenneth Hopkins, *Portraits in Satire* (London, 1958), p. 273.

> Are the true secrets of the commonweal
> To make men wise and just. . . .   (ll. 6–10)[2]

> . . . If Satire's scourge could wake the slumbering hounds
> Of Conscience, or erase the deeper wounds,
> The leprous scars of callous Infamy;
> If it could make the present not to be,
> Or charm the dark past never to have been,
> Or turn regret to hope. . . .   (ll. 17–22)

He finally denies outright the validity of 'Satire's scourge':

> This cannot be, it ought not, evil still—
> Suffering makes suffering, ill must follow ill.
> Rough words beget sad thoughts, . . . and beside,
> Men take a sullen and a stupid pride
> In being all they hate in other's shame,
> By a perverse antipathy of fame.   (ll. 35–40)

Satire seems only to make things worse. Shelley expresses a deep regret for these 'bitter waters' which flow from 'the sweet fountains of our nature' and opts for a more positive and charitable method of reform:

> If any friend would take Southey some day,
> And tell him, in a country walk alone,
> Softening harsh words with friendship's gentle tone,
> How incorrect his public conduct is,
> And what men think of it, 'twere not amiss,
> Far better than to make innocent ink. . . .
>   (ll. 44–49; 'The Fragment' breaks off here)

Although there is an element of jocularity in the particular application of these words, it can be shown that Shelley maintained the same basic attitude towards satire elsewhere with some consistency. It seems, for example, to lie behind his occasional reservations about the work of his friend, Byron: after enthusiastically praising Julia's letter in canto I of *Don Juan* in a letter to Byron dated 26 May 1820, he adds,

. . . I cannot say I equally approve of the service to which this letter was appropriated; or that I altogether think the bitter mockery of our common nature, of which this is one of the expressions, quite worthy of your genius. The power and the beauty and the wit,

2. All quotations of Shelley's poetry are from Thomas Hutchinson (ed.), *Shelley: Poetical Works*, 2nd edn, rev. G. M. Matthews (Oxford, 1970) [*Poetical Works*].

indeed, redeem all this—chiefly because they belie and refute it. Perhaps it is foolish to wish that there had been nothing to redeem. (*Letters*, ii. 198)[3]

He takes up the same point again in his letter of 21 October 1821, after receiving cantos III–V of *Don Juan*:

. . . You unveil and present in its true deformity what is worst in human nature, and this is what the witlings of the age murmur at, conscious of their want of power to endure the scrutiny of such a light.—We are damned to the knowledge of good and evil, and it is well for us to know what we should avoid no less than what we should seek. (*Letters*, ii. 357–8)

In this last sentence Shelley seems to be persuading himself as much as praising Byron: he is sure *Don Juan* is a great poem but he is not absolutely happy about the extent to which it is a negative poem, a poem which gives representations of evil and folly—in other words, a satire. His ambitions for Byron are very much an expression of his own views about poetry, and his occasional hints that Byron has not yet achieved the really stupendous poem of which he is capable can be referred to his own fundamental conviction that the greatest poetry must be positive.

In this way Shelley frequently implies a judgement about satire without directly discussing the genre as such. In his 'Essay on the Devil and Devils' of 1819 (itself something of a satire) he stresses the greater difficulty, and hence the greater merit, of 'positive' poetry:

Misery and injustice contrive to produce very poetical effect, because the excellence of poetry consists in its awakening the sympathy of men which among persons influenced by an abject and gloomy superstition is much more easily done by images of horror than of beauty. It requires a higher degree of skill in a poet to make beauty, virtue, and harmony poetical, that is, to give them an idealized and rhythmical analogy with the predominating emotions of his readers than to make injustice, deformity, and discord and horror poetical. (*Prose*, p. 273)[4]

This is also very much the theme of his 'Defence of Poetry' of 1821, in which the case for poetry as an instrument of moral

---

3. All quotations of Shelley's letters are from F. L. Jones (ed.), *The Letters of Percy Bysshe Shelley* (Oxford, 1964) [*Letters*], 2 vols.

4. All quotations of Shelley's prose are from David Lee Clark (ed.), *Shelley's Prose* (Albuquerque, New Mexico, 1954) [*Prose*].

good depends largely on the poet's power to represent beauties and ideals in such a way as to excite admiration and imitation. Shelley's fervent support for this traditional argument leads him into overstatement on the positive side, as when he says unequivocally that 'Poetry is the record of the best and happiest moments of the happiest and best minds' (*Prose*, p. 294). There is obviously no place for satire in such a theory, and indeed the only reference to it in the 'Defence' is somewhat oblique and highly critical: Shelley generalizes from what he sees as the degradation of the arts in the time of Charles II to say that

At such periods . . . Comedy loses its ideal universality; wit succeeds to humor; we laugh from self-complacency and triumph, instead of pleasure; malignity, sarcasm and contempt succeed to sympathetic merriment; we hardly laugh, but we smile. Obscenity, which is ever blasphemy against the divine beauty in life, becomes from the very veil which it assumes, more active if less disgusting; it is a monster for which the corruption of society forever brings forth new food, which it devours in secret. (*Prose*, p. 285)

From all this, it is clear that the critic looking for the satirical element in Shelley's poetry must be prepared to shift his categories slightly, for the poet himself obviously thinks in terms of positive and negative poetry as defined by social and ideological utility rather than by literary genres. Some critics would say that to shift one's categories in this particular way is to take oneself outside the realm of 'proper' satire altogether, but the definition of satire has never been very rigid anyway. Dryden provides a good basic starting-point in his *Discourse Concerning the Original and Progress of Satire* (1693) when he quotes Heinsius on Horace:

Satire is a kind of poetry, without a series of action, invented for the purging of our minds; in which human vices, ignorance, and errors, and all things besides, which are produced from them in every man, are severely reprehended; partly dramatically, partly simply, and sometimes in both kinds of speaking; but, for the most part, figuratively, and occultly; consisting in a low familiar way, chiefly in a sharp and pungent manner of speech; but partly, also, in a facetious and civil way of jesting; by which either hatred, or laughter, or indignation, is moved.[5]

Most people would accept this definition of satire in terms of its

5. W. P. Ker (ed.), *Essays of John Dryden* (Oxford, 1900), ii. 100.

subject-matter, its purpose and its methods. Its subject-matter is 'human vices, ignorance, and errors', its purpose the 'reprehension' of these failings, and its methods 'figurative and occult', by which it is implied that a satire is characteristically not a straightforward and utterly transparent account of the human vice and folly it describes, but more often an indirect and fictionalized account which makes use of a certain range of literary devices in order to make its 'reprehension' both powerful and attractively readable.[6] Within this general framework I should now like to consider some of Shelley's satirical poems, expecially *Swellfoot the Tyrant* (1820) and some of the 1819 poems. I shall confine myself to political satire since there will not be room for a discussion of the literary satire of *Peter Bell the Third* or for such secondary issues as the element of satirical irony in poems like *Julian and Maddalo* and the 'Letter to Maria Gisborne'.

Swellfoot the Tyrant (1820) is something of an oddity in the group of poems I have chosen for consideration and indeed in Shelley's work as a whole. It is perhaps more simply and obviously 'a satire' than anything else he ever wrote, in that it is, like *Absalom and Achitophel* or *Animal Farm*, a fictitious but easily recognizable version of contemporary political events presented in such a way as to exaggerate and throw into relief the viciousness and folly of those cast by the author into the roles of villains. Not only is the work conventional in terms of the literary tradition, but, as N. I. White has shown,[7] it bears very close relation to the political satire of its own period: the parallels between Shelley's treatment of the Queen Caroline scandal and various contemporary cartoons and pamphlets are too numerous to be merely coincidental. Its second and perhaps more interesting claim to unique status in the canon of Shelley's political poetry lies in the comparative triviality of its subject-matter and purpose: it is clear from his references to *Swellfoot* in his letters that Shelley found the whole affair ludicrous and did not take his pro-Caroline partisanship very seriously.[8] This is indeed obvious from the last scene of the play when the triumphant

6. The 'fictionality' of the genre is discussed very interestingly by Maynard Mack in 'The Muse of Satire', *Yale Review*, xli (1951), pp. 80-92.

7. N. I. White, 'Shelley's *Swellfoot the Tyrant* in Relation to Contemporary Political Satire', *PMLA*, xxxvi (1921), pp. 332-46 [White].

8. See *Letters*, ii. 207, 216, 218, 220, 236.

Iona Taurina gleefully encourages her supporters to wreak revenge on her enemies crying 'Give them no law . . . But such as
they gave you'—hardly a vision of 'reform' that Shelley could
have seriously approved! For him, it is lighthearted at the end
because the satirical 'reprehension' applies to both sides: although he earnestly desired the defeat of the Queen's enemies
(see *Letters*, ii. 216), he was also aware of the absurdity of presenting her as an innocent victim, let alone a potential saviour.

By contrast, the subject-matter and purpose of the political
poems of 1819 is deeply serious and important for Shelley, and
not without objective justification. In his *Social Origins of Dictatorship and Democracy*, Barrington Moore Jr writes of the period
from the latter years of the French Revolution to about 1822 as
a conspicuously reactionary phase in English politics:

The gathering movement to reform Parliament was placed outside
the law, the press muzzled, associations that smacked of radicalism
forbidden, a rash of treason trials initiated, spies and *agents provoca-
teurs* let loose among the people, the Habeas Corpus suspended *after*
the war with Napoleon had ended. Repression and suffering were
real and widespread, only partly mitigated by some continued
articulate opposition.[9]

Shelley certainly wanted to contribute to that opposition. If the
poem itself were not sufficiently impressive one could refer again
to the letters to prove how intensely moved Shelley was by the
events lying behind *The Mask of Anarchy*.[10] But here we begin
to run into problems of definition: in his *Politics in English Romantic Poetry*, Carl Woodring introduces his discussion of the
poem in this way:

The Mask of Anarchy is the longest and most imaginative, most visionary, of the poems for the people. It has seemed much too long to
those interested in it only as satire. Political it certainly is, but less
satiric than prophetic.[11]

And after two pages of analysis of the prophetic elements he
concludes that '*The Mask of Anarchy* breaks down the neoclassic
walls of genre'.[12] Without objecting to anything in his reading
of the poem I would quarrel with the conclusion: why should

9. Barrington Moore Jr, *Social Origins of Dictatorship and Democracy: Lord
and Peasant in the Making of the Modern World* (Harmondsworth, 1967), p. 443.
  10. See *Letters*, ii. 117, 119, 120, 136.
  11. Carl Woodring, *Politics in English Romantic Poetry* (Cambridge, Mass.,
1970) [Woodring], p. 265.   12. Ibid., p. 268.

the prophetic element stop us from calling it a satire? Prophecy has been a traditional ingredient of satire from at least *The Dunciad* to *Brave New World*, and the form of the apocalyptic dream-vision which Shelley uses antedates *Piers Plowman*. I think it is not so much the fact that the poem is prophetic which seems to challenge the label as that, unlike such satires as *The Dunciad*, its prophecy is avowedly optimistic rather than pessimistic. Moreover this is exactly where one would expect to find the clash between the two ways of approaching the poem: the generic critic must shift or redefine his categories if he is attempting to take into account Shelley's own basic assumption that good poetry must be positive.

The Mask of Anarchy is a particularly interesting poem in which to locate this problem, since it does present a certain conflict between its positive and negative elements. Few would deny that the early part of the poem is conventionally satirical in a negative way—the Mask itself (the procession of the 'Tyrant's crew') reminds us of Langland's descriptions of the Seven Deadly Sins, or Dryden's of Achitophel and his followers, by its grimly witty portraits of viciousness and hypocrisy, such as

> Next came Fraud, and he had on,
> Like Eldon, an ermined gown;
> His big tears, for he wept well,
> Turned to millstones as they fell.
>
> And the little children, who
> Round his feet played to and fro,
> Thinking every tear a gem,
> Had their brains knocked out by them.
>
> (ll. 14–21)

The 'reprehension' is controlled hatred and the effect extremely pessimistic. We are not surprised that when Hope appeared to the dreamer she 'looked more like Despair'. But we are surprised, perhaps, that Shelley can bring the poem around to a positive ending with the final words of advice to the people:

> 'Rise like Lions after slumber
> In unvanquishable number—
> Shake your chains to earth like dew
> Which in sleep had fallen on you—
> Ye are many—they are few.'
>
> (ll. 368–72)

Quoting the beginning and ending of the poem like this illustrates the conflict in its crudest form and brings out an important problem in Shelley criticism: do we have to discount some
of the satire as melodramatic exaggeration in order to be able
to accept the positive ending, or do we remain convinced of the
monstrosity of Castlereagh and the rest of the government and
dismiss the ending as an example of the 'facile optimism' deplored in Shelley by earlier critics? Either way the poem falls
apart. Ideally one would like to be able to incorporate both elements in one's reading, but this may be difficult.

One possible approach is through a closer examination of
what kind of optimism it is that we are offered at the end. I do
not agree with Carl Woodring's interpretation on this point:
he seems to assume that the giving of positive advice to the
people represents an unambiguously triumphant finale, whereas
it seems to me that the advice is about as desperate as the satire
which preceded it, and hence not inconsistent. Shelley imagines
another situation like Peterloo in which troops are commanded
to attack an unarmed civilian crowd, and counsels passive
resistance:

> 'Stand ye calm and resolute,
> Like a forest close and mute,
> With folded arms and looks which are
> Weapons of unvanquished war.'
>
> (ll. 319–22)

In theory this display of calm non-violent resolution will shame
the soldiers into stopping the slaughter:

> 'With folded arms and steady eyes,
> And little fear, and less surprise,
> Look upon them as they slay
> Till their rage has died away.
>
> 'Then they will return with shame
> To the place from which they came,
> And the blood thus shed will speak
> In hot blushes on their cheek.'
>
> (ll. 344–51)

But does Shelley believe, or does he make us believe, that this is
likely to happen? We know from his other writings that Mary
Shelley's notorious statement that 'Shelley believed that man-

kind had only to will that there should be no evil and there would be none'[13] is a misleading oversimplification. *Prometheus Unbound* itself (begun the year before *The Mask of Anarchy* and finished the year after) stresses that the ideal society it envisages and celebrates will not be achieved quickly or easily, and 'A Philosophical View of Reform' (written in 1819 and containing an explicit discussion of Peterloo) acknowledges that any kind of concerted action, including passive resistance, by the mass of the people is unlikely while the prevailing mood continues to be one of abject apathy.[14] But Shelley believed that it is the poet who can excite people out of their apathy and convince them of the desirability of a new order, and it is here of course that his purpose diverges from that of the conventional satirist: he wishes not only to point out and criticize the evil he sees in society but also to imagine and encourage radical change. That he was not naively optimistic about his ability to do this seems to me clear from both the tone of *The Mask of Anarchy* itself, where his hope looks very like despair, and from the lines near the end of the 'Ode to the West Wind' (written, like the *Mask*, in the autumn of 1819),

> Drive my dead thoughts over the universe
> Like withered leaves to quicken a new birth!
> (ll. 63–64)

where the ambiguity is more explicit: on the one hand there is hope for the new growth of spring, but on the other the thoughts are described as 'dead' and we feel that it will take more than 'withered leaves' to revitalize the universe.

The balance between optimism and pessimism continues to be a significant factor in the shorter political poems of 1819. All of the three poems I want to look at, the 'Song to the Men of England', 'Similes for Two Political Characters of 1819', and 'England in 1819', are straightforwardly satirical in so far as they take a critical attitude towards the society they describe and do not hesitate to condemn those responsible for it. In terms of a more positive purpose, however, there is some variation between them. The 'Song to the Men of England' shares the bitterness of *The Mask of Anarchy* about the oppression of the

13. Note on *Prometheus Unbound* in *Poetical Works*, p. 271.
14. *Prose*, pp. 257–8.

lower classes but goes further towards questioning the structure of this society:

> Wherefore feed, and clothe, and save,
> From the cradle to the grave,
> Those ungrateful drones who would
> Drain your sweat—nay, drink your blood?
> (ll. 5–8)

More than passive resistance is advised:

> Sow seed,—but let no tyrant reap;
> Find wealth,—let no imposter heap;
> Weave robes, let not the idle wear;
> Forge arms,—in your defence to bear.
> (ll. 21–24)

It is not surprising that the poem was distributed secretly by the Chartists in their earlier, more radical phase,[15] despite the gloomy and bitter irony with which it ends:

> With plough and spade, and hoe and loom,
> Trace your grave, and build your tomb,
> And weave your winding-sheet, till fair
> England be your sepulchre.   (ll. 29–32)

The other two poems are more negative in general tone, and hence nearer to the conventional definition of satire. The well-known sonnet on 'England in 1819' ('An old, mad, blind, despised, and dying king,') is very perfunctory about its optimistic ending, here almost a technicality: after building up a complex dark picture of corruption in the monarchy, the government, the army and the church, Shelley declares suddenly in the concluding couplet that all these evils

> Are graves, from which a glorious Phantom may
> Burst, to illumine our tempestuous day.

He gives no reason as to why or how this could happen, and his use of 'may' in such a strong position seems to imply that the 'glorious Phantom' is very unlikely to appear. The 'Similes' are without any relief of this kind at all. They are comparable to the beginning of *The Mask of Anarchy* in presenting a series of repulsive images for the political characters in question, but in this case there is no attempt to introduce any kind of opposition or

15. See Woodring, p. 263 and note on pp. 352–3.

alternative to the evil described. As with a great deal of other satirical poetry, the positive is implied rather than presented.

The comparatively straightforward and traditional nature of the 'Similes' makes them a good starting-point for a discussion of Shelley's satirical technique. The most striking thing about them is how grotesque and sinister they are:

> I. As from an ancestral oak
>   Two empty ravens sound their clarion,
> Yell by yell, and croak by croak,
> When they scent the noonday smoke
>   Of fresh human carrion   (ll. 1–5)

The politicians (shown to be peers by the use of 'ancestral') are compared here and throughout the poem with 'gibbering', obscene birds of prey waiting for 'human carrion'; other reputedly vicious animals are mentioned in the third and fourth stanzas (sharks, dog-fish, scorpions, wolves, vipers) but the vulture-images are most numerous and powerful. Although the creatures are said to be waiting and therefore passive, Shelley builds up a sense of horrible, hysterical excitement: they are 'sick for battle', obsessed by the scent of prey. Like the opening of *The Mask of Anarchy*, it is an outburst of political hatred, and its methods and tone have likewise been accused of melodramatic exaggeration. George Santayana sees this as the natural counterpart of Shelley's idealism when he says,

as [Shelley] seized upon and recast all images of beauty, to make them more perfectly beautiful, so, to vent his infinite horror of evil, he seized on all the worst images of crime or torture that he could find, and recast them so as to reach the quintessence of distilled badness.[16]

But for him this is too crude: 'His pictures of war, famine, lust, and cruelty are, or seem, forced,' and the extreme, doctrinaire position implied by the images is proof of 'a certain moral incompetence in his moral intensity'.[17]

Shelley's mode of representing vice is somewhat too vehement for the gentle reader of the twentieth century, but a certain aggressive violence in thought and expression is of course

16. 'Shelley: or The Poetic Value of Revolutionary Principles', in N. Henfrey (ed.), *Selected Critical Writings of George Santayana* (Cambridge, 1968), i. 164.

17. Ibid., i. 164, 170.

a very traditional element in the genre from Juvenal's 'si natura negat, facit indignatio versum' (*Satires*, 1. i. 79) through his English imitators such as Marston down to Shelley's own day. Moreover Shelley was not writing for academics but for the English working class at a time when the country was passing through a reactionary and repressive phase of considerable intensity. It is clear from Mary Shelley's Note on *The Mask of Anarchy*[18] that he was deliberately practising a plain style for this purpose; hence the absence in the poems of the difficult and abstract imagery we find in a work like *Prometheus Unbound*, which, as Shelley acknowledged, would have a much more limited readership.[19] Nevertheless, the poems are not straightforward political propaganda or 'preaching'. I said above that the characteristic methods of a satire are 'figurative and occult' and that it is usually 'an indirect and fictionalized account which makes use of a certain range of literary devices in order to make its "reprehension" both powerful and attactively readable', so I would like now to look at Shelley's use of the 'figurative and occult' in these poems. I shall centre my remarks on the problematic area of the violent and almost melodramatic nature of his imagery.

The sheer extremity of Shelley's images of evil must be related to the vogue for the Gothic in literature during the late eighteenth and early nineteenth centuries as much as to the allegedly manichean nature of Shelley's mind. On the one hand he used the Gothic paraphernalia of castles, monks, tombs, torture, and so on to provide sensational settings for fictional poems from *Original Poetry by Victor and Cazire* (1810) to *The Cenci* (1820), but he also adapted the Gothic for political purposes. We find this as early as 1810 in the *Posthumous Fragments of Margaret Nicholson* where the poem entitled 'War' begins,

> Ambition, power, and avarice, now have hurled
> Death, fate, and ruin, on a bleeding world.
> See! on yon heath what countless victims lie,
> Hark! what loud shrieks ascend through yonder sky. . . .

>   (ll. 1–4)

---

18. *Poetical Works*, p. 588.

19. See his references to it in *Letters*, ii, especially pp. 174 and 263. It is also worth noting how he stresses that *The Mask of Anarchy* is offered for publication in Hunt's *Examiner*, not the *Indicator*, implying that it is a piece of political ephemera rather than a strictly literary offering (*Letters*, ii. 152).

The representation of political oppression through the image of a tyrant torturing his victim occurs again even more explicitly in Shelley's poem 'To the Republicans of North America' of 1812, where he exhorts them to

> Shout aloud! Let every slave,
>   Crouching at Corruption's throne,
> Start into a man, and brave
>   Racks and chains without a groan;
> And the castle's heartless glow,
> And the hovel's vice and woe,
> Fade like gaudy flowers that blow—
>   Weeds that peep and then are gone
> Whilst, from misery's ashes risen,
> Love shall burst the captive's prison.
>   (ll. 11–20)

We have here a combination of images which is very typical of Shelley, and it becomes clear why the Gothic had such an appeal for him as a source of political metaphors: it provides an area in which images of restraint and freedom can be combined with images of death and rebirth, as we shall see later.

The stanza from 'To the Republicans of North America' is a rather crude example of Shelley's political use of the Gothic, which is more sophisticated in the poems of 1819 and 1820, partly through the use of a more generally fictionalized approach. There is something faintly ludicrous in the application of the 'medieval' details (racks, chains, castles) to North America in 1812 which is avoided in the opening sequence of *The Mask of Anarchy* where the dream-vision form sanctions the movement away from naturalism. The representation here is Gothic in providing horrific and monstrous images of tyrants while the people are 'slaves', 'pale as corpses', 'ankle-deep in blood', and so on. The imagery is consistently maintained throughout the poem, serving to emphasize the horrors of oppression and the desirability of freedom without implying any claim to literal truth. The same could be said of the 'Similes for Two Political Characters of 1819', where the vulture-images I have already discussed are decidedly Gothic in their evocation of the deathly, the predatory and the archaic.

Swellfoot the Tyrant, set for the most part in 'a magnificent Temple, built of thigh-bones and death's heads, and tiled with scalps', is more extravagant and outrageous in its use of the

Gothic, as befits its lighter tone: this is nearer to comic fantasy than to serious political comment. Some critics have found this comedy resistible—N. I. White for example describes it as 'the hysteric sort of grotesquerie which was Shelley's nearest approach to humor'[20]—but it seems to me that the play contains a wide range of genuinely comic effects, from the parody of political rhetoric in the speeches of Mammon and Purganax to the almost surrealist fantasy of the worship of the goddess Famine by the congregation of pigs.[21] *Swellfoot* is nearer to the comic end of the Gothic spectrum, but its imagery can be seen as a deliberately exaggerated version of a set of metaphors Shelley uses quite seriously elsewhere, not just in the satires but to describe, for example, the tyranny of Jupiter in *Prometheus Unbound* (for example, I. 159 ff., II. iv), or the cruelty of Keats's enemies in *Adonais* (ll. 244 ff.). And at the other extreme we find the fantastic side of the Gothic exploited for the tragic effects of fear and meaninglessness in 'The Triumph of Life'.[22]

The representation of political oppression in terms of prisons and graves is an aspect of the use of Gothic imagery in satire which existed as a tradition before the rise of the Gothic novel and is evident, for example, in the poems of John Oldham. The extravagance and self-indulgence of the Gothic might seem alien to the astringent spirit of satire but can also be seen as the logical result of the satirist's desire to paint the evils he sees as black as possible. Shelley is unusual in the extent to which he counters the images of oppression with positive ones of freedom and rebirth. It is here that his satire is again less like other

20. White, p. 332. Shelley perhaps redeems himself from the charge of humourlessness by being aware of his reputation in this respect: in the Preface to *Julian and Maddalo* (1818) he introduces his fictionalized self-portrait with the tongue-in-cheek comment 'Julian is rather serious', and in 1819 we find him saying of *Peter Bell the Third*, 'Perhaps no one will believe anything in the shape of a joke from me' (*Letters*, ii. 164).

21. The visually grotesque details we find more prevalent here than elsewhere in Shelley's satrical writing can be attributed at least in part to the influence of the political cartoons of the period, which often exploited the visual effects of the Gothic, as can be seen in the illustrations included in M. Dorothy George, *English Political Caricature 1793–1832* (Oxford, 1959).

22. There is, unfortunately, insufficient space for a discussion of 'The Triumph of Life' in this essay. I agree with several recent critics that it would probably have had a 'positive' ending, in accordance with Shelley's views about poetry outlined above, but it seems to me that the optimism would have been even more desperate than that of *The Mask of Anarchy*, judging by the uncertainty and pessimism of his final letters.

people's satire and more directly related to the rest of his own non-satiric poetry. He is able to exploit the element of mystery and the potential for supernatural intervention which are built into the Gothic tradition in order to represent the transition from evil to good which is such a crucial problem if optimism is not to appear facile.

Most characteristically he does this through an image of a rebirth, at once organic and miraculous. In 'To the Republicans of North America' we find Love rising from the ashes of misery —an early version of an optimistic image which will recur many times in later works: the 'withered leaves' quickening 'a new birth' in the 'Ode to the West Wind' are a less confident version of this life-from-the-grave image, while the appearance of the 'Shape' in *The Mask of Anarchy* (ll. 102 ff.) combines triumph with mystery. The image is not confined to the satirical poetry: the whole of *Prometheus Unbound* might be seen as an extended version of it. Its occurrence in 'The Cloud' (published with *Prometheus* in 1820) is particularly interesting: the whole poem celebrates the continual change, movement and renewal of nature, and ends with the Cloud about to destroy the perfect 'blue dome of air':

> I silently laugh at my own cenotaph,
>   And out of the caverns of rain,
> Like a child from the womb, like a ghost from the tomb,
>   I arise and unbuild it again.   (ll. 81–84)

The equivalence of the 'child from the womb' and the 'ghost from the tomb' in this ambiguous image of creation and destruction (the 'blue dome' will be destroyed but the rain is life-giving) helps us to interpret the ending of the sonnet 'England in 1819', where the context is one of gloomy political oppression until the final couplet (quoted above). For Shelley it is not an exaggeration to say that the evils of his time are 'graves', and therefore capable of implying a potential for rebirth.

One might say that the 'figurative and occult' in Shelley, as exemplified by his use of Gothic imagery, is the result of his intense awareness of the tragic gap between the possible and the actual. It does not seem to me a sign of 'moral incompetence' to believe in the innate potential for goodness in the human soul and to attempt to use poetry as an instrument for attaining this potential. Since Shelley's philosophy assumes that the individual, once free, and given proper instruction by leaders such as poets, will choose the best patterns of life and society, it is first imperative that freedom be gained. Hence the intensity of his horror of oppression and the importance of images of release. Given the genuinely alarming and reactionary political climate of the period it is not surprising that images of liberation from prison are capped by more daring and desperate-hopeful ones of rebirth from the grave.

In their imagery, then, as well as in their general tenor, Shelley's satires are unconventional in suggesting an extreme positive as well as an extreme negative. Despite his own misgivings, he does write satire as if it had the power to

> make the present not to be,
> Or charm the dark past never to have been,
> Or turn regret to hope.
> ('Fragment of a Satire on Satire', ll. 20–22)

The poems I have been considering are in fact distinguished from the general run of traditional literary satire by taking a much more active and radical role in their situations: usually the satirist deplores but cannot change his society, or the kind of change he wants is basically conservative or reactionary: he wants to restore an ideal which prevailed in the past. Shelley's philosophy of poetry, on the other hand, leads him logically to assume a responsibility for the progress of society towards hitherto unimagined goals. Since part of the poet's duty is to 'awaken sympathy' by the strength of his convictions and the intensity of his language, one would not expect Shelley to present, in his verse at least, a cool analysis of the evils of society and a few sober suggestions towards moderate reforms. Rather, the whole is presented in highly contrasting terms and the bitterness of Satire's scourge is, in intention, counterbalanced by the brightness of Hope's vision.

Keats's *Endymion* and Shelley's 'Alastor'

MIRIAM ALLOTT

I

'The one thing the Romantics had in common was that
they were different from each other.'

This engaging *aperçu*, struck off some years ago by an under-
graduate in the heat of wrestling with a three-hour examination
paper, may come home to students of this period with the daz-
zling light of truth. Certainly it is at least arguable that Shelley,
as a representative of the second generation of the Romantic
poets, was in a sense putting in a plea for the individuality of his
own and his contemporaries' imaginative gifts while acknowledging how much they possessed in common when he wrote in
1818, in the Preface to *The Revolt of Islam*,

> there must be a resemblance, which does not depend upon their own
> will, between all the writers of any particular age. They cannot
> escape from subjection to a common influence which arises out of an
> infinite combination of circumstances belonging to the times in
> which they live; though each is in a degree the author of the very
> influence by which his being is pervaded.[1]

The interaction of these influences and circumstances, which
throw into relief simultaneously resemblance and disparity,
means that we tread on eggshells wherever we pursue it, and in
the case of the poets of the period which we still think of as the
Romantic Revival, especially those of the second generation, we
have to step with peculiar circumspection.[2] The matter is particularly complicated when we come to the relationship between Keats's *Endymion* and Shelley's 'Alastor', since the authors

1. T. Hutchinson (ed.), *Shelley: Poetical Works*, rev. G. M. Matthews
(Oxford, 1970) [*Poetical Works*], p. 35.
2. As a *caveat* see Timothy Webb's 'Coleridge and Shelley's "Alastor": A
Reply', *RES*, NS xviii (1967), pp. 402–11.

were still at the outset of their struggle to discover and preserve an individual poetic identity while contending with their responsiveness to the poetry of their older contemporaries. The publication of Wordsworth's *The Excursion* in 1814 coincided with the dawning of their creative powers—their salute to it is explicit in these youthful poems—and Wordsworth's seminal effect on their work can hardly be overstated. That they responded with comparable enthusiasm to the same kind of literature sharpens rather than eases the problem in the case of *The Excursion* because what was unresolved and ambiguous within this failed 'philosophical poem' in turn produced ambivalences in their reading of it. In the event, the use which they made of what they found in Wordsworth was still more individual than the use which they made of other shared (and for both of them less long-standing) youthful enthusiasms, such as the 'wonders' discovered in various 'Gothick' tales and in the ornate oriental journeyings of Landor's *Gebir* (1798) and Southey's *Thalaba the Destroyer* (1801) and *The Curse of Kehama* (1810), three lengthy narrative poems which left a strong impress on the pictorial details and narrative structure of 'Alastor' and *Endymion*.[3]

We owe to A. C. Bradley—in 'The Long Poem in the Age of Wordsworth' and 'The Letters of Keats', written during the period 1903–5 and collected in his *Oxford Lectures on Poetry* (1909)—the first substantial attempt so to draw *Endymion* and 'Alastor' together that they shed light on each other, on the literary relationship of their authors and on certain contending strains in particular types of Romantic creativity. 'The first longer poem of Shelley which can be called mature was "Alastor" . . . The first long poem of Keats was *Endymion*', he says in 'The Long Poem in the Age of Wordsworth', and diagnoses in each, as in *The Prelude*, a response to the 'infection of the time':

And what is its ['Alastor's'] subject? The subject of *The Prelude*; the story of a Poet's soul, and of the effect upon it of the revelation of its ideal . . . The . . . subject of *Endymion* is again the subject of

3. References to these and other source materials occur in K. N. Cameron's article on 'Alastor' and *Rasselas* (see n. 27 below), Desmond King-Hele, *Shelley: His Thought and Work* (London, 1960) [King-Hele], N. Rogers, *Shelley at Work* (Oxford, 1967), *passim;* Miriam Allott (ed.), *The Poems of John Keats* (Longman Annotated English Poets, London, 1970) [*Keats: Poems*], pp. 116–17.

The Prelude, the story of a poet's soul smitten by love of its ideal, the Principle of Beauty, and striving for union with it . . .[4]

In the later essay, Bradley returns to his theme of the 'great differences' and the 'very close affinities' between the types of creative imagination which produced these poems, each being 'the first poem of any length in which the writer's genius decisively declared itself'.[5] In his Note to the essay, which is in effect a brief but indispensable survey of verbal and thematic parallels in the work of Keats and Shelley, he repeats his argument that the resemblances 'are largely due to similarities in the minds of the two poets, and to the action of a common influence on both', the strongest influence being that of Wordsworth in *The Excursion*.[6] But he now finds in addition that Keats was almost certainly affected by his reading of 'Alastor' ('Alastor' appeared in March 1816 and *Endymion* was written during the seven months from April to November 1817). Certain of the resemblances between the two poems appear to him to be very close indeed, especially, as he singles out with his customary perceptiveness, 'The descriptions in "Alastor" [ll. 192–222] and *Endymion* Book 1 [ll. 672–710] of the dreamer's feelings on awakening from his dream, of the disenchantment that has fallen on the landscape, and of his "eager" pursuit of the lost vision.' At the same time, 'Everything is in one sense different, for the two poets differ greatly . . .'[7] He adds at the close, 'Keats, of course, was writing without any conscious recollection of the passages in "Alastor" ', but this naturally is a more controversial statement and will need to be looked at again later.

II

'All little children are Platonists and it is
their education that makes men Aristotelians'
(F. D. Maurice, 1836)[8]

The fascination of teasing out the likenesses and dissimilarities between Keats and Shelley had been felt, we know now, by many of Bradley's predecessors in the nineteenth century. We are a good deal better informed than we used to be about movements

4. A. C. Bradley, *Oxford Lectures on Poetry* (1909; Macmillan paperback edn, London, 1965) [Bradley], pp. 186–7.   5. Bradley, p. 227.

6. Bradley, pp. 240–4.   7. Bradley, p. 241.

8. F. Maurice, *The Life of Frederick Denison Maurice* (London, 1884), i. 206–7.

of Victorian critical opinion and, thanks to G. M. Matthews's editorial care in his *Keats: The Critical Heritage* (1971), we at last have ready access to the most telling and substantial of the earlier commentaries on Keats and Shelley, including those by Arthur Hallam in 1831, George Gilfillan in the 1840s and 1850s, Aubrey de Vere in 1849, and David Masson in 1860. Playing in and out of almost everything that these critics have to say is an interest in the conception of an 'undissociated sensibility' which Keats's native gifts constantly aspire to and sometimes triumphantly attain, while Shelley's poetic genius, in spite of the keen sensibility which serves it, is felt to move in another direction, though it is not necessarily implied that such unity remains therefore permanently out of reach. 'His body seemed to think', says Aubrey de Vere in 1849 of his 'integrated Keats' (in Mr Matthews's phrase),[9] echoing William Howitt's astonishing description of Keats's poetry, in an essay published two years earlier, as a 'vivid orgasm of the intellect'.[10] Keats, for de Vere, has 'masculine energy' and 'intensity', Shelley 'a fiery enthusiasm':

Rushing through regions of unlimited thought, Shelley could but throw out hints which are often suggestive only. His designs are always outline sketches . . . Shelley admired the beautiful, Keats was absorbed in it . . . That deep absorption excluded . . . every intrusion of alien thought; while the genius of others, too often like a double-reflecting crystal, returns a twofold image, that poetic image which day by day grew clearer before Keats . . . was whole and un-broken . . .[11]

Whatever our view of its rights and wrongs, the belief that since the days of the Elizabethans 'feeling' and 'thought' had somehow suffered a fatal disjunction was a critical commonplace long before T. S. Eliot renewed its currency in 1921.[12] It is discussed by the brilliant Arthur Hallam in his extensive essay on Tennyson's poetry. This was written in 1831, not so long before his tragic death at the age of 22, and includes his analysis of

9. From de Vere's unsigned review in *Edinburgh Review*, xc (October 1849), pp. 388–433, reprinted in G. M. Matthews, *Keats: The Critical Heritage* (London, 1971) [*Heritage*], pp. 341, 343.

10. From William Howitt's *Homes and Haunts of the Most Eminent British Poets* (1847), reprinted in *Heritage*, p. 311.

11. *Heritage*, pp. 341–2.

12. In 'The Metaphysical Poets', *Selected Essays, 1917–1932* (London, 1932).

Shelley and Keats and their effects on the poetry of the new age. The close of the eighteenth century is, he declares,

an era of reaction, an era of painful struggle, to bring our over-civilised condition of thought into union with the fresh productive spirit that brightened the morning of our literature. But repentance is unlike innocence . . . Those different powers of poetic disposition, the energies of Sensitive, of Reflective, of Passionate Emotion, which in former times were intermingled, and derived from mutual support an extensive empire over the feelings of men, were now restrained within separate spheres of agency. The whole system no longer worked harmoniously, and by intrinsic harmony acquired external freedom; but there arose a violent and unusual action in the several component functions, each for itself, all striving to reproduce the regular power which the whole had once enjoyed. Hence the melancholy, which so evidently characterises the spirit of modern poetry; hence that return of the mind upon itself, and the habit of seeking relief in idiosyncrasies rather than community of interest. In the old times the poetic impulse went along with the general impulse of the nation; in these, it is a reaction against it, a check acting for conservation against a propulsion towards change.[13]

Matthew Arnold was only 9 years old at the time, but it is his voice that we think of when we read this. For Hallam, however, both Keats and Shelley are poets whose faculties wrestle energetically towards achieving what we are now accustomed to call a unified sensibility. If they are 'both poets of sensation rather than reflection', the sensation is such that it is eventually inseparable from reflection:

So vivid was the delight attending the simple exertions of eye and ear, that it became mingled more and more with their trains of active thought, and tended to absorb their whole being into the energy of sense. Other poets *seek* for images to illustrate their conceptions; these men had no need to seek; they lived in a world of images . . . This powerful tendency of the imagination to a life of immediate sympathy with the external universe, is not nearly so liable to false views of art as the opposite disposition of purely intellectual contemplation.[14]

13. From Hallam's signed review, 'On Some of the Characteristics of Modern Poetry, and on the Lyrical Poems of Alfred Tennyson', *Englishman's Magazine*, i (August, 1831), pp. 616–21, reprinted in *Heritage*, p. 271. Hallam notes of his use of 'Sensitive', 'We are aware that this is not the right word, being appropriated by common use to a different signification'; he suggests the substitution of 'sensuous' as 'a word in use among our elder divines, and revived by a few bold writers in our own time'.

14. *Heritage*, p. 267.

Hallam's role is that of apologist for his friend and fellow poet, whose earliest work proclaims its Keatsian allegiance (though the allegiance is to Keats's 'natural magic' rather than the quality which prompted Howitt's unforgettable phrase). Consequently he identifies in Tennyson, Keats, and Shelley qualities regarded as correctives for prevailing 'false views of art'. Even so, 'Shelley and Keats were, indeed, of opposite genius': Shelley is 'vast, impetuous, sublime' and has the patience 'for minuter beauties' only if 'they can be raised to a general effect of grandeur'; Keats, on the other hand, seems to have been 'fed with honey-dew' and through 'tenderness' cannot sustain 'a lofty flight'. But, says Hallam, 'He does not generalise or allegorise Nature.'[15] Hallam overlooks the robust realism which in 1819 was already toughening Keats's style and subduing his prettiness and his taste for 'honey-dew', but I have emphasized this last remark because it represents the central and most enduring strain in the history of Keats's critical reputation.

From where we stand now, it is easy to see that the exploration of Keats's poetry primarily for whatever systematically abstract 'allegorical' meanings it may yield dates only from the later decades of the nineteenth century and lasts—alongside the main tradition—in its purest and most influential form until about twenty years or so ago (extreme examples include, at each end of the period, Mrs Frances Owens's readings of Keats's *Endymion* in her *John Keats* of 1880 and Earl Wasserman's readings of Keats's major poems in *The Finer Tone* of 1953). The period more or less concides with the banishing of a 'fiery' in favour of a 'feminine and etherial' Shelley. The phrase is David Masson's in 1860 and anticipates by twenty years Arnold's 'beautiful and ineffectual angel' (Masson failed to find in Shelley what he found in Keats, that is, evidence even in very early poems of 'the presence of a keen and subtle intellect' which would eventually inform and work in harmony with 'the extraordinary keenness of . . . bodily sensibility').[16] Nowadays, alongside our robust Keats, whose truths reside in the concrete particulars and mingled bliss and bale of individual human

15. *Heritage*, p. 267.
16. From 'The Life and Poetry of Keats', *Macmillans Magazine*, iii (November 1860), pp. 1–16, reprinted in *Heritage*, pp. 373, 382. Arnold's phrase occurs in his essay on Byron (1881), reprinted in R. Super, *The Complete Prose Works of Matthew Arnold* (Ann Arbor), ix. 237.

existence, we have, *pari passu*, an increasingly tough though still musical Shelley, whose style is seen to have become in his short writing life relatively disciplined and urbane and whose imagery, so far from being vague and imprecise (as F. R. Leavis argued in 1936), is rooted in accurate observation of external nature and reinforced by a firm grasp of scientific fact.[17] But the robust realism of the one poet and the accurate observation of the other are still seen to be at the service of different kinds of vision, though the differences are perhaps of the kind that Coleridge would call 'opposites' rather than 'contraries', since 'opposites' can move towards each other while 'contraries' cannot.

Our fondness for placing mankind into one or other of the two categories has a long history, as David Newsome recalls in his *Two Classes of Men: Platonism in English Romantic Thought* (1972), where he cites Arnold's Hebraists and Hellenes and Heine's anticipation of Arnold in his 'all men are either Jews or Greeks' (a celebrated twentieth-century extension of these distinctions is to be found in the 'hedgehogs' and 'foxes' of Isaiah Berlin's essay on Tolstoy).[18] To our own purpose are two further instances, which are also used by Mr Newsome: Coleridge's pronouncement (recorded in his *Table Talk* for 2 July 1830) that,

Every man is born an Aristotelian, or a Platonist. I do not think it possible that anyone born an Aristotelian can become a Platonist; and I am sure no born Platonist can change into an Aristotelian. They are the two classes of men, besides which it is next to impossible to conceive a third . . .,

and F. D. Maurice's reply to this six years later,

All little children are Platonists and it is their education which makes men Aristotelians.[19]

As a historian of ideas, Mr Newsome's first interest is not the

17. See F. R. Leavis, 'Shelley', *Revaluation* (London, 1936), pp. 203–32, and King-Hele, pp. 213–18.

18. Isaiah Berlin, *The Hedgehog and the Fox: An Essay on Tolstoy's View of History* (London, 1953).

19. See S. T. Coleridge, *Specimens of Table Talk*, ed. H. N. Coleridge, 3rd edn (London, 1851), 2 July 1830, pp. 100–1; n. 7 above; and David Newsome, *Two Classes of Men: Platonism in English Romantic Thought* (1972), pp. 1, 8.

individual texture, tone and style of the poets of his period; but his charting of the erosions and accretions in the contours of Platonic thought in England during the so-called 'Flight from Reason', which took place in the later eighteenth and early nineteenth centuries, is a warning to anyone tempted to take a short cut by labelling as 'Platonic' and 'Aristotelian' respectively what Masson, for instance, described as the 'entirely opposite schools and tendencies' represented by Shelley and Keats.[20] But if we permit ourselves to adopt 'idealism' and 'empiricism' as working terms for ways of thinking more or less associated with the traditions which descend from Plato and his pupil—'solider Aristotle' as Yeats called him—it is not hard to see, even as early as in their 'Alastor' and *Endymion*, a process at work in Keats and Shelley which accords with Maurice's shrewd observation of characteristic stages in individual development.[21] What the two poems also tell us is that the process got under way earlier in Keats than in Shelley, in a manner which is in keeping with the general consensus about the native bent of his mind and imagination.

III

. . . there seems to be a change discernible in Shelley's thought and poetry between 1815 and 1822. His philosophic disquiet during these years is plainly manifest in his prose and letters. Its focus is always the problem of evil in the world. His early method of circumventing that problem was to embrace an Idealism whereby the contingent world could be divinised by the human imagination. He was never completely comfortable with such an approach . . . By 1821 . . . his estrangement from his 1815 Idealism was quite pronounced . . . The old Idealistic contraries of divine (good) and natural (evil) values broke down when Shelley finally rejected supernature as something to be sought in the temporal world. They are supplanted by the contraries of human existence. The necessary divisiveness of the former pair and the equally necessary communion of the latter were obvious to Keats, but Shelley had to wrench himself from the one and struggle slowly toward the other. He died before his new vision

20. *Heritage*, p. 373.
21. The process does not, of course, depend on direct influences from philosophical reading. Shelley's close study of Plato dates from after 'Alastor'; Mary Shelley notes that his responsiveness confirmed an affinity (*Poetical Works*, xxii). Masson contrasts in Keats 'his passing spurts of speculation, but . . . no system of philosophy' (*Heritage*, p. 373).

was able to assume complete control over his poetry. (Joseph McGann, 'The Secrets of an Elder Day: Shelley after "Hellas"' (1966)).[22]

Few passages could be more pertinent than this to a discussion of 'Alastor' and *Endymion* as stages in their authors' groping journeys, by different routes and at a different pace, towards a similar goal, and it is quite on the cards that Keats himself would have approved of it. What we know about his not particularly intimate association with Shelley—from the first encounter at Leigh Hunt's in December 1816 (after which they ran across each other fairly frequently through the following two years at social gatherings of the Hunt circle), to his refusal of Shelley's invitation from Italy when his health was finally failing in 1820[23]—shows that he was not only resolute, in his habitual manner, to remain his own man, but was also conscious of a want of *rapport* with this member of the trio of 'Young Poets' whose advent Hunt had celebrated in the *Examiner* for 1 December 1816 (his feelings towards John Reynolds, the third member, were entirely different). Keats and Shelley first met, then, some nine months after the publication of Shelley's 'Alastor' and were in each other's company on and off during the period when Keats was conceiving, and planning to begin, *Endymion*. Contrary to Bradley's view, it is quite as certain that in the course of composing his narrative, he found himself consciously recollecting and replying to 'Alastor', even in some sense using it as an 'anti-model' (this could well have been in his mind, among other unsorted ideas, at an early stage in 1817), as it is certain that he was consciously recollecting *The Excursion*—'one of three things to rejoice at in this age', as he told Leigh Hunt in January 1818[24]—when he wrote his individual celebration of 'the principle of Beauty in all things' with which he opens his own long poem.[25]

Bradley in 'The Letters of Keats' sketches the common narrative ground of 'Alastor' and *Endymion*:

Both tell the story of a young poet; of a dream in which his ideal

---

22. *The Keats–Shelley Journal*, xv (1966), reprinted in R. B. Woodings (ed.), *Shelley: Modern Judgements* (London, 1968), p. 270.

23. H. E. Rollins (ed.), *The Letters of John Keats, 1814–1821* (Cambridge, 1958) [*Letters*], ii. 322–3.

24. *Letters*, i. 203.   25. See *Keats: Poems*, p. 120.

appears in human form, and he knows the rapture of union with it; of the passion thus enkindled, and the search for its complete satisfaction.[26]

To these broad resemblances can be added the densely packed 'Romantic' properties of the scenery through which the hero's journey takes him. In both poems he encounters vertiginous cliffs, forested mountain-heights, torrential rivers and waterfalls, deep caverns encrusted with gems, burning volcanoes, and wide uncharted seas; voyages from north to south and on to the Far East, through weather which is variously tempestuous, brilliant, or bitter with ice and snow; finds nature at one moment prodigal with fruit and flowers and at the next, withdrawing her favours, forbiddingly stark; and sees above him in the limitless sky the spectacle of stars, moon, and sun, which arouse in him intense feeling and reflection whether they wax or wane, shine out or remain veiled in cloud. Such resemblances, whatever the degree of incidental literary borrowing, are obviously fostered by 'common influences belonging to the times', though we shall have to glance in a moment at the different use made of this prodigal natural imagery by Shelley, since in 'Alastor', as not in *Endymion*, it is designed to carry a systematic symbolic reference, in particular to the Odyssean nature of speculative human thinking. What this pictorial imagery reflects in both poems, even if more intermittently in *Endymion* than in 'Alastor', is the strain of Romantic feeling which sets man against vast forms of nature in order to dramatize at once the scale of his longing, his solitariness, and his ineluctable limitations. The feeling finds an outlet here and there before these 'times', for example at the beginning of *Rasselas* (which Shelley had read not so long before writing 'Alastor' and returned to later),[27] and it reappears after them with intensity in certain Victorian writers, most noticeably perhaps (among novelists) in Emily Brontë and Hardy. It signals in Keats and Shelley an affinity—whose presence in themselves they confront in different ways—with one movement of feeling in *The Excursion*, that is to say the feeling which brings into being the Solitary and which finally fails to 'correct' his 'despondency' (it is stoicism

26. Bradley, p. 227.
27. See K. N. Cameron, '*Rasselas* and "Alastor": A Study in Transmutation', *Studies in Philology*, xl (1943), pp. 58–75.

more than anything else which provides the prevailing closing temper of Wordsworth's poem). Peacock, we know, claimed to have chosen Shelley's title for him—'Shelley was at a loss for a title, and I proposed that which he adopted: *"Alastor"* or the spirit of *Solitude*. The Greek word ἀλάστωρ is an evil genius'[28] —and some think that Shelley's prefatory description of 'the fury of an irresistible passion' pursuing his hero 'to speedy ruin' was written as a kind of afterthought prompted by this suggestion of 'Greeky Peaky's'. 'The furies', says Desmond King-Hele, taking the term literally, 'are not mentioned in the poem and are best ignored.'[29] But the furies are there none the less, for Shelley is certainly concerned, as his preface indicates, with the destructive effects of 'self-centred seclusion' and he shares his worries with Wordsworth and Keats. The subject inspired the truest voice of feeling in Keats two years after his trial run in *Endymion*, that is in late 1819 with 'The Fall of Hyperion', when he made his supreme imaginative effort to separate the self-absorbed 'dreamer' from the 'true poet', on the one hand, and the humanitarian man of action, on the other. 'Self-centred seclusion' had been a worry for Johnson, too, as (chronologically speaking) a 'pre-Romantic' man, and it remains naturally enough a constant theme in later literature, penetrating modern English and European imaginative writing from Stendhal through the major Russians to Conrad and beyond.

When we turn from the setting of the hero's quest, with its complex overtones of Romantic desire, to look at the 'dream in which his ideal appears in human life', and at the consequences of the dream, we can see that, if both poets were responding to 'common influences', Keats was also responding to their individual manifestation in Shelley and obliquely providing a commentary upon it. At this stage the different scale of the two poems calls for attention as an index to their wide differences of approach. *Endymion*, which has the sub-title 'A Poetic Romance' and runs to four books of some thousand lines apiece, was regarded by Keats as 'a trial of my Powers of Imagination

28. T. L. Peacock, *Memoirs of Shelley* in *Fraser's Magazine* (June 1958, January–March 1860, March 1862), reprinted in H. F. B. and C. E. Jones (eds), *Works* (1924–34).

29. King-Hele, p. 62.

and chiefly of my Invention . . . by which I must make 4000
lines of one bare circumstance and fill them with Poetry'.[30]
Shelley's poem is shorter than any single book of *Endymion* (it
runs to 720 lines) and its author saw it as 'allegorical of one of
the most interesting situations of the human mind': the situation of a youth 'of uncorrupted feelings and adventurous
genius' who 'drinks deep of the fountains of knowledge', remains
'joyous and tranquil' so long as his desires 'point towards objects . . . infinite and unmeasured' but is 'blasted by disappointment' and 'descends to an untimely grave' once he seeks a
human prototype of his ideal conceptions.[31]

Although our recent debates about the Intentional Fallacy
have left us at a point not far from where we were before it
began, its post-operative effects include a lingering uneasiness
about trusting the teller as well as his tale. Of course there is a
recognizable 'allegorical' component in *Endymion*, though not
quite in the sense implied by Professor Bate in his seductive
description of the poem as an 'allegory *manqué*' where the intention 'becomes thinned, distracted and ultimately divided' by
its author's wish to snatch at 'embellishments as mere filler'
in order to complete his programme.[32] Equally, there is, if we
like to put it so, a snatching at 'embellishments' for their own
sake in 'Alastor'. To express this another way, it is true that
Shelley's musical sense commands his blank verse; that this
sense combining with his delight in exotic names gives their
haunting resonance to his catalogues of distant countries, ancient civilizations, and 'awful ruins'—'the lone Chorasmian
shore', 'Arabie, / And Persia, and the wild Carmanian waste
. . .', 'Athens, and Tyre, and Balbec, and the waste / Where
stood Jerusalem . . .'; and that his loving observation of external
nature guarantees immediacy and vivacity for certain of his
incidental passages of description. At the same time, what these
tellers have to say about the nature of their poems is essentially
accurate. It is clear that Shelley's natural imagery operates
throughout 'Alastor' as an allegorical representation of the
movements of a human mind (it is of a piece with a metaphori-
cal habit which Shelley himself regarded as his most individual

30. Letter to Benjamin Bailey, 8 October 1817 (*Letters*, i. 169–70).
31. *Poetical Works*, pp. 14–15.
32. W. J. Bate, *John Keats* (London, 1963, rev. 1967), p. 174.

poetic innovation).[33] His hero's pursuit of 'nature's most secret steps' and visits to 'awful ruins of the days of old' picture an intellectual journey in a manner alien to *Endymion*, which is altogether a more hybrid affair and embodies ideas currently of importance to its author while allowing him at the same time to invent a self-contained, variegated world, a 'Region', as he said, which the reader could wander about in and appreciate for its own sake.[34] Not all his readers have been duly grateful and some have found this free enterprise damagingly self-indulgent (Matthew Arnold deplored the space which the poem occupied in its author's work),[35] but it is understood that we owe to this flexibility examples of Keats's finest early writing, notably the Hymn to Pan in Book I and certain of the passages describing Glaucus's undersea world in Book III.

This level of poetic achievement in itself offers a comment of sorts on the Faustian pursuit of knowledge which occupies Shelley's doomed poet-hero before the advent of his 'dream'. He leaves

> His cold fireside and alienated home
> To seek strange truths in undiscovered lands,

and the casualties of his single-minded search include the human ties figured in lines 129–39 by the lovelorn 'Arab maiden' who brings him food and tends his sleep and for her pains returns '. . . to her cold home / Wildered, and wan, and panting . . .' Nemesis, for Nemesis it is, arrives thousands of leagues on in the 'Vale of Cashmir' (ll. 145–91) when 'The spirit of sweet human love' sends

> . . . a dream of hopes that never yet
> Had flushed his cheek . . . (ll. 150–1)

The 'veiled maid' in the vision speaks with a voice like that of 'his own soul', and after her swift disappearance—leaving a memory of her 'lofty' song and her brief ecstatic embrace—she becomes the new, and finally unattainable, object of his quest.

By contrast, Keats's hero, as Bradley long ago pointed out, is

33. See Mary Shelley, 'Note on *Prometheus Unbound*' in *Poetical Works*, pp. 272–3.

34. Letter to Benjamin Bailey, October 1817 (*Letters*, i. 170).

35. Letter of 26 June 1887, quoted in E. V. Lucas, *The Colvins and their Friends* (London, 1928), p. 193.

not 'self-secluded, or inactive, or fragile, or philosophic'.[36] In reworking the myth about a young man visited and beloved by the goddess of the moon, Keats follows a tradition which presents Endymion as a shepherd king and so allows him to portray a robust youth with a companionable sister and a friendly clan, whose members are anxious about him at the Festival of Pan precisely because he is not himself, being withdrawn and troubled. Moreover Keats's dream-girl is much more mettlesome than Shelley's Narcissistic mirror-image of the hero, who like him (and like his creator) is a poet and is similarly impassioned by themes of 'knowledge . . . truth . . . virtue / And lofty hopes of divine liberty' (ll. 158–9): in the dream the lovers are transported at the same instant by the same ideas and simultaneously rise to face, and dissolve into, each other in an embrace hardly more fleshly than Catherine's final encounter with her *alter ego* Heathcliff in *Wuthering Heights*. Shelley's ideal figure has 'dark locks floating in the breath of night', while Endymion's is shiningly fair, since she is the moon goddess. But there is nothing philosophic or bardic or spiritually elevated about this divinity. She has 'pearl-round ears, white neck and orbed brow', and her impassioning characteristics are not 'lofty hopes of divine liberty', but 'delicious' embraces which leave Endymion 'fainting' with delight.[37] As Keats has it in 'Lamia', with an admirable grip on actuality but with one of his unembarrassed lapses into bathos seemingly relished by some recent readers,[38]

> There is not such a treat among them all
> Haunters of cavern, lake and waterfall,
> As a real woman . . .   (1. 330–2)

Endymion nudges the reader into recognizing these contrasts by taking over from 'Alastor' and putting to different uses some of its incidental narrative details, notably the intermingling of the dark and the fair in the hero's mysterious female visitors and the device of the well in whose depths he is permitted to see (as Robert Frost saw in *his* well) 'for once, then, something'. Shelley's hero, after the dream,

36. Bradley, p. 241.
37. *Endymion*, i. 616, 636–53.
38. Among them Christopher Ricks in his *Keats and Embarrassment* (Oxford, 1974).

> . . . eagerly pursues
> Beyond the realms of dream that fleeting shade,
>   (ll. 205–6)

but his creator—following probably unconsciously the reversal
of the roles of hunter and hunted in his father-in-law's *Caleb
Williams* (1797)—transforms his pursuer into one pursued, and
from this moment, though the narrative pace quickens, it is
ambiguity which pervades the poem. A 'passion . . . like a fierce
fiend' drives him across seas and over mountains to peer at last
at his reflection in the well. 'Dark, gleaming, of most translucent
waves',

> . . . as the human heart,
> Gazing in dreams over the gloomy grave,
> Sees its own treacherous likeness there.
>   (ll. 472–4)

The Spirit which suddenly appears to stand beside him is at first
identifiable with nothing 'the visible world affords / Of grace,
or majesty, or mystery' (ll. 482–3). But on looking up he sees
'Two starry eyes, hung in the gloom of thought'. They may or
may not belong to the dark-haired girl of the dream—they seem
to be blue, for they beckon 'with . . . serene and azure smiles'—
and a question mark is left hovering over the episode. The anti-
nomies of Shelley's sorrowing 'Arab maiden', dark-haired
visitant in Kashmir and mysterious 'starry' and 'azure' eyes at
the well remain unresolved; and it is hard not to believe that
these lodged themselves in Keats's imagination which there-
upon 'alchemised'[39] them into his dual-natured heroine, who is
a blonde goddess in one guise and a dusky mortal Indian
maiden in another and leads Endymion in the end to a happy
unambivalent position where he can eat his cake and have it.
For Shelley's hero this is out of the question: whether the Spirit
at the Well is the Spirit of Nature, Intellectual Beauty, Uranian
or Pandemian Love, or each and all these, what matters is that
the reconciling of the ideal and the actual cannot be effected by
his pursuing his 'good' in the temporal world. He travels on,

39. *Endymion*, i. 777–80,

> Wherein lies happiness? In that which becks
> Our ready minds to fellowship divine,
> A fellowship with essence, till we shine
> Full alchemized, and free of space . . .

but now only to look for a suitable place in which to compose himself for death.

This will not do for Endymion, whose own experience at his well represents one stage in his resolute pursuit of 'A hope beyond the shadow of a dream' (a line obviously echoing the passage from 'Alastor' (ll. 205–6) quoted above). For the Keats of 1817, 'Thinking makes it so' ('The Imagination may be compared with Adam's dream', he wrote in the November, 'he awoke and found it truth').[40] This outlook, more youthfully optimistic, but not more determined to come to grips with actuality, than his outlook in 1819, lends buoyancy to his attempt in *Endymion* to accomplish two things which Shelley's 'Alastor' fails to do: to make his hero get the best of both worlds and to do so by acting according to the humanitarian principles which Shelley glances at in his preface, as we shall see before leaving this subject, but does not illustrate in his poem. Endymion is disconsolate when the dream fades, but he is not pursued by 'furies', his well is a friendly place whose waters reveal

> The same bright face I tasted in my sleep
> Smiling in the clear well . . .,   (i. 895–6)

and the experience remains firmly tactile as he looks up and is showered 'refreshfully' by dew-drops and extremely solid 'dewy buds and leaves and flowers'. His spirit is bathed,

> . . . in a new delight,
> Aye, such a honey-feel of bliss
> Alone preserved me from the drear abyss
> Of death, for the fair form had gone again.
>   (i. 902–5)

Delight in 'sensations' afforded by the 'fellowship with essence' which the temporal world affords through nature, friendship, art and love (four grades of his 'pleasure-thermometer' which Keats sets out in Book I, lines 777–842), preserves Keats's hero from destruction as it cannot preserve Shelley's, though for both, of course, the first awakening from the 'dream' is equally bleak. The sequence from delight to pain, as in the placing of man by both poets against a huge natural setting, is again characteristic of one strain in Romantic sensi-

40. Letter to Benjamin Bailey, 22 November 1817, *Letters*, i. 185.

bility, for it expresses in its most graphic form anguish at the
gulf between what is longed for and what is. When the dream
ends, 'how crude and sore', says Keats in Book II, lines 275–6,
'The journey homeward to habitual self!'. Behind Shelley's
description of the stark real world in lines 193–4, beginning,

> The cold light of morning, the blue moon
> Low in the west, the clear and garish hills,

and Keats's outcry at the painful disappointment of the real
world in Book I, lines 681–2, beginning,

> . . . Ah, my sighs, my tears,
> My clenched hands! . . .,

lies an urgency anticipating Emily Brontë's passionate recollection of the visions which 'rise, and . . . kill me with desire', and
her despair at the aftermath,

> O! dreadful is the check—intense the agony
> When the ear begins to hear, and the eye begins to see;
> When the pulse begins to throb, the brain to think again,
> The soul to feel the flesh and the flesh to feel the chain.[41]

But if the anguish is keen so is the sense that for the purposes of
ordinary life this temperamental habit simply will not do. It is
no accident that a major literary preoccupation from the later
eighteenth century onwards is contention with the 'Romantic
dream' and the 'common influences' which encourage it. This
road is thickly populated with fictional figures: Catherine
Morland and Catherine Linton, Julien Sorel and Emma
Bovary, Dorothea Casaubon and Eustacia Vye, Isabel Archer
and Lord Jim, are in their different kinds and degrees incapaci-
tated by the 'dream', and their creators, being novelists (whose
gifts flower later than those of lyric poets, as Auden celebrates
in his poem 'The Novelist'), are empiricists to a man, for
reasons which F. D. Maurice would have understood and which
have fascinated at least one modern critic of the novel.[42]

If we follow the movements of Shelley's thought and feeling
after 'Alastor' through 'The Revolt of Islam', *Prometheus Unbound*

41. 'Julian M. and A. G. Rochelle' ('Silent is the House . . .'), C. W.
Hatfield (ed.), *The Complete Poems of Emily Jane Brontë* (New York, 1941),
pp. 238–9.
42. For example Lawrence Lerner in his *The Truthtellers: Jane Austen,
George Eliot, D. H. Lawrence* (London, 1967).

and the songs for 'Jane' to his unfinished poem 'The Triumph of Life' we can trace the outlines of an attitude which
might have led him in time to make his own highly individual
contribution to this central concern of modern imaginative
literature. The closing paragraph of his preface to 'Alastor',
with the quotation from *The Excursion*, is in a sense ahead of the
poem (as Keats's early letters are ahead of his early poems) and
anticipates the debate in 'The Fall of Hyperion', for which it
unquestionably provided some degree of inspiration. The poet's
self-centred seclusion may be dangerous, he says, but is to be
distinguished from that of 'meaner spirits', who,

deluded by no generous error, instigated by no sacred thirst of
doubtful knowledge . . . loving nothing on this earth, and cherishing
no hopes beyond, yet keep aloof from sympathies with their kind . . .
They are neither friends, nor lovers, nor fathers, nor citizens of the
world, nor benefactors of their country . . . Those who love not their
fellow-beings live unfruitful lives, and prepare for their old age a
miserable grave.

> The good die first,
> And those whose hearts are dry as summer dust,
> Burn to the socket![43]

These ideas provided Keats with his stepping-stones from the
first of the Books of *Endymion* to its remaining three. 'The playing
of different Natures with Joy and Sorrow' clarified itself as his
'major attempt in the Drama' during the writing of the passage
in Book I about the 'pleasure-thermometer',[44] where he introduces his first set of variations on Shelley's prefatory themes.
Thereafter, his hero adventures on land and sea, under the
earth and in the air, to identify himself at last as 'friend' and
'brother', with the sufferings of Glaucus and the distressed lovers
in Book III and again as a 'friend' and 'brother', and finally
also as a lover, the highest gradation in the 'thermometer', with
the unhappy Indian maid in Book IV. In taking on the identity
of this 'maid', moreover, Endymion's goddess herself submits to
the 'World of Pains and troubles' which Keats elsewhere describes as 'a Vale of Soul-making'.[45] Everyone wins a prize in

43. *Poetical Works*, p. 15. The passage quoted is taken from *The Excursion*,
I. 500–62.
44. Letter to John Taylor, 30 January 1818 (*Letters* i. 218–19).
45. Journal-letter to George and Georgiana Keats, entry for 21 April 1819
(*Letters* ii. 102–3).

this caucus race. By turning from the ideal world to an acceptance of actual human existence, the Indian maid is transformed into the deity of the early dream and both lovers look forward to their eternity of bliss.[46]

Two years later, in 1819, Keats took as the motto for one of his two sonnets on Fame, 'You cannot eat your cake and have it too'[47] and the cake at this time tasted like 'brass' upon the palate, a bitter image for the flavour of human life which Keats used three times in his last years.[48] In 1817 the case seemed different, and the cake then—a honey-cake, manna, moly—was magically endowed with properties to unite joy and pain and to transfigure them into that intense experience which would make 'all disagreeables evaporate'.[49] Shelley at a similarly early stage, had no such belief, and his flight from actuality in 1816 is rooted in a stronger sense of the bale of life together with a weaker sense of its potentialities for bliss. But his poem acknowledges that human affairs demand something more than the indulgence of this sensibility. As a major irony of literary history, each of these two poets made his most unflinching attempt to confront what Henry James called 'the Medusa face of life' in a poem which life did not permit him to complete. The astonishing fragments, 'The Fall of Hyperion' of 1819 and 'The Triumph of Life' of 1822, indicate the beginning of a remarkable new maturity in their authors. They make us wonder about the kind of poetry which Keats and Shelley would have written had they lived another thirty years. They would then have been men in their fifties, living in mid-Victorian 'times'

46. See Cynthia's promise to Endymion, *Endymion*, ii. 807–10,

> . . . I vow an endless bliss,
> An immortality of passion's thine.
> Ere long I will exalt thee to the shine
> Of heaven ambrosial . . .

47. *Keats: Poems*, p. 513.
48. See 'Hyperion', i. 189 and *The Fall of Hyperion*, ii. 33,

> Instead of sweets his ample palate took
> Savour of poisonous brass . . .,

and Keats's letter to Fanny Brawne, August 1820, 'The last two years taste like brass upon my Palate' (*Letters*, ii. 312).
49. Letter to George and Tom Keats, '. . . the excellence of every Art is its intensity, capable of making all disagreeables evaporate' (*Letters*, i. 192).

at the centre of the new set of 'common influences and circumstances' which helped to foster eminent Victorians. Carlyle and
Thomas Arnold, we suddenly remember, were born in the same
year as Keats, and Darwin and Tennyson only seventeen years
later than Shelley.

Barnaby Rudge:
Dickens and Scott

S. J. NEWMAN

I

No longer Dickens's most neglected novel, *Barnaby Rudge* has been persuasively presented in the most considerable recent studies[1] as a substantial historical novel, unified in theme and structure, essentially devoted to demonstrating the relationship between conflicting generations and public disorder. Each critic approaches this conclusion in a different way, but I think a remark by Jack Lindsay may be taken as representative: 'In the last resort we find that Dickens . . . was building on the ground that Scott had cleared with his strong sense of the dialectical interrelation of individual and society at a specific crisis-moment of national growth.' Such a reading does Dickens's intention no more than justice, for as Kathleen Tillotson points out in *Dickens at Work*, *Barnaby Rudge* was, in a way, Dickens's most ambitious youthful project, a novel designed to challenge 'comparison with Scott', the presiding deity of early Victorian fiction.

There is abundant evidence for this. Jack Lindsay remarks on the way in which Dickens sought to strengthen 'his sense of fellowship with Scott' during the years 1836–40 when *Barnaby Rudge* was germinating. The interval of time between the riots and the writing accords precisely with Scott's principles in chapter 1 of *Waverley*. The choice of subject inevitably recalls the Porteous riots in *The Heart of Midlothian*. No one who has pursued Dickens's sources can accept without qualification Humphry House's statement in *The Dickens World* that he 'had

1. J. Lindsay, '*Barnaby Rudge*' in J. Gross and G. Pearson (eds), *Dickens and the Twentieth Century* (London, 1962); S. Marcus, *Dickens: From Pickwick to Dombey* (London, 1965;) A. E. Dyson, *The Inimitable Dickens* (London, 1970); J. Lucas, *The Melancholy Man* (London, 1970).

no exact historic sense, no desire to make his stories into accurate "period" records': Dickens ransacked his sources with an appetite for detail worthy of Jedediah Cleishbotham or Jonathan Oldbuck. Further, as the studies I cited at the beginning of this essay reveal, minds accustomed to Scott's rich and leisurely survey of the local manners and customs of an age, from which the historical theme shapes itself, will quickly find evidence of a similar approach in the first half of *Barnaby Rudge*.

Nevertheless, some qualifications are necessary.

Scott's historical art reaches its peak in an imaginative synthesis of private and public events, in a richly ambiguous vision of the past, compounding growth with decay, and in characters who convey what Lukács calls 'the totality of national life'.[2] Variables such as chance, or personal eccentricity, are subsumed into the general design. As a result, novels such as *Waverley*, *Old Mortality*, *The Heart of Midlothian*, and *Redgauntlet* communicate a discriminating vision of society as an inevitably evolving organism and yet avoid any suggestion of mechanical determinism or social uniformity. No novelist displays more of what Dryden calls 'the commonwealth genius' while at the same time penetrating the crannies and recesses of individual and social oddities. The opening of *Old Mortality*, in which Goose Gibbie precipitates the complex sequence of events leading to Morton's implication with the rebel Cameronians, is a paradigm of Scott's historical method.

Dickens's attempt at a similar vision in *Barnaby Rudge*, however, can only be justified if we ignore or (worse) take seriously some extraordinary lapses in the execution.

Firstly, the murder intrigue is not only threadbare (its elaborately obvious secrets quickly become tedious), but often badly out of focus. Solomon Daisy's alarm cry at the end of chapter 1 is either the reddest herring in literature or damaging evidence that Dickens did not, even after he began publishing his serial, envisage an intimate relationship between the June riots and the climax of his intrigue. Neither does Dickens's use of the rioters, to effect an *éclaircissement* of the mystery by burning down the house which murder has thrown into ruin, seem consistent: *pace* Jack Lindsay and John Lucas, Dickens's

2. G. Lukács, *The Historical Novel*, trans. H. and S. Mitchell (London, 1969), p. 52.

rioters are very far from representing the new generation, as I hope to show later.

Secondly, Dickens's attitude to the past cannot sustain comparison with Scott's fertile ambiguity: wavering uncertainty seems the best he can offer. 'The London of 1775 is depicted as being worse, in every way, than the London of the 1840s', says A. E. Dyson: but a glance at the nostalgic portrait of Clerkenwell in chapter 4 or of the Temple in chapter 15 is sufficient to refute this statement. I sympathize with John Lucas's account of the Maypole in chapter 1 as an image of the moment when maturity becomes senility. But the equally prominent description in chapter 10 manages only to lurch from heavy satire on ancient grandeur to melancholy and falsifying nostalgia. And that nostalgia is overcorrected in turn by an increasing tendency to slip into an uncritical, ahistorical evocation of the Maypole's virtues:

All bars are snug places, but the Maypole's was the very snuggest, cosiest, and completest bar that ever the wit of man devised. Such amazing bottles in old oaken pigeon-holes, . . . so many lemons hanging in separate nets, and forming the fragrant grove, . . . suggestive, with goodly loaves of snowy sugar stowed away hard by, of punch idealised beyond all mortal knowledge. (p. 151)[3]

And, thirdly, the characters on whom we must chiefly rely, if we wish to argue that Dickens's theme of conflict involves the heart of eighteenth-century society as well as its lunatic fringe, are too often only smudged outlines. We have only to compare the inhabitants of the Maypole with Scott's provincials to see the extent of Dickens's failure here. John Willet is mildly amusing but his best moments (such as his Shandeian associations between 'Grace' and 'pickled pork and greens' in chapter 21, or his rococo snores in chapter 33) have nothing to do with either history or society.[4] And I find it impossible to consider seriously as historical types the wilderness of nonentities who flourish beyond the bounds of the Maypole: Edward Chester, Emma Haredale, Geoffrey Haredale, Mary Rudge are faded replicas,

3. Page references throughout are to the New Oxford Illustrated Dickens edition of *Barnaby Rudge* (London, 1954).

4. I cannot agree with J. Kincaid that Dickens's humour in the first half of *Barnaby Rudge* is 'on a level with that of *Pickwick*' (*Dickens and the Rhetoric of Laughter* (London, 1971), p. 110).

not living embodiments. Gabriel Varden alone of the 'normal' characters is endowed with sufficient vitality to represent (and fight for) society. But, apart from his great scene outside Newgate on which I comment later, he lacks the heroic stature necessary to sustain this role alone.

As a result the world of *Barnaby Rudge* totally lacks Scott's spacious solidity. Eighteenth-century England is reduced to an artificial back-cloth, its unreality only heightened by the guidebook prose in which Dickens laboriously attempts period authenticity (see chapter 16 for an example). Just how far, indeed, Dickens is from communicating 'the totality of national life' may be estimated from those moments when he imports into his narrative a vision that is more corporately aware. In chapter 66, for instance, closely following William Vincent's soberly responsible account,[5] he laments the destruction of Lord Mansfield's 'great Law Library, on almost every page of which were notes in the Judge's own hand, of inestimable value—being the results of the study and experience of his whole life' (p. 510). The outburst, natural from Vincent, is almost laughable from Dickens. This is partly because it is aimed at a mob which, we are told in chapter 49, was 'composed for the most part of the very scum and refuse of London, whose growth was fostered by bad criminal laws, bad prison regulations, and the worst conceivable police' (p. 374); but chiefly because it throws into sharp relief Dickens's failure elsewhere in the novel to envisage society other than as a bunch of vividly drawn eccentrics.

And the effect on the riots of this lack of density is to destroy their historical foundations within the novel. What makes Scott's treatment of the Porteous riots so impressive is the way in which he demonstrates their relation to society before and after 1736, whereas, for lack of sufficient 'geological' basis,[6] the riots became the be-all and end-all of *Barnaby Rudge*. The very intensity with which they are drawn may be compared unfavourably with Scott's cooler, more detached perspective.

5. W. Vincent [Thomas Holcroft], *A Plain and Succinct Narrative of the Late Riots and Disturbances* (London, 1780), p. 29.

6. G. W. Spence in his edition of *Barnaby Rudge* (London, 1973), p. 30: Dickens seems not to have 'read far in the history of the origins of the riots' and to have 'turned to the historical sources only for accounts of "the principal outrages" '.

Scott sees round and over his riots. Dickens can only see into the midst of his. *Barnaby Rudge* warrants the title of historical novel only in the rudimentary sense that it includes a vivid account of historic events.[7]

II

I said earlier that Scott's best historical novels combine orderly design with—to quote Walter Bagehot—'the strange varieties and motley composition of human life'.[8] And Dickens did not hesitate to imitate Scott in the latter qualities any more than in the former. But whereas his attempt to imitate Scott's structure led to imaginative inertness, his imitation of Scott's 'anomalous characters'[9] led to an imaginative triumph of a kind very different from his master's.

To understand the difference, it is illuminating to begin with Bagehot's penetrating criticisms in his studies of Scott and Dickens. Of Scott's 'eccentrics' he remarks:

Monstrosity ceases to be such when we discern the laws of nature which evolve it. . . . Just so with eccentricity in human character; it becomes a topic of literary art only when its identity with the ordinary principles of human nature is exhibited in the midst of, and as it were, by means of, the superficial unlikeness. . . . A writer must have a sympathy with health before he can show us how, and where, and to what extent, that which is unhealthy deviates from it; and it is this consistent acquaintance with regular life which makes the irregular characters of Scott so happy a contrast to the uneasy distortions of less sagacious novelists.[10]

Scott's mind is, like Chaucer's, that of a 'healthy sagacious man of the world':[11] his genius is 'symmetrical'. Dickens's, on the other hand, 'is essentially irregular and unsymmetrical':

An irregular mind naturally shows itself in incoherency of incident and aberration of character. The method in which Mr Dickens's mind works, if we are correct in our criticism upon it, tends naturally

7. Cf. W. Dibelius, *Charles Dickens* (Leipzig, 1916), p. 138: 'Er hat es mit Scottscher Technik bearbeitet, aber ohne Scotts Geist'—'He has treated [the subject] with Scott's technique but without Scott's spirit'.

8. W. Bagehot, 'The Waverley Novels', *Literary Studies* (London, 1916), ii. 139.

9. Ibid., p. 141.   10. Ibid., p. 142.

11. 'Charles Dickens', *Literary Studies*, ii. 168.

to these blemishes. Caricatures are necessarily isolated; they are
produced by the exaggerations of certain conspicuous traits and
features; . . . The original germ of *Pickwick* was a 'Club of Oddities'.
The idea was professedly abandoned; but traces of it are to be found
in all Mr Dickens's books. It illustrates the professed grotesqueness
of the characters as well as their slender connection.[12]

I think that in these distinctions between Scott's and Dickens's
'anomalies' Bagehot marks a crucial divergence of their gifts.
Dickens's eccentrics rarely blend unobtrusively with 'regular
life' like Baron Bradwardine, Cuddie Headrigg or Caleb
Balderstone. They belong to a world alien to 'the ordinary
principles of human nature': even their noble impulses (think
of Newman Noggs or Captain Cuttle) seem stranger than the
weirdest fancies of Scott's madmen. But there is more to the
matter than Bagehot's contrast allows. The 'anomalous' characters in *Barnaby Rudge* are not only unlike Scott's eccentrics, they
are unlike the majority of Dickens's other oddities. They reveal
for the first and last time a successful effort on Dickens's part
to fuse his sense of the absurd with a consistent moral vision.
With the possible exception of *A Tale of Two Cities*, the novels
which precede and succeed *Barnaby Rudge* allow their 'anomalies' too much licence for such a vision to be uniformly sustained. The vitality of characters such as Quilp or Mrs Gamp,
Micawber or Flora Finching arouses responses too complicated
and, in some cases, too elemental for it to be satisfactorily accommodated within the subtle but strict confines of moral art.
In *Barnaby Rudge*, however, this vitality is controlled. Delight,
which plays a great part in the complication of our response to
such monsters as Squeers, is excluded. Each of these characters
can be seen to fulfil a function. Each is isolated, subject to in-
ternal obsessive laws, and eccentric not only in the sense of
being odd, peculiar, but in the root meaning of the word, out of
centre. He inhabits the fringes of society—either literally like
Barnaby or psychologically like Miggs.

Dickens seems to have designed these characters to assault the
principles of what Henry James calls 'natural sense and natural
feeling'.[13] Chester and Gashford negate them (the one courteously malign like Milton's Belial, the other a man possessed);

12. 'Charles Dickens', *Literary Studies*, ii. 186.
13. M. Shapira (ed.), *H. James: Selected Literary Criticism* (London, 1963).

Gordon, Barnaby, and Hugh (two 'naturals' and a 'salvage man') unconsciously parody them; Miggs, Sim, and Dennis pervert them. This last and most monstrous group reveals in a particularly striking way Dickens's increasing concern with what he called the 'horribly ludicrous'.[14] We are forced to laugh at these creatures, but laughter brings the relief neither of delight nor of dismissive mockery. We see them as maimed, absurd, and distorted, pitiless and unpitiable. Wickedness (Gashford) or fanatic idiocy (Gordon) pale beside their appallingly funny deformity.

Of the three, Miggs, Sim, and Dennis, Miggs is the nearest to pure absurdity. She anticipates Mrs Gamp in her insistent monologues, her addiction to what Dickens calls 'the irrelative pronoun' (p. 546), and her evangelical no-man's language (though her tone is altogether shriller, thinner, more mincing and edgy than Mrs Gamp's gin-saturated stream of semi-consciousness). In *The Imagination of Charles Dickens* A. O. J. Cockshut draws attention to the strange relics of religious language that litter Mrs Gamp's speech and indicate a distorted religious sense. The same is true of Miggs, but in her case the 'volcanic', eccentric, isolated use that she makes of a common language and creed is more structurally relevant. It sheds light on the way tradition can become fossilized in the individual and thus on Dicken's contention in the Preface that 'what we falsely call a religious cry . . . is senseless, besotted, inveterate, and unmerciful'. And Miggs's ingrown religious faculty is more clearly a symptom of neurosis than Mrs Gamp's. We are told in chapter 7, in terms reminiscent of Shakespeare's 129th Sonnet, that she 'held the male sex to be . . . fickle, false, base, sottish, inclined to perjury'; her every utterance suggests the clenched rigidity of paralysed desire:

> 'Oh Simmun,' cried Miggs, 'this is worse than all. I know if I come down, you'll go, and—'
> 'And what, my precious?' said Mr Tappertit.
> 'And try,' said Miggs, hysterically, 'to kiss me, or some such dreadfulness; I know you will!' (p. 73)

The hiatus between 'try' and the anti-climactic 'kiss' makes Dickens's adverb seem clinically precise.

14. Dickens, 'Capital Punishment', *Miscellaneous Papers* (London, 1908) [*Papers*], p. 27.

Sim himself sublimates ungratified desire more successfully, though if possible less attractively. In his case personal impotence passes directly into fantastic grandiloquence; private spite and envy transubstantiate themselves into 'the noble shame and the divine discontent'. Jack Lindsay and John Lucas consider Sim a figure of fun too trivial to embody a serious function; in both cases their judgments are based on a misconception of Dickens's purpose. Sim does not represent underprivileged apprentices or journeymen, and his secret society is surely no parody of 1830s Unionism. He is a 'waterfly': absurd but capable of stinging nastily, and evidently based on Edward Oxford,[15] tried in 1840 for shooting at Queen Victoria. Dickens, analysing the similar case of Hocker, wrote of Oxford who was found guilty but insane, 'There is no proved pretence whatever for regarding him as mad; other than that he was . . . brimful of conceit, and a desire to become, even at the cost of the gallows (the only cost within his reach) the talk of the town'.[16] Tappertit epitomizes this sort of self conceit. There is a link between his fustian speech—'patience! I will be famous yet. A voice within me keeps on whispering Greatness' (p. 67)—and his plan for liberating the apprentices and society by restoring the 'good old English customs' (p. 65). He can create neither a plan nor a language to accommodate his desire for originality; inevitably he is thrown back on old forms which resist 'the innovating spirit of the times' (p. 65). Like Miggs, the only trace left of 'natural sense and natural feeling' lies in the morbid intensity

15. Oxford, a barman aged 'eighteen or nineteen years' at the time of his trial, belonged to a secret society called 'Young England' whose rules stipulated that every member should be 'provided with a brace of pistols, a sword, a rifle, and a dagger' and that every officer should 'have a fictitious name'. The sort of dangerous cloak and dagger nonsense it represented may be deduced from the following account of a meeting sent to Oxford by the secretary: 'Soon after he [a new member] was introduced we were alarmed by a violent knocking at the door; in an instant our faces were covered, we cocked our pistols, and with drawn swords stood waiting to receive the enemy. While one stood over the fire with the papers, another stood with lighted torch to fire the house. We then sent the old woman to open the door, and it proved to be some little boys who knocked at the door and ran away.' Oxford's mother testified at the trial that her son 'was in the habit of talking in a strain which exhibited a most anxious desire on his part to obtain celebrity in the world'. J. Rayner and G. Crook (eds), *The Complete Newgate Calendar* (London, 1925–6) [*Newgate Calendar*], v. 304–13.

16. Dickens, 'Capital Punishment', *Papers*, p. 27.

with which he communicates his fantastic ambitions. Unlike Dick Swiveller, Sim is possessed by his fantasy: he is on the road that leads to such vestiges of humanity as the Smallweeds.

But even Sim seems positively humane compared to Dennis. Indeed, perverted nature seems epitomized in this hideous creation. Not only does he represent all that is most repressive and reactionary in the English state, he does so in language which communicates the horrible intoxication of authority stripped of kindliness. I think Steven Marcus is right to call Dennis 'a kind of super-ego gone berserk'. By the end of the novel it is impossible to hear the words 'law', 'Protestant', 'constitution', 'Parliament' or 'civilization' without the accompaniment of a sickening jerk and a snap; Dickens speaks justly of the 'frequent prostitution of a noble word to the vilest purposes' (p. 285). And, by transmuting eighteenth- and nineteenth-century hangman's jargon ('turn off' or 'tuck up') into the altogether fiercer, more strenuous 'work off', Dickens suggests in Dennis an extraordinarily repulsive combination of sexual obsession and murderous frenzy: the repression of originally 'natural' reproductive instincts crystallized in this extreme example into the desire to kill. His attitude towards the abducted heroines makes Hugh's cave-man sexuality seem positively refined:

> 'You are an older man than your companion, sir,' said Emma, trembling. 'Have you no pity for us? Do you not consider that we are women?'
> 'I do indeed, my dear,' retorted Denis. 'It would be very hard not to, with two such specimens afore my eyes. Ha ha! Oh, yes, I consider that. We all consider that, miss . . . I tell you what though, brother,' said Dennis cocking his hat for the convenience of scratching his head, and looking gravely at Hugh, 'it's worthy of notice, as a proof of the amazing equalness and dignity of our law, that it don't make no distinction between men and women. . . . If you was to count up in the newspapers the number of females as have been worked off in this here city alone, in the last ten year . . . you'd be surprised at the total—quite amazed you would.' (pp. 455–6)

It is right that of these three perversions of humanity, Dennis alone, backed by the state itself and licensed to kill, should be at ease, regarding himself without tension as 'an artist—a fancy workman—art improves natur' that's my motto' (p. 298), and strolling amid the ruins left by the riots 'with his leather gloves clasped behind him' like 'a farmer ruminating among his crops,

and enjoying by anticipation the bountiful gifts of Providence'
(p. 535). The idea of nature could hardly be distorted further.

III

With such potent characterization on the periphery it is
curiously appropriate that 'the centre cannot hold', that the
heart of *Barnaby Rudge* collapses into the 'great Nether Deep,
of Bedlam, Fanaticism and Popular wrath and madness'.[17]
And Dickens undoubtedly intended to establish a connection
between these characters and the riots. A study of his sources
reveals the conscious skill with which Dickens fashioned his
reconstructions. For instance, several witnesses considered that,
to begin with, the mob consisted chiefly of 'persons decently
dressed, who appeared to be incited to extravagance, by a
species of fanatical phrenzy';[18] others looked back to the puritan
fanaticism that marked the inception of the Civil War. But
Dickens isolates religious fervour in the extraordinary figure of
Lord George Gordon. For the rest, 'No Popery' is a cry as
meaningful as Grip's 'Polly put the kettle on'. Dickens also
disposes quickly of rumours that the riots 'had been fomented
by foreign powers who sought to encompass the overthrow and
ruin of England' (p. 560). The character of his mob is summed
up in Gashford's report on the funds to Gordon:

'Forty scavengers, three and fourpence. An aged pew-opener of St
Martin's parish, sixpence. A bell-ringer of the established church,
sixpence. A Protestant infant, newly born, one-half-penny. The
United Link Boys, three shillings—one bad. The anti-popish prisoners in Newgate, five and fourpence. A friend in Bedlam, half-a
crown. Dennis, the hangman, one shilling.' (p. 273)

A comparison between *Barnaby Rudge* and Vincent's *Plain and
Succinct Narrative* clinches our understanding of Dickens's purpose. The use of Vincent's strong central account as the chief
source pays huge dividends in terms of narrative vigour (and
easily counters the local disruption caused by incorporating as
'fossils' some of Vincent's opinions). But there can be no question of Dickens's imagination being dominated by his borrowed

17. H. D. Traill (ed.), Carlyle, *The French Revolution* (London, 1898), iii. 88.
18. F. Reynolds, *The Life and Times of Frederick Reynolds* (London, 1826),
i. 125; see also Anon., *Sketches of Popular Tumults* (London, 1837), p. 55.

material: at every point his narrative is both more quiveringly alive than Vincent's and more concentrated. As he wrote to John Landseer, 'my object has been to convey an idea of multitudes, violence, and fury'[19] and 'idea' here sustains its Platonic meaning of 'paradigm'. *Barnaby Rudge* does more than provide a picturesque reconstruction of the Gordon Riots: it communicates, for the first time in Dickens's novels, a central vision of society. Historically, Dickens failed utterly to depict the significance of the riots; imaginatively, he finds in the event a symbol of a world at the mercy of its darkest, more anarchic and 'unnatural' elements. Instead of historical analysis we have a vision akin to that of the end of *The Dunciad*, the world become an inferno, sense and feeling dispossessed by 'a community of eccentrics', Barnaby's nightmare of faces that 'grin and chatter' come true (for example p. 386).

Jack Lindsay complains that Dickens's use of imagery to communicate this vision weakens his 'objective assessment of the social forces involved'; but it seems to me that by the time he reached the riots Dickens had abandoned any idea of impartial social analysis. This does not however mean that he escaped into impressionism. Jack Lindsay himself, in his excellent account of Dickens's method here, rightly uses the term 'pictorial precision': the great climaxes such as the burning of the Warren, of Newgate, of Langdale's distillery owe their stunning effect to their co-ordinated particularity, not to blurred suggestions. The more heated Dickens's imagination, the cooler and sharper grows his eye for details. The men 'who danced and trampled on the beds of flowers as though they trod down human enemies, and wrenched them from the stalks, like savages who twisted human necks', and the drunken lad on whose skull 'lead from the roof came streaming down in a shower of liquid fire, white hot; melting his head like wax' (p. 423) contribute to the central symbol of an inferno as minutely detailed as any by Bosch. Dickens earns the right to his concluding vision at Langdale's where, at last, the figurative meaning is allowed to emerge at the expense of detail and complication:

the reflections in every quarter of the sky, of deep red, soaring flames, as though the last day had come and the whole universe were burning;

19. M. House and G. Storey (eds), The Pilgrim Edition of *The Letters of Charles Dickens*, ii, *1840–1841* (London, 1969), pp. 417–18.

the dust, and smoke, and drift of fiery particles, scorching and kindling all it fell upon; the hot, unwholesome vapour, the blight on everything; the stars, and moon, and very sky, obliterated;—made up such a sum of dreariness and ruin, that it seemed as if the face of Heaven were blotted out, and night, in its rest and quiet and softened light, never could look upon the earth again. (p. 525)

Setting aside the matter of historical determinism, Carlyle's words in *Chartism* are enormously apt:

When the thought of a people, in the great mass of it, have grown mad, the combined issue of that people's workings will be a madness, an incoherency and ruin![20]

IV

If this were all, *Barnaby Rudge* would be an easy novel to assimilate: a Janus-faced fiction, looking uncertainly towards Scott and confidently towards the controlled grotesquerie of *A Tale of Two Cities*. But, in fact, the parts of the novel where Dickens's imagination is most active raise even greater problems for the critical reader than those where it is inert. The most brilliant episodes in *Barnaby Rudge* confuse and contradict the central vision I have been discussing just as vigorously as they promote it.

The confusion derives from the fact that Dickens's chief theme is compounded with another, the oppression of the individual, which both illuminates and obscures his central preoccupation. At times, of course, the idea adapts itself perfectly to the novel's predominant imaginative vision. Individuals such as Haredale in chapter 43, John Willet in chapter 54, and John Grueby— 'My cause is the cause of one man against two hundred' (p. 436)—enforce the idea of the rioters as alienated monsters by assuming the role of oppressed 'natural sense and natural feeling'. In the cases of Haredale and Willet this role is assumed momentarily and at the expense of their other, less satisfactory personae. In the case of Grueby it is consistent with his character of a 'square-built, strong made, bull-necked fellow, of the true English breed' (p. 265). In all cases the encounters are too brief to create a 'centre' to the novel of the kind I argued earlier

20. H. D. Traill (ed.), Carlyle, *Critical and Miscellaneous Essays* (London, 1899) [*Essays*], iv. 120.

was lacking, but perfectly adequate to throw the rioters into high relief.

But as we look more closely we realize that this secondary theme is tangential to the riot theme, not harmonious with it. The oppressors cease only to be the mob, but become constitutional authority as well. Thus, in chapter 47 Barnaby confronts the country squire, a symbol of authority who, confusingly, shares characteristics with Sim Tappertit, John Willet, John Grueby, and Dennis. In chapter 57, Barnaby again is the oppressed individual, imprisoned by soldiers for guarding the rioters' plunder, his situation rendered through prose that implicates us in his suffering consciousness:

. . . he could hardly believe he was a Prisoner. But at the word, though only thought, not spoken, he felt the handcuffs galling his wrists, the cord pressing his arms to his sides: the loaded guns levelled at his head. (pp. 440–1)

A still stranger moment of a similar kind comes in chapter 62 where the murderer Rudge, finally and rightly delivered into the arms of the law, is immediately generalized into 'the prisoner' and made the medium for a sensitive study of the cruelty of 'rotten-hearted jails' (p. 513). And to compound our confusion, Dickens brings the two themes tentatively together with Varden's defiance of the rioters in chapter 64. Of course if the reader regards Varden, as does A. E. Dyson, as the 'one great embodiment of virtue' in the novel, his nature crystallized in the description at the opening of chapter 41, there is no contradiction: 'There was nothing surly or severe in the whole scene. It seemed impossible that any one of the innumerable keys could fit a churlish strong-box or a prison-door' (p. 308). But Dickens himself must have been aware of the growing confusion for he evades the issue here. Varden's allegiances lie with the authorities who have imprisoned Barnaby:

'Lookye, Varden,' said Sim, 'we're bound for Newgate.'
'I know you are,' returned the locksmith. 'You never said a truer word than that.'
'To burn it down, I mean,' said Simon, 'and force the gates, and set the prisoners at liberty. You helped to make the lock of the great door.'
'I did,' said the locksmith. 'You owe me no thanks for that—as you'll find before long.' (p. 485)

Without going so far as John Lucas, who says, 'It is very hard to avoid feeling that [Varden's] request [to the keeper of Newgate] to "Keep 'em out, in King George's name" is wickedly ironic', I do think this scene marks the moment when the secondary theme begins to conflict with the primary theme of anarchy.

And in chapters 76 and 77, with the riots over, it emerges so fiercely that it buckles and nearly destroys the imaginative vision I was discussing earlier. For in this final section the leaders of the rioters become victims of an authority every bit as ugly as the mob they represented. The result is not only to cast a retrospective light of social justification over the riots— ' "Better be mad than sane, here," said Hugh' (p. 585)—but also to subject 'The hangman himself, the centaur, and the madman' to a massive change of significance.

The scene of their punishment is prepared with a concentration of technique that makes 'Fagin's Last Night alive' or Thackeray's 'Going to See a Man Hanged' seem like apprentice efforts. In eight terse paragraphs Dickens takes us from darkness and the sinister figures of the scaffold builders like 'shadowy creatures toiling at midnight on some ghostly, unsubstantial work' through the glimmer of dawn to a morning of Wordsworthian radiance:

A fairer morning never shone. From the roofs and upper stories of these buildings, the spires of city churches and the great cathedral dome were visible, rising up beyond the prison, into the blue sky, and clad in the colour of light summer clouds, and showing in the clear atmosphere their every scrap of tracery and fret-work, and every niche and loophole. (pp. 589–90)

But his purpose is not contrast, only intensification. This is no celestial city; the spires and dome symbolize not Christianity and mercy but church and state. They are allied to, not divided from, the prison. Daylight does not melt the scaffold like a dream, it seems to solidify it: '. . . it was better, grim and sombre in the shade, than when, the day being more advanced, it stood confessed in the full glare and glory of the sun, with its black paint blistering, and its nooses dangling in the light like loathsome garlands' (p. 590). Dickens's use of light as a Blakeian symbol of vitality has often been remarked; but he as often uses it for the reverse effect of cruel exposure (as in much of *Little*

Dorrit). The effect of this visionary light after so much of the novel has been shrouded in darkness is not to stabilize society but to plunge it from one extreme of cruelty to another. The radiance of these faces does not console:

> The hum grew, as the time drew near, so loud, that those who were at the windows could not hear the church-clock strike . . . Nor had they any need to hear it, either, for they could see it in the people's faces. So surely as another quarter chimed, there was a movement in the crowd—as if something had passed over it—as if the light upon them had been changed—in which the fact was readable as on a brazen dial, figured by a giant's hand. (p. 591)

And in this intolerable blaze Barnaby, Hugh, and Dennis attain a significance unequalled elsewhere in the novel. Even at the height of the riots Dickens's purpose extended, as he told Landseer, to lose[ing] my own dramatis personae in the throng, or only to see[ing] them dimly, through the fire and smoke', whereas here they form the focal point. In the case of Barnaby and Hugh this leads to plain disruption of their earlier identities. Barnaby becomes a holy fool rather than an instance of 'ordinary morbid idiocy'[21] and is movingly delineated as such. Hugh ceases to be a Caliban and becomes a social prophet as eloquent as Carlyle. In each case, the force of the portrayal shames into silence, at least while we read, our hankerings after consistency; and leaves us with the impression not of broken-backed characterization but of two powerful but conflicting double exposures on our mental retinas. With Dennis, however, something more complicated occurs. For he has been all along a representative, as Hugh and Barnaby have not, of 'the constitution'. Like Whitehead's John Ketch he looks 'upon our artificial state of society as a scheme, whereby all the individuals composing it were naturally predisposed to fall into his hands'.[22] And he creates an insoluble problem. If, following history, he is reprieved in order, to quote *The Newgate Calendar*, 'that he might hang up his brother rioters',[23] then he will force an interpretation of the law as anarchy before which even Dickens hesitates. If on the other hand he is hanged he will only reinforce our

21. G. Watson (ed.), Coleridge, *Biographia Literaria* (London, 1965), p. 194.

22. C. Whitehead, *The Autobiography of Jack Ketch*, 2nd edn (London, 1836), p. 38.   23. *Newgate Calendar*, iv. 147.

growing sense that the constitution is unjust and impersonal. This is in fact what happens. Dickens tries to contain Dennis by belabouring him with opprobrious epithets but the character is beyond such control. When he cries, 'have mercy upon a wretched man that has served His Majesty, and the Law, and Parliament, for so many years' (p. 594); when he explains to the authorities that hanging is 'worse, it's worse a hundred times, to me than any man. Let them know that, sir. Let them know that. They've made it worse to me by giving me so much to do . . . Don't hang me here. It's murder' (pp. 594–5), we can feel only horror at a law which treats him in this way. His appeal fuses into a coherent impression all the disparate scenes and phrases scattered through the novel that hint at the tyranny of the state.

I do not dwell on this confusion in order to resurrect Edmund Wilson's argument in *The Wound and The Bow* that Dickens's conscious intention was subverted by an unconscious exultation in what he described, which 'completely obliterates the effect of his right-minded references in his preface to "those shameful tumults" '.[24] I hope I have already sufficiently indicated the genuine horror with which Dickens responds to the riots (and we must beware of mistaking the imaginative delight he clearly experienced in portraying them for a moral delight at what he portrayed).

But neither can I accept Steven Marcus's argument (although his essay seems to me the most penetrating study there is of the novel) that there is no confusion, only ambiguity: '. . . it is exactly this kind of ambiguity—enlisting identical arguments in the service of opposite, or ostensibly opposite, purposes—which gives *Barnaby Rudge* its peculiar, though abstract, density'. Ambiguity is a slippery quality: plain or obscure meanings in literature are notoriously at the mercy not only of historical, social and linguistic changes, but also of each reader's sensitivity. The more refined the intelligence, the greater must be the temptation to 'rewrite' critically an imperfect work of art. 'Ambiguity' gives this temptation most scope because it allows complex order to be created out of contradictory disorder. And it is therefore important to insist that ambiguity does not lie only

24. E. Wilson, 'Dickens: The Two Scrooges', *The Wound and The Bow* (London, 1941; paperback, London, 1961), p. 18.

in the presence of qualities susceptible of various interpretations, but that there must also be shown to be a consciousness of the ambiguity, revealed by an attempt to synthesize it, on the part of the artist.

And in *Barnaby Rudge* there is no synthesis between the two contradictory visions, of anarchy and tyrannical authority: the novel is thematically at war with itself. The final chapters maddeningly evade the issues that have been raised. The more we are assured that 'it *was* a *very* long time before Joe looked five years older, or Dolly either, or the locksmith either, or his wife either' (p. 632), the more our awareness of the novel's unresolved contradictions is exacerbated. 'Few readers ever seem at ease with it' says Steven Marcus of *Barnaby Rudge*: this is true, but it is not, as he suggests, the reader's fault.

At the same time the fault should not automatically discredit Dickens. I think John Bayley is right when, arguing that 'the concept of unity' can 'get in the way of our judging how and why good novels are good', he asks, 'Might it be more helpful to praise the symptoms of disunity, the extent to which the contradictions in the novelist's consciousness have contributed to phase it out as a dominating presence, or divide it into parts whose mutual unawareness gives them the look of independent entities?'[25] I realize that to suggest *Barnaby Rudge* owes something of its power to its lack of synthesis, so that it strikes us less as a controlled symbolic reconstruction, more as an intolerably vivid experience, is to risk falling into what Yvor Winters calls 'the fallacy of imitative form'.[26] Nevertheless these contraries without progression or resolution embroil the reader's imagination in a way that largely accounts for the book's peculiar force.

As an emulation of Scott, then, the novel fails. But the failure is of a kind that should alert us to a significant transition in Dickens's career. Until he had begun *Barnaby Rudge* Dickens must still have believed that, with some chastening, his own genius could vie with Scott's 'symmetrical' genius. But (as I have tried to suggest by quotation) we can sense another influence emerging in the thick of the novel: that of Carlyle. From the evidence of *Barnaby Rudge* it seems likely that Dickens

25. *Times Literary Supplement*, 27 July 1973.
26. Y. Winters, *The Function of Criticism* (London, 1962), p. 54.

had already learnt from *The French Revolution* that 'incoherency of incident and aberration of character' were susceptible of more imaginatively unified treatment than he had accorded them in the exuberant improvizations of *Pickwick* and *Nicholas Nickleby* or the dream worlds of *Oliver Twist* and the *Old Curiosity Shop*. For Carlyle's vision of society in that work was not achieved, like Scott's, by a process so gradual and unobtrusive that it seems (until we look closely) artless, but by forging, through violent poetic rhetoric, 'The Bedlam of Creation'[27] into 'a broad, deep Immensity' where 'each atom is "chained" and complected with all'.[28] In its attempted synthesis of unruly elements into a coherent vision, *Barnaby Rudge* anticipates the ambitious designs of *Bleak House* and *Little Dorrit*, and shows Carlyle to have been a more potent influence than Scott and his subtle equipoise.

But, as I have shown, this vision of anarchy is itself anarchic. I do not think this to be a simple matter of moral ambivalence on Dickens's part but the symptom of an awareness that, in his attempt to discipline his material, he had come dangerously close to impoverishing it. (After all, Miggs cannot be compared with Mrs Nickleby, nor Barnaby's madness with that of Mrs Nickleby's lover.) The material that confuses the novel's essential idea also enriches it, though in a wildly uncontrolled way. It is as though Dickens's imagination rioted against the curbs that were applied to it. Synthesis comparable to Carlyle's is sought prematurely in *Barnaby Rudge*: it could not be achieved until Dickens had probed to its depths the 'Bedlam of Creation'. The synthesis he eventually created out of his 'brooding irregular mind'[29] was not attained by exclusion but by accommodation: *Martin Chuzzlewit* is the book's logical successor.

27. H. D. Traill (ed.), Carlyle, *Sartor Resartus* (London, 1901), p. 193.
28. Carlyle, 'On History' in *Essays*, ii. 89.
29. W. Bagehot, 'Charles Dickens', *Literary Studies*, ii. 195.

Victorian poetry and the legacy of Romanticism

KENNETH ALLOTT

I

A modern Oxford critic, F. W. Bateson, has argued ingeniously and with some plausibility that the amount of poetic talent remains fairly constant from age to age.[1] If, then, the poetry of different ages—the Elizabethan, the Augustan, the Victorian —is of distinctly unequal value, we must assume that some other factor than the genetic is involved. It is generally agreed, for example, that the outpouring of poetry, both dramatic and non-dramatic, between 1580 and 1630 cannot be paralleled in any later period of English literature. Moreover, this is not simply a matter of the luminosity of the major poets, Spenser, Shakespeare, Sidney, Marlowe, Donne, and the rest, but of the high level reached by talents of the second and third order of creative ability. So we have to look beyond the genetic factor for another, and this other factor is obviously environmental. Matthew Arnold, who took the idea from Goethe, spoke in

Miriam Allott writes: Before his death in 1973 my husband had planned to contribute a piece to this volume, probably on Matthew Arnold and Romanticism, and had agreed to act as one of the volume's editors. What follows is taken from notes for an introduction to a series of lectures on the Victorian poets delivered by him some years ago, as Andrew Cecil Bradley Professor of Modern English Literature, to students in the Department of English at the University of Liverpool. The informal origin explains an evident departure from the customary complexity and precision of his written style, and the relatively early date of the notes any difference from his later assessments of the range and quality of Victorian poetry. Alterations are confined to grouping in paragraphs sequences of sentences originally set out under individual headings, expanding some of the shorthand phrasing, rearranging or omitting passages which were designed to introduce information unfamiliar to new students, and supplying a title and footnotes.

1. See, for example, his *English Poetry and the English Language: an Experiment in Literary History* (Oxford, 1934), pp. 6–7.

1865 of the necessary equation between 'the man and the moment'.[2]

It is what a man makes of his talent—or, to speak more exactly, what he is allowed to make of his talent by his age—which determines the quality, and even to some extent the quantity, of the poetry he writes. This is a truism. It must matter whether the temper of the age is friendly or hostile towards the life of the imagination. It must matter whether or not the poet can count on a recognizable audience for his work. For example, the consistency even of uninspired Augustan poetry is connected with the poet's confidence in his audience. Equally, the extraordinary variations in tone and quality of all but the best work of the major Romantic poets suggest that they did not know where their audience was or what feelings and attitudes they shared with them. The isolated poet in talking to his contemporaries has the same disadvantages as the deaf man. Their unevenness is a result at least in part of a significant change in the poetic environment.

How does all this apply to the Victorian poets? I am going to assume that Mr Bateson is right in saying that the amount of poetic talent in the Victorian age is commensurable with that of other periods. I am also going to assume that in fact no Victorian poet reached the level of poetic achievement attained by Wordsworth, Shelley, or Keats in the previous age. There is a great deal of fustian in Wordsworth, of hermaphroditic shrillness in Shelley, of moony decorativeness in Keats. And yet there is no long poem by a Victorian to stand by *The Prelude*, no sustained lyrical vision comparable to *Prometheus Unbound* or Keats's great Odes.

Let us go a little further at the risk of provoking disagreement. The Victorian age is the first age in English literature in which the quality of the success in prose is superior to that in poetry: *Middlemarch*, let us say, is a greater achievement than *In Memoriam*. It is also the first age in which French poetry is superior to English. You can match Tennyson against Victor Hugo, and I will maintain that Tennyson is the better man and the finer poet. But where will you find the English equivalent

2. 'The Function of Criticism at the Present Time', *Essays in Criticism* (London, 1865), reprinted in R. W. Super (ed.), *The Complete Prose Works of Matthew Arnold* (Ann Arbor, 1962), p. 261.

of Baudelaire or Rimbaud? The question to be investigated, then, is what in the Victorian age stood in the way of the production of masterpieces of the first order.

To another audience I might be less candid. If I were preaching to the heathen—to those whose composite image of the Victorians is one of antimacassars, Sunday observance, sweated labour, and sexual prudery—I would stress the variety and the high level of success attained in Victorian poetry. I would do my best to surprise them by showing that Victorian poetry is not all sugary or escapist or religiose. Let me illustrate my point by two brief examples. The first is from the mid-Victorian period, which is taken to be moralistic and sentimental. A young man is in Rome during the siege of Rome by the French. English visitors are clustered for safety in the Maison Serny. What would he do if it came to actual violence?

> Now suppose the French or the Neopolitan soldier
> Should by some evil chance come exploring the Maison Serny
> (Where the family English are all to assemble for safety),
> Am I prepared to lay down my life for the British female?
> Really, who knows? One has bowed and talked, till, little by little,
> All the natural heat has escaped of the chivalrous spirit.
> Oh, one conformed, of course; but one doesn't die for good
>   manners,
> Stab or shoot, or be shot, by way of graceful attention.
> No, if it should be at all, it should be on the barricades there;
> Should I incarnadine ever this inky pacifical finger,
> Sooner far should it be for this vapour of Italy's freedom,
> Sooner far by the side of the damned and dirty plebeians.
> Ah, for a child in the street I could strike; for the full-blown
>   lady—
> Somehow, Eustace, alas! I have not felt the vocation.[3]

This is from a verse-novel, a form which was invented in the Victorian period and which includes Tennyson's *Maud*, Meredith's *Modern Love*, and Mrs Browning's *Aurora Leigh* as well as Arthur Hugh Clough's two poems, *The Bothie of Tober-na-Vuolich* and *Amours de Voyage*. It is also written in colloquial English and in accentual hexameters. (The form derives ultimately from Goethe's *Hermann und Dorothea*.) I hesitated between this passage from *Amours de Voyage* and another from

3. Arthur Hugh Clough, *Amours de Voyage* (London, 1858), II. iv. 64–78, reprinted in A. L. P. Norrington (ed.), *The Poems of Arthur Hugh Clough* (Oxford, 1968) [*Poems of Clough*], p. 189.

The Bothie describing dawn in Liverpool when they were building the railway station at Edge Hill.[4] (*The Bothie* was written in
a house, 51 Vine Street, now pulled down to make way for the
chemistry laboratories on the edge of the university precinct.
There is no plaque of commemoration.)

My second example is from the 1890s, which are thought to
be remote and unreal, and is by John Davidson. In this case it
is the totally unsentimental and honest reporting which is
'un-Victorian':

> Nature selects the longest way,
>   And winds about in tortuous grooves;
> A thousand years the oaks decay;
>   The wrinkled glacier hardly moves.
>
> But here the whetted fangs of change
>   Daily devour the old demesne—
> The busy farm, the quiet grange,
>   The wayside inn, the village green.
>
> In gaudy yellow brick and red,
>   With rooting pipes, like creepers rank,
> The shoddy terraces o'erspread
>   Meadow, and garth, and daisied bank.
>
> With shelves for rooms the houses crowd,
>   Like draughty cupboards in a row—
> Ice-chests when wintry winds are loud,
>   Ovens when the summer breezes blow.
>
> Roused by the fee'd policeman's knock,
>   And sad that day should come again,
> Under the stars the workmen flock
>   In haste to reach the workmen's train.
>
> For here dwell those who must fulfil
>   Dull tasks in uncongenial spheres,
> Who toil through dread of coming ill,
>   And not with hope of happier years—
>
> The lowly folk who scarcely dare
>   Conceive themselves perhaps misplaced,
> Whose prize for unremitting care
>   Is only not to be displaced.[5]

4. Clough, *The Bothie of Tober-na-Vuolich* (London, 1848), ix. 82–87,
reprinted in *Poems of Clough*, pp. 171–2.

5. John Davidson, 'A Northern Suburb', *New Ballads* (London, 1897),
reprinted in John Hayward (ed.), *The Oxford Book of Nineteenth-Century
English Verse* (Oxford, 1964) [Hayward], p. 904.

What I am getting at is that we have to steer between the
Scylla and Charybdis of over-estimation and under-estimation
of the Victorian poets. The range of Victorian poetry is wider
than is commonly allowed; it is capable of intelligence, sharp
observation, epigram, and colloquiality as well as of sentiment
and high finish. All this needs to be said. But at the same time,
of course, we must not exaggerate. Almost all the Victorian
poets until the 1880s and 1890s wrote too much. Browning's
plebeian loquacity is disgraceful and almost hides his real suc-
cesses as ivy hides the comeliness of early Victorian rectories
and villas. *The Ring and the Book* is a mistake. Tennyson is a
remarkable poet—he has, says Auden, the finest ear of any
English poet. But he could write (and is unhappily widely re-
membered for doing so),

You must wake and call me early, call me early mother dear;
Tomorrow'll be the happiest time of all the glad New-year;
Of all the glad New-year, mother, the maddest, merriest day;
For I'm to be Queen o' the May, mother, I'm to be Queen O' the
    May . . .,[6]

and,

    Hallowed be Thy name—Halleluiah!—
      Infinite Ideality!
      Immeasurable Reality!
      Infinite Personality!
    Hallowed by thy name—Halleluiah!

    We feel we are nothing—for all is Thou and in Thee;
    We feel we are something—that also has come from Thee;
    We know we are nothing—but Thou wilt help us to be.
    Hallowed be Thy name—Halleluiah![7]

Much later-Victorian poetry is a kind of evasion. It creates
a dream world, as in some of William Morris's poems. Even

6. 'The May Queen', *Poems* (London, 1832), ll. 1–4, reprinted in
Christopher Ricks (ed.), *The Poems of Tennyson*, Longmans Annotated
English Poets (London, 1969) [*Poems of Tennyson*], p. 418.
7. 'The Human Cry', one of the hymns making up—with 'The Two
Greetings' and 'Out of the deep . . .'—Tennyson's *De Profundis* (1880), re-
printed in *Poems of Tennyson*, p. 1283. In the margin beside these quotations
K. A. has written out Swinburne's remark about Tennyson's King Arthur:
'The snuffles of the Homeless king'. (For Swinburne's strictures on *Idylls of
the King* see E. Gusse and T. J. Wise (eds), *The Complete Works of Algernon
Charles Swinburne* (London, 1925–7), pp. 404–7.)

earlier it escapes into a medieval past as in Tennyson's *Idylls of the King*, or into a pseudo-Italian Renaissance as in Browning's 'Fra Lippo Lippi'. Loquacity, downright silliness, escapism: these are real faults. It is because of them that the readers, the intelligent and appreciative readers, of Victorian poetry are few. On the one hand there are those simple souls who go to poetry for burnt poker-work mottoes and texts:

> But tasks in hours of insight willed
> Can be in hours of gloom fulfilled.[8]

This is unexceptionable in sentiment and was written by Matthew Arnold. And if some lonely or discouraged or underpaid person draws courage from it, so much the better. But it is not good poetry and the pleasure drawn from it is not a poetic pleasure. On the other hand there are the new academics (many of them American) who have made Victorian poetry their field, their specialization. They bring a great apparatus of scholarship, textual, biographical, and critical to bear on it. They will do anything for Victorian poetry but evaluate it. They are ready to face anything except the real weight of the strictures brought in Victorian times, and since, on the faults of Victorian poetry: Yeats's criticism, for example, that the Victorians smothered their imaginations in moralizing, psychologizing, the purveying of information; or Santayana's profound criticism of Browning in his 'The Poetry of Barbarism'.[9]

So on the one hand, the simple souls; on the other hand the academics. These are two mistaken ways of reading the Victorians. There is another way, not so much mistaken as perverted. I mean the enjoyment of Victorian poetry which is a patronizing of its quaintness or oddity. This whimsical appreciation of what is highflown or absurd in the Victorian arts is more evident in some appreciation of Victorian architecture, music or the arts of applied design, but it also operates in poetry. Such readers will tell you that Patmore's *Angel in the House* is really more interesting than his later Odes.[10]

8. 'Morality', ll. 5–6, reprinted in Kenneth Allott (ed.), *The Poems of Matthew Arnold*, Longmans Annotated English Poets (London, 1965) [*Poems of Arnold*], p. 259.

9. George Santayana, 'The Poetry of Barbarism', *Interpretations of Poetry and Religion* (New York, 1900).

10. The first book ('The Betrothal') of *The Angel in the House* was published in 1854; *The Unknown Eros and other Odes* appeared in 1877.

We have reached this point circuitously: Victorian poetry has range and variety of excellence, but many serious weaknesses; it is hardly read today by anyone (but what poetry is today? As Auden says, the poet is lucky to get a corner of the kitchen table: the big desks are reserved for the wapping liars). And so we come back to the question I posed. Why did Victorian poetry fail to reach the highest standards of excellence? What was there in the age hostile to poetic development?

Let us stay immediate hunger for a reply with a quotation from an essay by Yeats written in 1901, the last year of Queen Victoria's reign. He says:

The Arts have failed; fewer people are interested in them every generation. The mere business of living, of making money, of amusing oneself, occupies people more and more, and makes them less and less capable of the difficult art of appreciation.[11]

Let us consider that—it is worth considering—while I attack the question obliquely from another angle.

II

Every year I say to my students that Queen Victoria's reign is the longest in English history and that the term Victorian must therefore be carrying a different sense when it is applied to 1845 and 1895. (Consider how many changes there have been in modern poetry since 1920.) The second longest reign in English history is that of George III, stretching from 1760 to 1820, but we do not speak of Georgian poetry, though we speak of Georgian houses and Georgian silver, because George III's reign is bisected by the gulf between decayed Augustanism and the rise of Romanticism. Critics have accordingly avoided a term which has to cover Churchill's satire, Cowper's didactic poems, Wordsworth's and Coleridge's *Lyrical Ballads*, and the poems of Byron, Shelley, and Keats. But the differences between early and late Victorian poetry are almost as great, and this is a fact which the use of the term 'Victorian' for all the poetry produced between 1837 and 1901 tends to conceal.

11. 'Ireland and the Arts', *Essays and Introductions* (1961), p. 203.

Yet there is after all a justification for this inclusive term. It seems to me that early and late Victorian poetry both deal with the same question but give different answers to it, whereas totally different questions were being asked in 1760 and 1820. This is perhaps a trifle gnomic in expression, so let me try to be more explicit, even at the risk of oversimplifying:

1. Romanticism puts an emphasis on individual experience and its uniqueness that was lacking in the Augustan period: why else did Wordsworth write about leech-gatherers and solitaries and gipsies?

2. Romanticism puts an emphasis on feeling and imagination at the expense of the analytical powers of the reason.

3. Romanticism is concerned with the greater environment at the expense of the immediate environment. Most men and women live in towns, they work in factories and offices, they enjoy themselves at clubs or dances, they make friends, fall in love and marry, quarrel with neighbours. This is what I call the immediate environment. But there is also the greater environment. There is the whole world of nature: friendly, hostile, or indifferent to man? There are the wide silent spaces of the universe which frightened Pascal. There are the vanishing perspectives of time. It is one function of the Romantic poet to recall the greater environment. 'What have I to do with routs, dinners, morning calls? With Mr Pitt or Mr Fox or the Westminster Election?', Wordsworth asked Lady Beaumont in his letter to her in 1807. And this placing of man in the greater environment is triumphantly done by Wordsworth and Shelley.

4. Two results need to be noted: the Romantic poets in their diction, imagery, metrical forms, develop a technique of poetic expression suited to the individual and solitary exploration of experience and the presentation of the 'great appearances of nature in the wider environment'; and they initiate a debate on the relationship between reason and imagination, the debate between 'head' and 'heart' which is carried on through the Victorian period.

In 'Empedocles on Etna', Arnold says through Empedocles,

> The brave impetuous heart yields everywhere
> To the subtle contriving head . . .,

and he speaks in 'The Scholar Gypsy' of the 'disease of modern life' with its 'sick hurry and divided aims'.[12] This is his Empedocles's own situation: 'Something', he tells himself,

> . . . has impaired thy spirit's strength,
> And dried its self-sufficing fount of joy . . .,

and now his 'heart will glow no more'.[13]

This conflict of 'head' and 'heart' is the key to the Romanticism of the Victorian age and its troubled art. When Tennyson says in *In Memoriam*,

> If e'er when faith has fallen asleep,
>   I heard a voice 'believe no more'
> And heard an ever-breaking shore
>   That tumbled in the Godless deep;
>
> A warmth within the breast would melt
>   The freezing reason's colder part,
> And like a man in wrath the heart
>   Stood up and answered 'I have felt',[14]

and when Browning makes Paracelsus realize that he has failed by not allowing love to speak with power and knowledge, we have this opposition. Tennyson and Browning, in the main and in the long run, subordinated the thinking power to the feeling power. They made the head less important than the heart because they feared that reason would end in scepticism, despair, and the end of civilization. Arnold's respect for truth and reason is greater. He tells Clough in a letter of October 1850,

I go to read Locke on the *Conduct of the Understanding*: my respect for the reason as the rock of refuge to this poor exaggerated surexcited humanity increases and increases. Locke is a man who has cleared his mind of vain repetitions . . .[15]

This appearance of Locke's name is extremely significant. Locke, after all, was not Arnold's favourite philosopher (Spinoza was). But Locke is the typical philosopher of the eighteenth-century Enlightenment. In *Sartor Resartus* Carlyle, through Teufelsdrock, addresses Voltaire (who follows Locke and uses his weapons):

12. 'Empedocles on Etna', II. [i]. 90–91, 'The Scholar Gypsy', ll. 203–4, *Poems of Arnold*, pp. 180, 342.
    13. 'Empedocles on Etna', II. [i]. 21–22, 327, *Poems of Arnold*, p. 188.
    14. *In Memoriam*, cxxiv. 9–16, *Poems of Tennyson*, p. 974.
    15. H. Lowry (ed.), *Letters to Clough* (Oxford, 1932), pp. 116–17.

. . . thou has demonstrated this proposition: that the Mythus of the Christian Religion looks not in the eighteenth century as it did in the eighth . . . but what next? Wilt thou help us to embody the divine Spirit of that religion in a new Mythus, in a new vehicle and vesture, that our souls, otherwise too like perishing, may live? (Book II, chapter ix)

Locke was himself a Christian, but his weapons of analysis employed by other hands led to a radical scepticism, to a universe in which will, the sense of beauty and the conscience were subjective only. Even secondary qualities of taste, colour, scent, were not 'real'. The extreme of this position is found in David Hume and it is from him that Kant takes off.

> Locke fell into a swoon
> The garden died
> God took the spinning-jenny
> Out of his side.[16]

The modern world, with its scepticism, its faith in science and its industrial processes, is the end-product of the mental revolution initiated by Locke, and, of course, by Descartes. Kant is really a sort of patron saint of Romanticism. The 'Lockean' view put imagination below reason, as possessing in the main only a decorative function. Kant held that reality lies behind the appearances which Locke and the scientists call solid reality. He followed Hume's scepticism in holding that it is logically unknowable but believed that in moral matters we have certitude of an instinctive kind. This certitude is ensured by insight into reality. The noumenal world is not approached by analytical reason but by a kind of intuition in which, in Newman's phrase, 'the whole man moves'. This thinking, as we know, was extended by other idealists and brought home to England by Coleridge and Carlyle. Coleridge uses it as a basis of a new apologetic for Christianity, Carlyle found in it the germ of his clothes-philosophy: the 'divine spirit of that religion' was morality and new clothes had to be found for it as the old mythology was unbelievable. (Arnold attempts something similar in his religious books: he wants to keep the 'Hebrew old clothes', but to recognize they are only clothing, a

16. W. B. Yeats, 'Fragments', *The Tower* (London, 1928), reprinted in *The Collected Poems of W. B. Yeats* (London, 1939), p. 240.

disguise, a poetic representation of eternally valid moral truths.)

To get back to the point. The analytic reason is the 'head', the 'heart' is the moral intuition, is feeling and imagination. But to an honest man, the process of trusting the feelings rather than the reason has a disreputable ring. Melville relates in *Moby Dick* the story of the whale tied to the ship. Since there is danger of capsizing, another whale is tied on the other side for balance:

> So, when on one side you hoist in Locke's head, you go over that way; but now, on the other side, hoist in Kant's and you come back again; but in *very poor plight* . . .[17]

Notice the last words. Carlyle, Tennyson, and Browning would never face this; Arnold tried to. The essential matter here is that what both he and Melville recognized is that imagination may give genuine insights into reality in the Kantian sense, but that imagination motivated by our strongest feelings may lead us to acclaim as insight what are merely our disguised wishes. So that we are forced, if we are honest, to recognize reason again. The master-faculty of the nineteenth century, Arnold says in *Essays in Criticism*, is the 'imaginative reason'. This mysterious entity appears to be a balance of man's powers. Carlyle, in *Sartor Resartus*, proclaims 'The Understanding is indeed thy window, but Fantasy is thy "Eye" ', and again, '. . . not our Logical, Mensurative faculty, but our Imaginative one is King over us . . .'.[18] As a poet Arnold must believe that the Imagination is important, but he is too aware of himself and his motives to have Carlyle's blind self-confidence in his feelings. He knows, too, that reason or understanding may seem like a drudge, but it is a faithful and useful one.

I may be grossly oversimplifying, but it seems to me that one source of Victorian weakness in poetry is that the poets inherit a technique of Romantic expression developed for this purpose of initiating the debate between reason and imagination, between the 'head' and the 'heart', and carry it on in an age which demanded that the poet should have an immediate

17. See the close of chapter 73, 'Stubb and Flash kill a Right Whale; and then have a Talk over him'.

18. Book III, chapter 3, 1897 edn, ed. J. A. S. Barrett, pp. 261–2.

social function. They inherit a technique, they do not modify it.
There is an incompatibility between, on the one hand, the
poetic techniques which Tennyson derives from Wordsworth
and especially from Keats and, on the other, the social needs
which he tried to satisfy in his verse. Tennyson was a singularly
pure and lonely poetic voice and his Romantic technique was
adequate to the expression of his individual poetic experience.
But the age told him this was not enough. If the imagination, as
Romantic aesthetics maintained, was an organ of truth, the
poet had a duty to come down into the market-place and teach.
But for the teaching, for any social end, Romantic techniques
of expression were inadequate. The situation is rendered para-
bolically by Tennyson in 'The Palace of Art':

> I built my soul a lordly pleasure-house,
>   Wherein at ease to dwell.
> I said 'O Soul, make merry and carouse,
>   Dear soul, for all is well'.[19]

All was not well. The missionary impulse favoured by the Victorian temper of social cohesiveness destroyed Tennyson's
pleasure in his ivory tower:

> So when four years were wholly finish'd
>   She threw her royal robes away.
> 'Make me a cottage in the vale', she said,
>   'Where I may mourn and pray.
>
> Yet pull not down my palace towers, that are
>   So lightly, beautifully built:
> Perchance I may return with others there
>   When I have purged my guilt.'[20]

I am speaking now of early and mid-Victorian poetry: of the
poets of the generation of Tennyson, Browning, and Arnold.
Their poetry is Romantic poetry, but it differs from that of the
great Romantics in having to serve two masters: the individually mediated and almost private vision of truth—the truth
of the imagination; and the social 'truth' of the market-place,
which, as good Victorians themselves, the poets did not feel
they could ignore. There is an unresolved conflict in the Victorian poet between his duty to his imagination and his duty

19. ll. 1–4, *Poems of Tennyson*, p. 401.
20. ll. 289–96, *Poems of Tennyson*, p. 418.

to his age. This results in a worried art. So that our question,
'Why did the early and mid-Victorians produce no master-
piece of the first order in poetry?', is now susceptible of a sort of
answer. They did not because their perception of imaginative
truth was cramped and distorted by the social pressures of their
age; and because for the kind of poetry they were able to write
they did not develop a verse-technique different from that of
the Romantic poets.

The only poetic forms developed in the Victorian period were
the verse-novel and the dramatic lyric or monologue. The first
is a simple attempt to recapture for poetry an audience that
has turned to fiction for its pleasure. The second evades the
problem of giving a personal view of reality by seeing reality
through the eyes of a hundred dramatic characters. Browning
in 'Pauline' and 'Paracelsus' attempts the personal vision, but
its quality is spoilt by conventional elements—very much of the
age and not of all time—and Browning obscurely recognizes
that he is working on the wrong lines: in *Men and Women* (1855)
he repudiates the personal viewpoint for the ventriloquist bril-
liance of his fifty 'men and women'. In sum, the Victorian
poets of the first half of Victoria's reign do not in Yeats's phrase
'think in a marrowbone'. They do not try to unify their experience of thinking and feeling by bringing it to an immediate
personal focus. As a modern American critic says: 'There was a
conflict, demonstrable in the work of the writers themselves,
between the public conscience of the man of letters who comes
forward as the accredited literary spokesman of his world and
the private conscience of the artist who conceives that his highest allegiance must be to his own aesthetic sensibilities'.[21] To
demonstrate this fully would involve one in a variety of pro-
jects, the most rewarding perhaps being a study of the diction
of Victorian poetry. Robert Lowell has said that the aims of
Victorian poetry are either to fortify or narcotize. This broadly
reflects the two influences of Wordsworth and Keats. Wordsworth, who influenced Arnold, had a theory of diction, but
ignored it in practice in all his best poems. Keats, far more influential even than Wordsworth in the Victorian period (he
influenced Tennyson, Browning, Rossetti, Arnold, and almost

---

21. E. D. H. Johnson, *The Alien Vision of Victorian Poetry* (1952), pp. ix–x.

all the poets in the second half of Victoria's reign), had no theory of diction. But his practice was eclectic. He borrowed from all the Elizabethans, and this pseudo-Elizabethan diction modified in various directions was the style of poetic speech until Pound, Eliot, and the later Yeats developed a new and more masculine diction, more closely related to actual speech, during and after the First World War. ('The Elizabethans are so up-holstered', said Lawrence, and Pound's admiration for Browning—besides being that which one vulgarian naturally has for another—was for the Victorian poet who was least influenced by Keats.)

I must leave this topic and address myself briefly to the poetry of the second half of the Victorian period. The prophet of this new poetry, its theoretician and apologist, is Walter Pater. The Gospel is preached in the Conclusion to *The Renaissance* and what bluntly it amounts to is the doctrine of 'Art for Art's Sake' and the seclusion of the artist in an ivory tower. He takes Arnold's definition of criticism, 'To see the object as it really is', and gives it a solipsistic twist. This means, he argues, 'to know one's impression of the object'. All views are therefore relative. Art cannot reach the truth, only 'the truth for me'. Experience is to be valued for its own sake: a sort of Eastern bazaar where one shops for interesting sensations.

I am putting this as an early Victorian would. For example, consider Browning on Rossetti:

Yes, I have read Rossetti's poems—and poetical they are—*scented* with poetry, as it were—like trifles of various sorts you take out of a cedar or sandalwood box: you know I hate the effeminacy of his school.[22]

But let us for a moment see it as those later Victorian poets saw it. They thought that the early Victorians had lost themselves in a Sahara of moralizing, psychologizing, and information. To repeat Yeats's criticism, 'Ideals make the blood thin and take human nature out of people'. Tennyson, Browning and Arnold had betrayed the imagination because they had felt uneasy about giving it the primacy over reason. They had also betrayed

22. Browning to Miss Isabella Blagden, 19 June 1870, in T. J. Wise and T. L. Hood (eds), *Letters of Robert Browning* (1933), p. 137.

it by admitting the demands the age made on them to teach and instruct. (Rossetti, seeing two camels at the zoo, said they were Wordsworth and Ruskin.) Wordsworth was in their view the only great poet who 'after brief blossom, was cut down and sawn into the planks of obvious utility'. With the lesson of the early Victorians before them, they repudiated the influence of the age and sought to pursue their art for art's sake. The criticism that the characteristic preoccupation of the Victorian poet was to create a dream-world applies mainly to the later Victorians. The 'medieval' world of Rossetti, the Greek, medieval, and Icelandic worlds of William Morris, the 'Irish legend' world of Yeats slightly later: all these worlds are dream-worlds. They bear little relationship to the real historical periods from which they are derived and to which they nominally refer; and the slow hypnotic incantatory rhythms the poets used in writing about these worlds show that they are preoccupied with weaving a spell, not with an objective portrayal of something that once existed. Favourite epithets are 'sad', 'weary', 'tired', 'melancholy'. The retreat from life to save the imagination from the pressure of the age ended in emasculating the imagination.

Take William Morris, a man of great physical vitality and mental energy, a socialist who unhorsed a policeman in a Trafalgar Square demonstration, a manufacturer and designer as well as a poet. His verse is thin and world-weary:

> Dreamer of dreams, born out of my due time,
> Why should I strive to set the crooked straight?
> Let it suffice me that my murmuring rhyme
> Beats with light wing against the ivory gate,
> Telling a tale not too importunate
> To those who in the sleepy region stay,
> Lulled by the singer of an empty day.

> Folk say, a wizard to a northern king
> At Christmas-tide such wondrous things did show,
> That through one window men beheld the spring,
> And through another saw the summer glow,
> And through a third the fruited vines a-row,
> While still, unheard, but in its wonted way,
> Piped the drear wind of that December day.

> So with this Earthly Paradise it is,
> If ye will read aright, and pardon me,
> Who strive to build a shadowy isle of bliss
> Midmost the beating of the steely sea,
> Where tossed about all hearts of men must be;
> Whose ravening monsters mighty men shall slay,
> Not the poor singer of an empty day.[23]

That is beautiful, but it is the wan beauty of a chlorotic and dispirited girl, not what might be expected from a man who would have given a good account of himself in a boxing ring. The poets of the second generation fail—fail, that is to say, to produce poetic masterpieces of the first order—because they empty too much of life out of their poetry, because dream usurps too much the place of the intellect.

It seems to me, therefore, that the Victorians were in a cleft stick:

1. If, like Tennyson or Arnold, they tried to deal with their age in poetry, their poetry was muddied: they continued to write delightful and imperfect poetry like Tennyson or they fell silent like Arnold.

2. If, like Rossetti and Morris, they repudiated their age, then they saved their poetry from social dilution, but this poetry became increasingly remote from life. 'Life', said Villiers de l'Isle Adam, 'leave that to the servants' hall.'

It took Yeats, who began in the school of Rossetti and Morris, until he was 50 to work his way out of these difficulties and create a daylight poetry not subservient to the social pressures of the age. Even Hardy, who was an early Victorian in temper, could not escape, even in rejecting its attitudes, the infection of the world-weary later Victorian style. Here is one of his poems of 1883, 'He Abjures Love':

> At last I put off love,
>   For twice ten years
> The daysman of my thought,
>   And hope, and doing;
> Being ashamed thereof,
>   And faint of fears
> And desolations, wrought
>   In his pursuing,

---

23. William Morris, 'An Apology for *The Earthly Paradise*', *The Earthly Paradise* (London, 1868), ll. 22–42, reprinted in Hayward, pp. 785–6.

Since first in youthtime those
　　Disquietings
That heart-enslavement brings
　　To hale and hoary,
Became my housefellows,
　　And, fool and blind,
I turned from kith and kind
　　To give him glory.

I was as children be
　　Who have no care;
I did not shrink or sigh,
　　I did not sicken;
But lo, Love beckoned me
　　And I was bare,
And poor, and starved, and dry,
　　And fever-stricken.

Too many times ablaze
　　With fatuous fires,
Enkindled by his wiles
　　To new embraces,
Did I, by wilful ways
　　And baseless ires,
Return the anxious smiles
　　Of friendly faces.

No more will now rate I
　　The common rare,
The midnight drizzle-dew,
　　The gray hour golden,
The wind a yearning cry,
　　The faulty fair,
Things dreamt, of comelier hue
　　Than things beholden! . . .

—I speak as one who plumbs
　　Life's dim profound,
One who at length can sound
Clear views and certain.
But—after love what comes?
　　A scene that lours,
A few sad vacant hours,
　　And then, the Curtain.[24]

One's confidence in dealing with a subject is inversely pro-
portional to one's knowledge of it. Victorian poetry has been my

24. *The Collected Poems of Thomas Hardy* (London, 1952), pp. 220–1.

concern for more than twenty years, but I have found this lecture extraordinarily difficult to prepare, and I remain highly dissatisfied with what I have said.

As I have stressed so strongly the inadequacy of Victorian poetry at the very highest levels of poetic achievement, let me end by saying that short of this level it offers pleasures of a much wider range and variety than is commonly supposed. Let me close with a roll-call: Tennyson, Browning, Arnold, Dante Gabriel Rossetti, Christina Rossetti, Swinburne, Clough, Morris, Hardy, Meredith, Patmore, Barnes, Hopkins, Yeats. None of these (except Yeats and he after 1914 only) is precisely a great poet. But equally half of them are more than minor poets. Even English poetry with all its glories is not so rich that it can afford to forget them.

Index

This index is primarily an index of persons. It includes however periodicals and titles of individual works when these are mentioned without reference to their authors and these authors are not named elsewhere in the volume. Main entries are in bold figures.

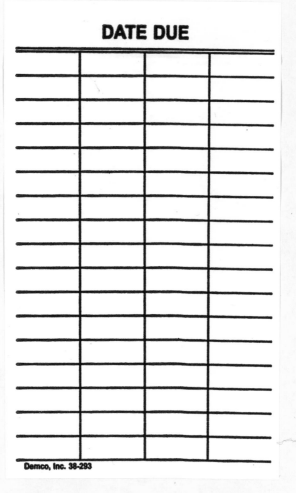